loving
PETER

D1589892

loving PETER

My Life with Peter Cook and Dudley Moore

JUDY COOK

with ANGELA LEVIN

piatkus

PIATKUS

First published in Great Britain in 2008 by Piatkus Books
This paperback edition published in 2009 by Piatkus

Copyright © 2008 by Judy Cook

The moral right of the author has been asserted

All rights reserved
No part of this publication may be reproduced, stored in a retrieval
system, or transmitted in any form or by any means, without the
prior permission in writing of the publisher, nor be otherwise
circulated in any form of binding or cover other than that in which
it is published and without a similar condition including this
condition being imposed on the subsequent purchaser

A CIP catalogue record for this book
is available from the British Library

ISBN 978-0-7499-2947-3

Typeset in Sabon by Action Publishing Technology Ltd, Gloucester
Printed and bound in Great Britain by Clays Ltd, St Ives plc

Papers used by Piatkus are natural, renewable and recyclable
products sourced from well-managed forests and certified
in accordance with the rules of the Forest Stewardship Council.

Mixed Sources
Product group from well-managed
forests and other controlled sources
www.fsc.org Cert no. SGS-COC-004081
© 1996 Forest Stewardship Council

Piatkus
An imprint of
Little, Brown Book Group
100 Victoria Embankment
London EC4Y 0DY

An Hachette UK Company
www.hachette.co.uk

www.piatkus.co.uk

Dedication

To my cousins John Drake and Francis Newcombe
and my half-brother Paul Gourju.

Picture Credits

Pg 2 (bottom) © of Rolf van Brandtzaeg; pg. 7 (bottom left) © United Press International

Every effort has been made to identify and acknowledge the copyright holders. Any errors or omission will be rectified in future editions provided that written notification is made to the publishers.

Contents

Acknowledgements

I should like to thank Robert Smith, my agent, for believing in me and my story; Angela Levin, my co-writer, who has written with deep insight, understanding and empathy; and Gill Bailey, my publisher and Helen Stanton, my editor, and all at Piatkus Books who have supported and guided me through to publication with such care.

The Real Peter Cook

I don't want to go to the dinner party. I tell Gaye Brown, a rather bossy friend, that her party is not my scene, but she persuades me to change my mind. She wants me to meet Peter Cook, who is also going. I say we have met twice before, very briefly. Peter is Britain's funniest man, a comedy genius, and one half of the country's most famous double act, along with Dudley Moore.

Although Peter is the man of the moment, sought after and fêted wherever he goes, Gaye tells me that privately he is very unhappy. His marriage is on the rocks and his wife, Wendy Snowden, spends most of her time abroad. I can sympathise as I am going through a bad time too, and my husband, Sean Kenny, a phenomenally talented stage designer, is currently working out of the country.

It's 1967 and London is swinging. There's a feeling of freedom in the air and everyone is supposed to believe that anything and everything is possible, especially if you're a woman. Hippies are leading the way. They dress in kaftans, wear flowers in their long hair and believe that rock music, drugs and free love can change the world. The buzz slogan is 'Make love, not war', and we are all encouraged to throw off our inhibitions along with our clothes.

Gaye's party won't be anything like that. She is a renowned hostess and tonight she is taking over her grandmother's smart terraced house in Fulham to entertain about twenty friends. Gaye, whom I met when she was an assistant stage manager and I was in the chorus of *The Lord Chamberlain Regrets* revue, refuses to take no for an answer and eventually I agree to come to the party. I feel she is trying to set me up with Peter, even though we are both married, but I tell myself there are lots of dishy men about, just as there are many beautiful girls, and you don't have to fall in love every time you meet one.

It is a gentle May evening as I drive to Fulham in my white soft-top E-type Jaguar, with the roof down. The car is a present from Sean. The rooms are filling up when I arrive, and nearly everyone is smoking. Instead of one long table, buffet-style, small round tables are dotted around. They are all beautifully laid with crisp white tablecloths and Gaye's grandmother's silver cutlery.

I am about to pass a table where Peter is sitting when he catches my eye, points first to the chair next to him, then at the place setting, where my name, Judy Huxtable, has been carefully written. A thought flies through my mind: if I stay, it is unlikely that I will ever get away. I sit down. From the way Peter smiles at me, I know we will hit it off. We begin with the usual social pleasantries. He says it's good to see me again and admires my dress. I have tried to look my best, but all I can now recall about that night is that I am wearing high boots. Nevertheless, I can remember everything about Peter.

He looks as if he has lost weight since appearing in his hit revue *Beyond the Fringe*. His hair is no longer fogeyish and drooping over one eye. Instead it's layered and rather tousled. He is wearing a tight-fitting navy pinstriped suit and a periwinkle-blue silk shirt. He radiates charisma. I find him incredibly good-looking but am most fascinated by his eyes. They are large and dark with long lashes, and gaze at me with a mixture of sparkling humour, defiance, intensity and sadness. They are so mesmerising that from then on I barely notice anyone else in the room. He concentrates entirely on me too. I feel flattered but not entirely surprised, as he was extremely attentive on both occasions when I met him before. Although I don't have a fraction of his talent, I know how intoxicating it can be to be the centre of attention.

People meeting me usually assume that I have everything: I've been a deb, am twenty-three years old, petite and pretty with large green eyes and long, ruffled blonde hair, and have a burgeoning acting career of my own. My outer confidence, however, contrasts sharply with how I feel inside. I live in fear of Sean, who is a violent drunk and regularly unfaithful, and I have as much self-esteem as a battered housewife. I only married him a year ago because I didn't have the courage to break off our five-year relationship. Somehow I feel Peter understands all this, which scares and pleases me in equal measure. I think of what Gaye has told me about Peter's own current marital difficulties: he and his wife, Wendy, are living separately a lot of the time.

For the rest of the evening we are locked in with each other. Neither of us speaks to anyone else, even the others sitting at our table. We talk for hours but I barely remember a word apart from the fact that he tells me Wendy has bought a house in Majorca, where she stays with their two daughters, Lucy and Daisy, while he remains in their large family house in Hampstead, north-west London, on his own.

He doesn't try to touch me, not even semi-accidentally; it's the reserved public schoolboy in him. As the evening wears on, I become aware that some people get up to dance in another room or swap tables, but no one approaches us. Perhaps they instinctively realise that they will get short shrift.

At about midnight, I tell him I have to go home. Sean will be ringing from Canada and I must be there. Peter says he will follow me in his car and pop in for a drink. I climb into my E-type, and Peter clambers into a battered old Citroën that he tells me he bought second-hand two years ago. We set off to Chelsea, where I live. Now I am on my own, though, I start thinking a fraction more rationally. I tell myself that there is no way I am going to bed with him tonight, and wonder what will happen.

I park outside the Henry VIII hunting lodge that Sean rents for us at 14 Cheyne Row. It's like a doll's house, with one up and one down. I take Peter into the sitting room and offer him some whisky. I don't touch alcohol because I have experienced the horrors of both my parents, not to mention Sean, drinking too much. We sit on different sofas, one on either side of the fireplace, and as he downs his whisky, he tells me about his unhappy marriage and that they both see other people. I talk about Sean's habit of going on benders and confess I am frightened of him. They are things I previously haven't told a soul, but I feel comfortable telling Peter because he knows and likes Sean and understands he is a difficult character. On one level, our confessions are a code to let each other know that we both want to continue to see one another.

At around 3 a.m. Peter suddenly announces he is tired and is going to bed. I expect him to leave, but instead he goes upstairs to find the bedroom. It is a tiny house so he can only mean my bed. I am taken completely by surprise and think to myself, You can't do that in someone else's house. But he does, as if it's perfectly normal.

I manage to say, 'All right, then. I'll stay downstairs on the sofa.' I don't know if he expects me to behave any differently, particularly because our meeting has been so intense and this is the Swinging Sixties after all, but that isn't my style. My nightwear is upstairs, but I stay downstairs and sleep, or rather doze, in my dress. Sean hasn't made the phone call I have been expecting and I begin to worry in case he will ring sometime during the night and suspect something from my tone of voice. Luckily he doesn't call. My self-confidence has been so shattered by Sean that it seems extraordinary that *the* Peter Cook, the man who is single-handedly changing the direction of British comedy, is upstairs sleeping in my bed.

There is not a peep out of Peter all night. I get up at about seven and make both of us a breakfast of freshly squeezed orange juice, coffee and toasted soda bread, and take it upstairs on a tray.

Peter is sitting up in bed, rather tousled, and asks, 'Where am I?' He looks as bemused as Dr Who when he lands somewhere new.

I tell him Cheyne Row, Chelsea. I put the tray on the bed and perch on the edge. He is very thirsty, and as soon as he has finished eating and drinking, he says he has to get back home to Hampstead. It is suddenly rather awkward between us, partly because our evening together was so loaded. He gets dressed and joins me downstairs. As he walks by the house phone, he picks up a pen and writes down my number on a piece of paper. I would never have offered it to him – I would have been too terrified of what might happen if Sean found out – but I don't stop him.

He says he will ring me and then leaves. We don't kiss, not even chastely on the cheek. I understand why. What is happening between us is far too powerful for that and I know I am not going to be able to stop it. It is obvious that Peter has fallen for me in a big way, just as I have fallen for him. And as strange as it may seem, equally obvious that he is going to keep in touch with me wherever I am and whatever I do.

He rings the same evening and asks what I am doing and if I am all right. It is as though we talk every day. He calls again the following morning and again that evening. None of the conversations lasts very long, but there is no awkwardness between us. I do feel guilty, though. I don't know how I will handle what we are going to do and wonder when and how it will happen.

A few days later Peter invites me round to his home for dinner. When I arrive at 24 Church Row, I feel rather nervous, but laugh when he tells me that he has the whole evening sorted. He is a great fan of Tottenham Hotspur and they are playing a match he wants to watch. It reveals an unexpected homely side to him, one that we both share, and quickly binds us together. It's also a relief that the intensity of our first evening can be translated into something more normal. He then shows me round his house. It's an amazing early Georgian terraced mansion over five floors. There's William Morris wallpaper in the hallways, Tiffany lamps, heavy silk drapes at the windows, and it's stuffed to the gills with both antiques and knick-knacks. Peter's study is on the top floor and has the most stunning views of London. He also takes me into the garden to show me his roses. He doesn't pluck one to give me as a romantic gesture. I can already tell he isn't like that.

Back inside, he cooks us scrambled eggs with smoked salmon and brings it up on a tray from the ground-floor kitchen to the drawing room, one floor above. He has a glass of wine and I drink water. When we finish eating, Peter takes me upstairs to the fourth floor and goes into a spare room, which has a large bed with a brass bed head. He removes his clothes, gets under the covers and gestures for me to join him. It seems very natural and I am totally captivated. We make love together. He is sensitive, sensual and tactile and I need him both physically and spiritually. He has clarity of soul, an air of mystery and physical beauty.

Time flies and all too soon I have to leave him. I don't want to, but I must in case Sean phones. I also need to feed my cats, Ophelia, a Siamese, and Yogi Bear, a Burmese. I get home at 11 p.m. and know that what has happened between us is both profound and serious. I haven't felt anything remotely like it before and understand instinctively that my life is never going to be the same again. It's a consolation that both our marriages are unhappy and neither of us set out to destroy something that was good. I know I can't stay for ever in a relationship run by fear and vow never to have sex with Sean again.

Meeting Peter coincides with both of us being extremely busy. Peter along with Dudley has agreed to write a new series of *Not Only ... But Also*, but this time for ITV and under a different name. It will consist of four one-hour specials and be called *Goodbye Again*. He and Dudley had previously turned down the BBC's request for a further series, but impresario Lew Grade was keen to poach the series and made them an offer they couldn't refuse. The programmes are scheduled to be broadcast during the summer of 1968.

They are slightly changing the format, too, and instead of having short sharp sketches, they drop the punch lines and sketches now flow into one another like a long stream of consciousness. They also invent a more upmarket version of Pete and Dud, named Peter and Dudley, and at one point talk about their love lives and become rather personal.

Peter is also working with Dudley on the film *Bedazzled*, one of nearly twenty films he will make over his career. Peter is writing the script and will play wily George Spiggott, the Devil, who runs a Soho club, while Dudley is Stanley Moon, a hamburger cook who has a secret desire for Eleanor Bron, who plays a waitress. Peter grants Dudley seven wishes in return for possession of his soul. He explains in the film, 'It's the standard contract. Gives you seven wishes in accordance with the mystic rules of life. Seven days of the week, Seven Deadly Sins, seven seas, seven brides for seven brothers.' Dudley's wishes include being an intellectual Welsh bore, a pop singer, a knighted millionaire and a leaping nun. There is also a bedroom scene in which Raquel Welch plays Lust. Peter wants the film to be called *Peter Cook and Dudley Moore in Raquel Welch* and is disappointed when the distributors turn down his suggestion.

It is released in autumn 1967, but despite Peter's brilliant one-liners, which include 'You realise that suicide's a criminal offence? In less enlightened times they'd have hung you for it,' the reviews are only lukewarm. Cecil Wilson of the *Daily Mail* says, 'Despite some brilliant flashes, a full-length film seems to have overtaxed a pair who are accustomed to getting their laughs in short, sharp bursts.' It later becomes a cult classic and in 2000 is remade with Elizabeth Hurley taking on Peter's role as the Devil.

It's the busiest and most exciting time of my acting career too. I have been given the lead role in *The Touchables*. It's a comic film about four rich, exotic girls who are supposed to represent today's modern female. I play Sadie, the leader of the four. Appearing with me are Ester Anderson, Marilyn Rickard and Kathy Simmonds. I think I was chosen because the director, Robert Freeman, saw a sort of fragile resilience in me. The four of us kidnap a young pop singer, played by photographer David Anthony, and take him to our sixty-foot-high plastic pleasure dome, where we live. Our furniture largely consists of a giant bed in the shape of a fair-ground merry-go-round and some slot machines that we compete on to see who is going to have him first!

I love going off to the film studios early in the morning and watching London wake up. The light is so different, and I enjoy seeing people going about their basic duties, whether it's street-cleaners working away or the Household Cavalry clopping along the road before the day begins. It heightens all my senses.

Despite everything that is going on, Peter and I try to get together as much as we can, and sometimes manage to meet four times a week. It's all incredibly complicated as I have to be in the studio at 5 a.m. and often work very late. We are lucky that Sean and Wendy are spending so much time abroad.

It goes without saying that we can't be seen in public together, in case someone takes our picture and it gets into the newspapers. I can't tell anyone about him either. I find some relief by writing down my thoughts in my diary. Because I live in fear of Sean finding it, I write in code by composing what could in theory become a short story: 'It is 3 a.m. and I am driving home in a confused state, feeling as if I am travelling from one planet to another. Before I go to sleep, I tick off in my mind the minutes and hours until we are together again. And I wonder, Does he just go to sleep, or does he feel the same?'

When we can't see each other, Peter rings me several times a day. He likes to find out what I am doing, or just tell me he loves me. The problem is, he continues to ring even once Sean comes home from working abroad. I put the receiver down the second I hear his voice, but it's awkward as Sean keeps asking who's on the line and I keep saying it's a wrong number.

Even when Sean is away, Peter doesn't come to my house, partly because Mick Jagger of the Rolling Stones and his singer girlfriend Marianne Faithfull live round the corner, so there is usually a photographer hanging around. Instead we meet at Peter's home, or at actor Tom Courtenay's house. Peter and Tom are friends and Tom agrees to lend us his home while he is away filming. He is an adorable man and has recently received an Oscar nomination for his role as Pasha in David Lean's 1965 classic *Doctor Zhivago*. Sometimes I sit in my car outside Tom's house waiting for Peter to arrive and feel such passionate intensity for him that it's as if nothing else in the world matters.

Our times together are very precious. We usually go straight into the bedroom and stay there for hours. We need each other at every level. Peter is so exotic-looking and has a fine body and soft skin. I find him extremely fanciable. He is very sensual but sexually quite straightforward, almost polite. We talk endlessly too. He tells me that he and Wendy met when he was at Cambridge, that she was an art student and he married her when she was pregnant. He says that although she's been very supportive of his career, they have outgrown each other and he wants out. I reveal that sexually Sean and I no longer have a relationship.

We always stay together until the last possible minute; then I usually drop him off wherever he needs to go and continue home. If Sean is in London, it takes a supreme effort to gather myself psychologically so I look as if I have done nothing in particular. I hope it works, but I suspect my eyes give me away, as they inevitably mirror my true thoughts and feelings. It is so hard to give a believable account of my day, particularly as Sean tends to ask probing questions. All I can remember is being in bed with Peter and I find the effort it takes to wipe that from my mind quite exhausting.

It is difficult living a dual life, particularly when Sean and I are invited to the annual summer party given by Sir Donald Albery, a theatrical impresario. Peter is also invited and comes without Wendy, who is still in Majorca. Our affair remains a secret, so we have to be very careful not to arouse suspicion. Not that it seems to bother Peter. Whenever we see each other in public, which isn't very often as I don't go to many parties, he is always sociable and charming but you would never guess his feelings for me; it's only when I look in his eyes and see the intensity there that I can read how he really feels. I long to look back at him in the same way but force myself not to. I find the electricity between us is so powerful and obvious that I worry that others, and particularly Sean, might notice it too. He is such a jealous man.

When dinner is announced, I hang back in the first-floor drawing room, hoping that Peter will be able to have a quick word with me. Sean has left early to set up the lighting for a show, so I feel safe enough to steal a few moments with Peter. I sit on an antique chesterfield and almost immediately a gentleman comes up and asks if I mind if he joins me. It's Noël Coward. I say, 'Please do.' We start talking about how we are letting everyone get to the food first. I am secretly hoping that Peter will appear when suddenly there is an ominous creaking noise and the chesterfield collapses, leaving Noël and me on our bottoms with our legs in the air. We can't stop laughing and wonder aloud whose weight caused the chesterfield to break. We help each other to our feet and then go into the dining room to eat. I don't get my few private minutes with Peter.

It's not long after meeting Peter that he introduces me to Dudley, the most important man in his life. I instinctively understand that it is vital if my relationship with Peter is to grow that I get on with Dudley and that we become friends. Peter arranges for us to have a discreet meal in a restaurant, and Dudley arrives with Suzy Kendall, the beautiful actress he later marries in June 1968. They have recently moved to a Regency house round the corner from Peter. Peter introduces me to Dudley as if to say, 'This is what I've got. Isn't she fanciable? But she's mine and you can't have her.'

There is a huge difference in their height. Peter is over six foot, Dudley barely five. Although Dudley has a club foot, and is quite overweight, there is something very loveable and cuddly about him, and I like him immediately. Other ladies will soon start calling him 'Cuddly Dudley'. He is also very funny and has a naughty twinkle in his eye. They both crack jokes throughout the meal and it's obvious they are showing off. Dudley is hilarious and I can see what a marvellous foil he is for Peter. Each time Peter says something funny, Dudley comes straight back with an equally witty comment. I spend the whole evening in fits of laughter. I really like Suzy too. She is stunning to look at, with long blonde hair, huge eyes, sensual lips, a big smile and a great figure. She seems very gentle and looks at Dudley so lovingly. We talk a little together, but mainly we're the audience to Peter and Dudley's skilled performance.

I decide to tell my mother that I am having an affair with Peter. I have a strange relationship with her at the best of times, so her reaction is no surprise to me. She says, 'Ugh, Judy. He's married.' I knew she wouldn't approve but there is still an element of the little girl in me and I feel I have to obey her demand of telling her everything that I am doing.

After Peter and I have been together for about two months, I realise I have missed my period and start to feel sick and lethargic. Peter and I have played Russian roulette with contraception. I thought about going on the pill, but it has only just become available and there are many rumours about the risks involved, so I decided not to use it. I go to my doctor, who examines me and confirms I am expecting a baby. I feel shattered. I have already aborted a baby conceived with Sean because he didn't want it. I long to keep Peter's, but it has happened so early in our relationship. Luckily Sean is away. I phone Peter and tell him the news.

Peter waits until it is dark, to minimise the risk of being spotted by a photographer, then comes round to Cheyne Row. I know that because of his old-fashioned upbringing, Peter would do the right thing by me and the baby. We discuss it for hours, but I know what I must do. Single mothers are given the cold shoulder in the 1960s, and illegitimate children are shunned. Peter married Wendy when she was pregnant and I don't want to put him in the same position. I find it traumatic even to think about having another abortion, but I have been brought up to put on a good front and pull down my emotional curtains in any difficult situation and I know that whatever happens I can't fall to pieces. Instead I must put on my make-up, go out and face the world. I am also affected by the mood of the times. Mid-1960s women are supposed to be emancipated, take their own decisions, be responsible for themselves and not expect a man to do things for them.

Almost despite myself I decide to do the independent thing and show Peter I am not going to corner him. Soon after, I tell him I have arranged an abortion. He is quite passive about it all. He lets me take control, and goes along with what he thinks are my wishes. He also tells me we will have a baby together one day. I feel I have to be brave and take myself off to have my abortion as quickly as possible to show I can be self-reliant.

It is something I grow to regret, as I wonder later if Peter might have let me have the baby. If I had, I know Peter would have been besotted by him or her. The reality, though, is that we are both married, and my parents will be devastated if I have a baby out of wedlock. I have also been put under contract for seven years by 20th Century Fox and I have to be available to make films for them, especially as I am on the first rung of the ladder. That wouldn't be possible if I was pregnant or had just had a baby.

I arrange to have the abortion on a day when I am not filming. Peter pays but doesn't come with me. The following day I go back to work but feel emotionally and physically drained. I keep telling myself, I've got to get on with it and put what's happened behind me. It sort of works at the time. When I am feeling a little better, I am fitted with an IUD contraceptive coil.

Being extremely busy helps me recover. I start work on a thirty-minute film called *Les Bicyclettes de Belsize*, which is shot in and around Peter's favourite local restaurant, the Villa Bianca in Hampstead. It is based on the charming hit French film *Les Parapluies de Cherbourg* and is about a young man, played by Anthony May, who falls in love with a fashion model – that's me. There's no dialogue. Instead I mime to a soundtrack. The title song of the film becomes a hit for Mireille Mathieu and Engelbert Humperdinck. There are posters of me all over Belsize Park, and later it wins the award for 'Best Short Film' at the Venice Film Festival.

After we have been together for about a year, Peter tells me he wants me to leave Sean and says he will leave Wendy. I want to be with Peter and love him dearly, but am terrified of dealing with Sean. I keep going over it in my mind and finally decide that the best time to tell him I am leaving is after I get back from America, where I am promoting *The Touchables*, but I know it won't be easy.

2

Living with a Genius

Peter's star is in the ascendant. He is inundated with offers of work and mixing with lots of glamorous people. Everyone wants to meet him, especially women. I'm not surprised. He looks so lean and sexy. Peter is keen to expand his repertoire and made his film debut in 1966, a year before we met, starring with Dudley in *The Wrong Box*, in which they played two cousins out to grab an inheritance. It's a hilarious black comedy directed by Bryan Forbes and based on the novel by Robert Louis Stevenson. Many of the best comedy actors at the time were also in the film, including Michael Caine, Tony Hancock, John Mills, Ralph Richardson and Peter Sellers.

The critics never think he is at his best in a film and much prefer his television work, like *Not Only ..., But Also*, but soon after we meet he appears in another film, playing a foppish British agent called Prentiss in *A Dandy in Aspic*. This is a Cold War thriller based on a novel of the same name by Derek Marlowe. Laurence Harvey stars as a double agent with the task of hunting down and killing his alter ego. Tom Courtenay is a cynical British agent, and Mia Farrow plays a London-based photographer who has an affair with Harvey.

Good things are happening to me too. I am booked to fly off with my co-stars in *The Touchables* in October 1968 to open the Twelfth San Francisco International Film Festival.

The premiere of the film is scheduled to close the festival on 2 November. The four of us will then go on a promotional tour of America. I'm particularly excited as I hear Disney is interested in me, which could mean my career might take off in the States.

The timing is particularly apt. Although I am very much in love with Peter and don't want to leave him, I feel under enormous pressure. He wants me to be with him all the time, while Sean doesn't know I am about to end our marriage. It's a welcome relief to put all these life-changing decisions behind me and fly off to do something new and different. Just before I leave, Peter tells me he doesn't want me to go and fears he will lose me. I tell him not to worry.

Ester, Kathy, Marilyn and I turn up at Heathrow Airport specially dressed for the occasion in different-coloured hot pants. Mine are black, trimmed with gold and extremely short. I wear them with long black boots, a black waistcoat and a silk shirt. We are caught in a maelstrom of press attention. It's intoxicating, particularly as we are being promoted as 'four English swinging chicks'. We are rather like the 1960s version of the Spice Girls, except we don't try to sing.

Our first stop is San Francisco and we are invited on to several chat shows. The first is *The Tonight Show Starring Johnny Carson*. He says to us, 'Well, girls, are you the epitome of swinging London?' and we cry in unison, 'Yes!' I'm not entirely sure what swinging London is supposed to be, but I do know that young people and especially girls like me feel that the world is opening up for us in a way it never has before.

All four of us are involved in romances. Ester is having a relationship with Marlon Brando, Kathy is going out with Harry Nilsson, who wrote the song 'Everybody's Talkin' At Me', and Marilyn is seeing Christopher Blackwell of Island

Records. Christopher has recently divorced and has an eye for a pretty girl. We become friends and I later introduce him to Peter, who eventually goes on to record the first *Derek and Clive* album with him.

On another chat show we meet Timothy Leary, a psychology lecturer and LSD guru for the hippy generation. His catchphrase is 'Turn on, tune in, drop out', and as soon as he meets us, he tries to get us to smoke dope and try LSD. None of us takes him up on his offer. We couldn't even if we wanted to. We are being very closely chaperoned by 20th Century Fox and have male guards with us all the time to make sure no one harms us and that we don't get up to mischief.

After San Francisco we move on to Los Angeles, Detroit and New York. I have arranged with Peter that he will not phone during the tour but we will speak once it's over. Despite the excitement I miss him dreadfully.

The tour is amazing, but just before we are due to return home, I suddenly get cold feet about everything. I don't know if I have the courage to leave Sean. I worry if it will work out with Peter. I don't know how I will cope with the divorce proceedings and wonder whether I will continue to be able to earn a living. I'm also concerned about what will happen between Peter and Wendy. It all seems so overwhelming that I decide to remain in New York for another week and stay at a friend's flat.

Once Peter knows I am no longer travelling but staying in one place, he keeps ringing me, sometimes as often as five times a day, asking why I'm not coming back. I try to explain I need space to sort out my life and come to terms with what is happening, but with each day I stay away, he becomes more frantic.

I decide to buy a house when I return to England with the

money I've earned from *The Touchables* to give myself some stability. The decision is a turning point for me and makes me feel more independent and better able to tackle everything that is going on in my life. So although I fly back in November 1968 full of trepidation about leaving Sean, I feel more in control. While I try to find somewhere to buy, I arrange to rent a flat in Roland Gardens that is owned by Annabel Davis-Goff, the continuity girl on *The Touchables*, who is off to work abroad. Annabel later marries Mike Nichols, who directed Dustin Hoffman's first major film, *The Graduate*.

Then over a couple of weeks I transfer my clothes and some possessions to Annabel's flat, which is not far from Cheyne Row. I pile everything into my Camara, an American sports car that has replaced my E-type, timing each trip for when Sean is in his studio. I still haven't told Sean and spend my time working out what I am going to say to him. I know I need to be clear-headed, speak concisely and not say too much. A misplaced word could trigger enormous anger and possibly violence.

I face it one day and tell him that our marriage isn't working, that I am renting Annabel's flat and am moving out because I need to be on my own for a bit. I can't tell Sean about Peter because I fear he might attack me. He is desperate for me not to go, tells me how much he loves me, begs for a second chance and says he will never hurt me again. It's very hard to tell someone that you're leaving when they're being nice to you. I haven't expected Sean to be gentle and break down in tears, but I know deep down that I am doing the right thing. Sean knows Annabel and agrees to look after the cats until I am settled, as the flat doesn't have a garden. Unfortunately almost as soon as I have gone, my Siamese cat, Ophelia, climbs up the chimney, gets stuck, and when she tries to get down, falls and breaks her leg. Luckily the cleaning lady is there and takes her to the vet.

Peter phones me continually to ask if I have told Sean about him and says he wants me with him straight away. Although we speak on the phone, I don't feel I can see him or have a sexual relationship until I have sorted myself out.

I organise my final move out of the marital home while Sean is at work, but when he discovers I have gone, he comes round to Annabel's ground-floor flat, thumps on the door and screams through the letterbox that he will kill me if I don't go back to him. While he's shouting, windows in the surrounding houses open and people peep round their net curtains to see where the noise is coming from. Sean is a proud and possessive man, and is devastated that our marriage is over. It is the start of a pattern of destructive behaviour that becomes a nightmare. Some nights Sean comes round to Roland Gardens and dismantles my car so I can't drive it. I only discover what he's done when I leave home and try to use the car. I'm going to auditions and it's extremely awkward to find at the last minute that I don't have any transport. On other nights he fiddles with the wires under the bonnet and drives it away. When I wake up and discover the car's not outside the flat, it means Sean has taken it back with him to Cheyne Row. So when I have an audition to go to, I get up especially early, check if I have a car, and if not, go round to Cheyne Row and drive it back. It becomes a ludicrous and exhausting game, and many nights Sean stands outside banging on the door until 4 a.m.

In addition, Peter keeps wanting to come and stay, but I can't risk him being there if Sean comes round, as he will only shriek and bang on the door even louder. I tell Peter he must be patient and wait. The stress is getting to me. I stop eating and lose a lot of weight, but I don't think Peter will mind as he likes me thin. It also improves my chances when I audition for film work and commercials. To help myself feel better, I put my efforts into searching for somewhere to buy. One day Peter tells me he wants to spend Christmas 1968 in Majorca with Wendy and his daughters, Lucy and Daisy, who are four and three. I tell him I understand. When he returns in the new year he says he's told Wendy that he loves me and wants to be with me. I am angry beyond measure that he has taken this step without discussing it with me first. His impulsive behaviour has put me in a very difficult situation at a time when I am still recovering from my separation from Sean. The break-up has been overwhelmingly tough and I don't feel ready to cope with the fallout of Peter's relationship with Wendy or the effect his actions will inevitably have on his children.

Life gradually becomes calmer and in the late spring I find exactly the home I am looking for – 2 Ruston Mews, a two-up, two-down Victorian house, off Ladbroke Grove. It is in the rough end of Notting Hill but still trendy, and I discover the feminist writer Germaine Greer lives just down the mews. I tell Peter about the property and he wants to come to see it with me. I don't think it will be his cup of tea because his home in Church Row is so spacious and beautiful, whereas Ruston Mews is a small, simple house and needs a coat of paint and a new kitchen. Fortunately, though, he loves it and I'm thrilled. I purchase it in June 1969 for £12,000 through the trendy 1960s estate agent Roy Brooks and move in.

In the late 1960s it's still unusual for a woman as young as me to buy her own property. I decide to invite Sean to see it too, to try to move our relationship on to a more even keel, so we can be normal and friendly. By doing so I also hope to have his goodwill when we go through our divorce. He doesn't say much but points out that the lid to the drains is actually in the house and seems to delight in telling me that it could overflow at any minute. I don't take any notice.

At about the same time my parents decide to sell their homes in London and in the countryside and move to Jersey. My father is unwell and my mother says it is the only place they want to retire to. She buys a large, elegant house surrounded by beautiful gardens and overlooking a bay. I have taken it for granted that they will always be near me so I can call round at any time, so it is a great shock. I feel I now have to be totally responsible for myself. I understand I can fly over to Jersey when I'm not working, but it's not the same as just popping in to see them.

Shortly after I have moved a letter arrives at my house addressed to Peter. I ring him at home to tell him. He asks me to open it and stays on the phone. It is from a solicitor representing a Swedish au pair who worked for Peter and Wendy. It announces that Peter had an affair with her, that she is now pregnant and will be taking him to court. Wendy then comes on the line. It's strange that she wants to talk to me. She tells me she already knows about the affair with the au pair but can't keep her husband under control. She then puts the phone down. Peter tells me that he did have an affair with the au pair but assures me that she isn't pregnant. He's right and we don't have to worry for long. The au pair isn't pregnant and there won't be a court case.

Initially I feel quite angry that he has had a relationship with her, but I tell myself it's happening at the end of his marriage to Wendy and is part of the life he is trying to leave behind. I also accept his explanation that it was a casual fling and meant nothing. In any case I hate confrontation and guess that such incidents go with the territory of being with Peter. I know I have two choices: walk out and slam the door on our amazing relationship or cope with all that being with Peter brings, even if at times it seems too much. The truth is, I love him passionately and completely, so in practice I have no choice. In a way I understand how the au pair situation has happened. It must be very tempting for him to be left in the house with a pretty au pair while Wendy is in Majorca. As he is such an attractive and successful man, these girls are also bound to fall under his spell. I suspect she isn't the first and nor will she be the last.

Peter keeps pushing to move in with me, but I tell him he must live on his own for a few weeks first to be sure of what he is doing and to prove he is really serious about me. One day he turns up at my door with a present of a record player and speakers. He knows I love listening to music and it is very generous of him.

Peter decides to stay at Church Row when Wendy is in Majorca, and rents a serviced flat in central London when she is in Hampstead. He is absolutely miserable in the flat and rings me every night to tell me he is lying on a bed on his own, that he doesn't understand what he is doing there and feels so lonely that he needs me to go round and see him. I do of course. I don't have sex with him – I'm not ready for that again yet – but I lie on the bed beside him and we hug. He's not someone who wants to be on his own but he's even more susceptible to loneliness than I imagined.

A few days later he rings me sounding much brighter and asks if it's OK for him to take Joanna Shimkus out to dinner and to see a film. She is a very beautiful Canadian actress, who later marries the actor Sidney Poitier. I immediately feel threatened and for a short while again think I've made a mistake and should pull up the drawbridge on our relationship, but despite myself I tell him it's fine. He is a stunningly attractive TV and film star at the height of his career and beautiful women are bound to want to meet him, not least because he makes them laugh. It's also in his nature to want to be seen out and about with a glamorous female. I tell myself it doesn't necessarily mean he is linked with them emotionally or romantically.

I stay at home, and halfway through the evening he rings again. In those days audiences watched two films in one sitting, and Peter tells me he first watched *Twisted Nerve*, a Roy Boulting horror film with Hywel Bennett, Hayley Mills and Billie Whitelaw, and that the other film was *Les Bicyclettes de Belsize*, the romantic short film that I recently made. Peter says that he can't stop thinking about me, that he wants to come round and be with me, but he must be polite and take Joanna out to dinner first and will be as quick as he can. He is true to his word.

Although I still worry about us living together, about six weeks after I moved in, I tell him he can join me. Once he is with me day after day, all the stresses and strains we have been under totally drop away. It's usually quite difficult adapting yourself to somebody new, but with Peter it seems we are two halves coming together. If I feel like sleeping, he feels like sleeping. If I feel like going out, he does too. He even loves my cats and, from the moment he meets them, treats them as individuals and talks to them.

Peter is a genius, but no one can be a genius all the time and I can tell he feels very peaceful with me. We have the same sense of humour and laugh at the same things. We can look at something that isn't particularly funny in itself and both spontaneously burst out laughing – without either of us saying a word.

He isn't the least difficult over food. I ask him what he wants to eat, he tells me quite precisely, and either he goes out to buy it or I do. He enjoys trotting off and getting to know the locality and finding shops he likes. His tastes in food are quite simple. He is keen on meat and particularly steak or lamb cutlets, which he has with salad and a baked potato. If we are at home during the evening, Peter has about half a bottle of champagne with our meal and perhaps a little wine. The only time he comes back a little worse for wear is when he spends a gossipy evening with Frankie Howerd, whose career has been resurrected since he appeared at Peter's the Establishment, a club founded in 1961 by Peter and his Cambridge pall Nick Luard as a venue for the new wave of comedians and satirists. Peter and Nick also have a controlling stake in the satirical magazine *Private Eye*, so he is kept particularly busy by his various work interests.

I don't have a washing machine and Peter handles his own smalls. As soon as he takes something off, it goes straight into the bath to be washed. I can hardly believe he is happy to do these domestic things for himself. The one thing he is bad at is opening his mail. He often leaves it unopened in piles around the room.

Peter is also so easy to live with because there is a childlike quality to him, just as there is to me. We are a couple of kids having a good time and spend endless hours together. Sometimes we listen to music. Peter is quite sentimental and particularly loves the Beach Boys, Johnny Cash and Elvis Presley. Although he's not that keen on jazz, he is quietly respectful of Dudley's passion for it. He knows Dudley is in his element when he is playing the piano and often makes comments about him 'tinkling on the ivories again'.

I find Peter wonderfully funny and so life-enhancing. He can tell instantly if I am stressed or anxious and immediately change my mood by turning whatever is worrying me into something humorous. Shortly after he moves in, some major building work starts on a patch of land opposite our house.

It means there will be an awful lot of noise and will be very disruptive. Peter composes a letter to the builder pointing out that under the ancient Cobblestones Act of 1892 – which he invents – builders are not allowed to build houses on this particular site because the River Lad runs underneath where they are working. He dictates it to me and we laugh so much we immediately feel better. A few days later the builder writes back saying that we have missed a section of the act that gives them special permission to build. We start to correspond with each other and soon afterwards meet up and find we get on really well. As a result we feel better about the noise and the builder tries to keep it to a minimum.

Peter is quite idiosyncratic in his choice of clothes. At one point he fancies an army jacket and we spend hours searching through army surplus shops. At another he decides he wants to wear lots of cheap jewellery, often in the shape of dogs and roses, which he pins on to his jacket lapel. He has two favourite types of footwear: one is expensive brown crocodile shoes, which he replaces with an identical pair as soon as they wear out; the other is bright red trainers, which he often wears with suits.

There is such pressure on him to perform when he is with other people, and when he does, he works himself up to a level that is difficult to come down from and makes him stressed, but he is very different at home with me. He is relieved to be natural and not to have to put on a show. He is invited to loads of parties, but even though he is gregarious, we don't accept many invitations. There are exceptions of course. One day he is at a recording studio and meets the girls in the dance group Pan's People. At the end of the day he goes back to one of their flats. He rings me and from the background noise it's obvious that there is a party going on. He says he loves me and will be back in the morning. I let him get on with it because realistically there is not a lot I can do.

When he is at home, he likes to be quiet and thoughtful and reads a lot. He buys every newspaper each day and a stack of magazines, including *Newsweek*, the *Economist* and the *Spectator*, all of which he goes through very carefully. When he's not reading papers, he has his head in a book, particularly biographies and books on politics or history. Sometimes in the afternoon he lies on the sofa with his feet up, with the cats on top of him, surrounded by newspapers and reading a book, or snoozing. If neither of us is working, we often curl up together and go to sleep. These are precious times.

Our favourite way to spend an evening is to go to bed early and for Peter to read to me. I always wear a T-shirt and bed socks because I like to feel cosy if I am in for a long night's reading. Peter wears nothing. He reads me beautiful poetry and wonderful whimsical stories he has written and a biography of the Marx brothers, which we laugh at for hours.

Peter has a season ticket and a regular date at White Hart Lane to watch Tottenham Hotspur play. He is very emotional about Spurs and gets quite depressed if they lose. He watches matches with Dr Sidney Gottlieb, who lives just round the corner. He also occasionally plays golf with Sidney's son, Peter. Sidney specialises in alcohol and drug addiction. He is only five foot five, but very attractive and a great character. He has a large show-business clientele and is the official doctor to Ronnie Scott's nightclub. Peter met him at a party and Sidney has since become like a father to him.

Overall it is an idyllic time for both Peter and me. We are completely compatible and at ease with each other. He needs a total emotional experience when we make love. He wants to hold me tight and for us to feel very close. In turn I understand how important it is for him to be fully relaxed before he can loosen up. He needs the right ambience and to laugh a lot. He spends hours tickling my back. Sometimes when he is stroking my hair, the cats jump on to the bed to join us.

We are getting over the stage of just fancying each other and have moved to feeling so comfortable together that we want each other completely. I even cut his nails and sometimes his hair. In fact our only problem is that the house is too small for all our books, so we have to keep lots of them in packing cases.

I tell Peter that my parents are rather eccentric and in July 1969 take him to Claremont Court in Jersey to meet them. I mention my mother will lay on a superb welcome dinner served by the cook and will ply him with drink. She has had a heated swimming pool, lined with mosaic, installed just outside the drawing-room window, and I tell him she will turn all the lights on in the garden after dark, then ask him if he would like a swim. She will be very flirtatious, but sometime after this she will find a reason for an argument and, when it's really late, demand he leaves.

As I predicted, our visit plays itself out to the letter. My parents' house is medieval and beautiful with engraved roses on the ceilings and wood panelling. The dining room has pale green striped Regency wallpaper and a Georgian oval table and matching chairs. The table is exquisitely laid for dinner, as I knew it would be, with lots of silver and Venetian wine glasses. The wine itself is in cut-glass decanters on a beautiful antique side table. After dinner, at about 11 p.m., when my father is squiffy with drink and reciting French poetry, my mother asks me to come to the kitchen, where she tells me that Peter is an alcoholic. I ignore her comment and instead tell her to stop plying him with brandy. She then goes back to the drawing room and tells Peter to his face that he is a drunk. This ends in a blazing row between me, my mother and Peter. At one point she is so unpleasant and provocative that Peter taps her on the face to get her to stop. It gives her the excuse she's been looking for and she yells at him to leave the house. She enjoys being manipulative and making people lose their temper when she wants a feeling of power. I tell Peter not to pay any attention and we go upstairs to our bedroom.

He undresses completely and gets into bed. He then lights a cigarette and watches me take off my make-up as I sit at the dressing table. Suddenly my mother comes in. She has also had a lot to drink, but is acting as if nothing has happened, and certainly no furious argument. She sits on the bed as though she knows Peter intimately, calls him 'darling' and starts flirting outrageously.

Astonishingly Peter seems to be enjoying the spectacle, but it is absolutely not the way for a mother to behave when a man who is a guest in your house and is involved with your daughter is lying naked in bed and I am furious. She then starts telling him what he should and shouldn't be doing with his life, including what she thinks of him being married to Wendy and living with me. 'Darling,' she drawls, 'are you still married? And if so, what are you going to do about your wife? Are you getting a divorce?'

This is not the sort of discussion to be had so late at night and I can tell she has deliberately started trying to needle him again. I know that if Peter was dressed he would get out of bed and have a full-scale argument with her, but he can't do much with no clothes on. He's her captive audience, quite drunk after all the wine and brandy she has pressed on him and more concerned about getting his cigarette into his mouth than answering her probing questions. The problem is, once my mother gets going she can continue arguing for hours, hurling question after question without waiting for a single reply. I find it a form of torture. I can tell she is settling in for the night, and after about twenty minutes I decide I've had enough and escort her to her bedroom.

I am frightened that Peter won't want to continue being with me after such an experience, but he is intrigued and seems to take on board very quickly just how much I need him at a very deep level to help me cope with the mix of pain and humour that is part of dealing with my family. Peter perfectly understands all the nuances of what's going on. Spending time with my family is a bit like being in a Pinter play, especially when my grandmother, who trained as an opera singer, and who has moved to Jersey with my parents, and thankfully gets on well with Peter, follows her habit of bursting into song in the middle of a meal when my parents are arguing. Her favourite is the hymn 'O God, Our Help in Ages Past'. I feel much relieved when we get home and back into our own routine.

Peter leaves notes for me all over the house, particularly on the bed or sofa, saying he loves me or he has just popped out to do something. He always signs them with funny names, like Lord Whirleypokes or Rook the Greek. One day in late 1969 when I come back from an audition I find he has drawn a huge circle on the wall and inside has written in letters two feet high, 'Marry me.' I write underneath, 'Yes.' I am completely over the moon. I cannot imagine loving anyone more and know I want to spend the rest of my life with him.

From then on he continually asks me when my divorce is coming through, but Sean, it seems, has gone to Ireland and doesn't answer any of my solicitor's letters. He has also stopped paying the rent on Cheyne Row. Consequently the arrears build up until the bailiffs break in and take most of our furniture. When I discover what has happened, I try to buy some of it back.

Problems with Sean aside, I am the happiest I have ever been. I feel so close to Peter that there seem to be no barriers between us, which is a wonderful feeling. It will be a while before my life starts to crash in on me, and before that happens, I take on a new and exciting role.

3

Dudley, Peter and Me

One afternoon soon after Peter and I start living together, Wendy turns up unexpectedly at Ruston Mews. She is with the children. We invite her in but she refuses. Instead she starts shouting, saying Daisy has asthma because of Peter's relationship with me. She goes on and on until suddenly she grabs the children's hands and goes back into the taxi that has been waiting for her. Peter stands at the door for a while, and when he comes in, he tells me he feels crucified by what she is doing to the children. Shortly afterwards he reveals he wants us to move. He thinks Ruston Mews is too small for us to live in long term. It is also my house, and he wants us to live together in a house he owns.

A few days later he goes off to see a property and comes home looking very pleased with himself. He has found an idyllic cottage near Hampstead Heath, opposite Highgate Ponds. 'I can't believe my luck,' he says. 'I saw it advertised and I was the first to call. The owner has told me he doesn't like strangers tramping over his house and would like to sell it to me.'

He takes me to see it and I fall in love with it too. Kenwood Cottage is an idyllic sixteenth-century chocolate-box cottage that was originally an old farmhouse. It has three double bedrooms, two bathrooms, three reception rooms, a garage and a very pretty garden. The kitchen has wonderful old wooden beams, and there are cow hooks in the garage where the animals were once tethered. Peter does the deal, which is quite complicated because the family home in Church Row will have to be sold and somewhere has to be found for Wendy and the children. He discusses it with Wendy, who declares she doesn't want to leave Church Row. Peter buys Kenwood Cottage anyway and we decide I'll keep Ruston Mews and at some point perhaps rent it to friends.

Peter discovers an interest in DIY and starts chipping away at the plaster in a couple of rooms and discovers a mass of beautiful oak beams, which we varnish. He also knocks down a wall. 'I never thought I'd become an owner of a Black and Decker,' he jokes. We move the kitchen to the back of the cottage, turn what was the kitchen into a dining area and paint the walls cream. We move in with just a bed, a cooker and a fridge, but gradually we cover the stripped floorboards with rugs and some of Peter's antique furniture. Dudley gives Peter a table-tennis table, which we put up in the garage.

During our first few weeks at the cottage Peter reads me books by the humorist S. J. Perelman when we go to bed and doesn't sleep unless he is wrapped tightly around me. We settle in very quickly, which is important as Peter has a lot to do. He is working with Dudley on the third series of *Not Only ... But Also*, this time for the BBC. The original series was dreamt up by the BBC as a vehicle for Dudley when the *Beyond the Fringe* four – Peter, Dudley, Alan Bennett and Jonathan Miller – returned from New York in 1964. Dudley was the 'Not Only' part of the series and the 'But Also' was intended to be filled by a different personality each week. Dudley asked Peter to make the pilot. The BBC promptly commissioned seven episodes and it was decided that Peter would stay in the show permanently. The first series was broadcast in January 1965. It was ground-breaking and ingenious comedy, with Peter and Dudley collapsing into giggles almost as much as their audience. It introduced the world to Pete and Dud in a series of routines that became known as the 'Dagenham dialogues'. Pete and Dud are two know-all characters who dress in cloth caps and crumpled raincoats and discuss all manner of subjects. Pete turns banality into an art form, while Dud is credulous and dim-witted. Their characters have become national icons and their sign- off song 'Goodbye-ee' entered the charts in 1965 and has become a much-loved signature tune.

The second series was made a year later. Both men are hoping the one they are now working on, the third, will be as good as if not better than the previous two and the specials they made for ITV. Peter is also trying to complete a book of children's stories and verses and the synopsis for a film idea.

Peter and Dudley work together every weekday. Dudley is fanatical about punctuality, so Peter makes sure he is always ready for him. He gets up early, showers and has black coffee for breakfast. I have tea and fruit. He then sits ruminating while waiting for Dudley to arrive. He has a low table in front of him on which he places a notebook, where he scribbles ideas, and a tape recorder, to record their conversations. He may seem laidback and relaxed as he drinks his coffee and smokes, but I know that he is actually very alert. Dudley always looks immaculate and wears the same outfit every day – jeans, a black crew-neck sweater and his specially made boots – unlike Peter, who tends to put on the nearest thing to hand when he gets up, which is usually jeans and a T-shirt.

Dudley is also very finicky about what he eats and brings with him all sorts of delicacies, like seaweed biscuits and dandelion tea. He unpacks everything ceremoniously from a bag and lays it out on a tray so that it's all ready for him. He is obsessed about his figure, is trying to lose weight and prefers to eat small amounts at frequent intervals. Peter, on the other hand, is happy gulping down gallons of black coffee and chain-smoking. The dangers of passive smoking are not yet known, so Dudley, who doesn't smoke, makes no complaints. I open the windows when the room gets too smoky.

It's obvious that Peter loves Dudley, but not in a homosexual way. His love is that of a brother. I find Dudley very attractive too. You'd have to be from another planet not to. He is good-looking, naughty and flirtatious, and knows how to use his charm. Peter often tells me how devious he can be, so I am also a little wary.

The buzz between them as they work is highly charged and my role is to be their audience of one. When they take on a character and start a sketch, they watch me intently to gauge my reaction to whatever they say. I quickly learn that I can't be as free with my responses as I might like. They want me to laugh at what they are saying, but not loudly enough to disturb them. The length of time I laugh is important too. If it's too brief, they assume what they've said isn't funny, and if it goes on too long, I break their train of thought. They are both hilarious and sometimes I can't manage it and end up weak with laughter. I think of Peter as an alpha male and Dudley as a court jester.

Peter is particularly funny as Sir Arthur Streeb-Greebling and I remember watching one exchange in which Dudley asks him questions about his wife. Sir Arthur replies, 'She blew into the sitting room with a bit of shrapnel and became embedded in the sofa and one thing led to her mother and we were married within the hour.'

The sketch that really has me shaking with laughter is the

one in which both Dud and Pete are besieged by stunning film stars like Jane Russell and Greta Garbo who are after their bodies. Pete describes how he's gone to bed and is just about to drop off when he hears a tap, tap, tap on the window and sees Greta Garbo, 'stark naked' apart from a see-through nightie and 'of course' her signature dark glasses, clinging on to the windowsill and desperate to be with him. He tells Dud, 'I say, "Get out of it, bloody Greta Garbo." She wouldn't go, so I had to smash her down with a broomstick.'

I feel very lucky that I am in the unique position of seeing how they work and create such hilarious comedy together. They know each other so intimately it is closer than a marriage and they don't need to talk to understand what each other is feeling. Dudley can walk into a room backwards and Peter will still know what he's thinking. It is Peter's business to read Dudley like a book and vice versa, because that's how they perform best together.

Peter is brilliant at encouraging Dudley to take on a character. If things are going a little slowly, he often asks him about his mother. Dudley has inherited being pernickety from her. A sketch might begin with Dudley imitating his mother, laced with maternal innuendo. It's a voice he is very comfortable with and one that always makes Peter smile. Peter then seamlessly slips into the role of the son, encouraging Dudley and feeding him lines. Likewise when Peter is trying out a character, Dudley seems to know exactly when to tuck in behind Peter with a reply and feed him.

A power play always starts between them after just a few sentences. One short encounter I remember begins with Dudley, as his mother, saying, 'Well, dear, now you sit down and be comfortable. Don't you worry about me – my legs aren't as bad as they used to be.'

Peter, as the son, replies, 'Oh, Mother, I have been worried about you. I spoke to Dr Growack about you and he's very worried about your chest.'

Dudley quips back, 'There's no need to worry about me, dear. I'm getting on very well without you.'

It is just one example of how in their sketches, as in their lives, neither of them wants the other to get the upper hand. Once the sketch begins, Peter starts the tape recorder. He will also raise his voice and let his character become more aggressive, as he likes to change the tone of the sketch and play around with it, almost challenging Dudley to keep up.

Sometimes Peter puts the mother, played by Dudley, down or gets angry with her, saying, 'Now, Mother, I told you not to do that.' Dudley will then try to take the lead back. Depending on how the sketch develops, he'll do whatever he can to get ahead of Peter, be funnier than him or just sharpen him up.

They both find each other and themselves uproariously funny, and Peter leaves the tape on for hours. Equally they soon realise if a sketch isn't working, particularly when Peter rambles on a bit. Peter and I both love it when Dudley goes into his old-woman routine, because it means he is in a good mood and it softens the atmosphere. If he's in a bad mood, uptight and tight-mouthed, Peter describes his eyes as being 'like a hen's arse'. It's then harder for Peter to get warmed up and he has to rootle around to get Dudley to laugh. Once they've finished a sketch, they rarely edit it straight away. They prefer to wait until they are in front of a live audience, so they can see when the laughs are coming and edit as they go along.

I can sit for hours with them – apart from quietly slipping out of the room to make them coffee or tea – and whenever they do anything particularly funny, both their heads swivel round to look at me as if to say, 'Aren't we clever?' They see

I'm laughing, but I also give them the thumbs-up, knowing I mustn't speak and break the momentum. It's a unique privilege to watch two such brilliant people at work, and I absolutely love it.

When they want a break, they play table tennis. Sometimes I play as a twosome against one of them, but whoever I play against always does his best to ace me off the table. Although I am quite a good player, I don't stand a chance. There is no 'Let's be nice to her because she's a woman.' Instead it's always 'Let's thrash her'! They are never interested in having an enjoyable game. It's purely how quickly they can beat each other, and a game often consists purely of aces. When Dudley wins, Peter immediately announces the whole thing is a fraud and demands a rematch. He repeats his allegation until he wins.

There are, however, a couple of problems, which I don't at the time see as being particularly significant. One is that Peter has a cruel streak. I don't think he is purposely cruel, but it is inherent in him and he can be very sharp. For example, he keeps calling Dudley 'a walking example of Preparation H', which is a haemorrhoid cream. Peter has a supreme ability to force you to laugh at something that is basically rather nasty. Dudley realises it is a put-down, but because it comes from Peter, he finds it funny. He in turn calls Peter 'a long streak of piss'. Trading insults is a part of their relationship and they're not taken seriously.

The other problem is Peter's increasing love of gambling on the horses. First thing each morning he goes out to buy a copy of the *Sporting Life*, then rings up Ladbrokes with bets. I don't know what he puts on a horse – he never talks about how much he wins or loses, and I never ask because I think it is his business – but he bets so often it must add up to a considerable sum.

He also insists on keeping the television on in the background while he and Dudley work. When the race starts, he leaps up and shouts at a horse to encourage it to win, then cheers or shrieks in dismay according to whether it has won or lost. He also stops working to look through the *Sporting Life* and put on additional bets. Dudley gets tetchy and frustrated, as the racing delays them from finishing their sketches. He keeps saying to Peter, 'Turn the bloody thing off,' but Peter ignores him. To start with, I think this rather bizarre scene is just a bit of fun. I assume Peter will eventually realise that Dudley is genuinely fed up and stop, but he doesn't. I feel frustrated on Dudley's behalf and gradually grasp that it is a serious problem and something Peter does compulsively. It doesn't help that Joyce, our cleaning lady, who is a character, comes in, stands behind Peter and, waving her feather duster, shouts, 'Go on, go on, Mr Cook – you put your money on that one.'

I also notice that Peter's drinking is on the increase, but I don't worry about it. Dudley leaves in the late afternoon and sometimes Peter starts to drink the moment he goes and carries on through the evening. When I mention it to him, he replies that drinking is the best way for him to unwind and stop thinking about work. Occasionally I say to Peter, 'Hang on, do you realise you had a whole bottle of wine and then fell asleep?' but Peter doesn't respond, so that's the end of it. I tell myself he can take his drink because he is young and healthy. I then cook something for us to eat and everything seems to return to normal.

They are both under pressure. As well as writing what will be the third, and last, *Not Only ... But Also*, they need to prepare for touring Australia with *Behind the Fridge*. They choose the name for the show because an Italian restaurateur greeted them when they were in *Beyond the Fringe* with the words 'Ah, zee men from be'ind zee freege.'

Sometimes in the afternoon, when Peter and Dudley don't need me as an audience, I go to Ruston Mews for a few hours to tidy up or do some decorating. It is empty at the moment and I find working there rather therapeutic.

The winter is so cold that Peter buys me a combat coat. It's ridiculously big but I wear it everywhere. He gives me other thoughtful presents from time to time too, including a beautiful Victorian etching of a gentleman, who looks remarkably like Peter, reclining on a sofa and looking longingly at a lady.

Peter is desperately keen to have as much contact as possible with his daughters. He adores them, is very proud of them and is anxious about the effect his separation from Wendy will have on them. It is therefore particularly important when they are in London for him to go round to Church Row in the late afternoon to help bathe them, read them a story and put them to bed. Unfortunately he often comes back very stressed because he's seen and heard things that he's not happy about. It also hurts him deeply that the two girls spend so much time in Majorca. He tells Wendy he wants them to go to school in the UK and after consulting a lawyer to see if she could fight his demands, she reluctantly agrees to live in London.

His access to the children gradually becomes a bone of contention between himself and Wendy, and the conflict upsets him enormously. On one occasion Wendy isn't at home when he arrives to see the children, so he lets himself in with his key. He's barely said hello to them and the nanny when there is a knock on the door and two policemen arrive. I never find out for certain who called the police but I know that Wendy is convinced Peter wants to get custody of the girls. The policemen ask him what he is doing and if he is intending to abduct the children. He tells them he is not and they eventually go away. Peter is so angry and upset he decides in future to make all arrangements regarding the children through his solicitor. Even that doesn't work as sometimes, despite firm agreements on dates and times, the children are not there. One afternoon when he arrives for his pre-arranged visit and finds no one at home he loses his temper and breaks in through a bedroom window. Inevitably, the police turn up again.

Eventually, though, we work out a way of dealing with his visits. Each time Peter leaves to see his daughters I ring the police and tell them that Peter Cook, the father of Lucy and Daisy Cook, is coming to see his children at their home address in accordance with an arrangement that has been made through the solicitor and is not intending to abduct them. This works better, but it is still stressful.

At the time Wendy won't let the girls visit us at our home, but she does agree that I can come with Peter to see them. I feel very nervous about meeting her and the children properly for the first time, but it goes remarkably well. We sit in the kitchen and have tea together and try to look and act normally for the sake of Lucy and Daisy. Happily, I love them from the word go.

At one point I sense that Wendy and Peter want to talk in private, so I go upstairs to the children's playroom and ask them to show me their Wendy house. They are very well brought-up girls and, although they are only five and four, extremely well behaved. I think they are adorable and particularly special because they are Peter's. They are very easy to get on with too. Daisy in particular responds to me very positively, but I worry about her asthma. It's obviously inherited from Peter, but luckily something he has grown out of by the time we meet. Daisy is also like Peter in personality, whereas Lucy is more like her mother.

Peter wants his divorce to be as amicable as possible and, when he gives an interview, tells the newspaper reporter, 'I hope we will be one of the few couples of this or any century who will do this without bitterness.' Soon afterwards Wendy echoes his words by saying, 'Peter has said we must be civilised about this and I agree entirely. I don't regret the years together at all.'

One of the quickest ways to get a divorce at the time is for one partner to cite adultery. Although Wendy has admitted she has not been faithful to Peter, he asks me if I will agree to be named as the guilty party and I do. It is a foolish decision.

Peter tells Wendy, and because these things have to be done officially, she hires a private eye to follow us to prove that Peter is sleeping with me. Initially the detective gets it all wrong and takes pictures of me going in and out of our neighbour's house. He is Crispin Woodgate, a photographer. He is tall, thin and dark, and if you didn't know Peter, you could mistake Crispin for him. The private eye writes a report, which Peter and I see. It makes us laugh as he has it all so utterly wrong. It has to be thrown away and he has to start again. Peter and I agree to be at home one evening so he can photograph us coming into the house. We leave the curtains open so he can take more photographs a few hours later to show Peter is still there.

The decree nisi comes through shortly before the end of 1970 and is reported in all the papers. Judge Curtis-Raleigh cites me but exercises discretion over Wendy's admitted adultery. My parents are so upset that I have publicly been named as sleeping with a married man that I really regret my decision. They are respectable people who have been married for many years and it is shocking for them to see their daughter named in a divorce case. Although morals are looser and many young people barely think twice about having a sexual relationship, for my parents' generation, who lead very proper lives, such behaviour is scandalous. It had been Peter's idea to push the divorce through so he could marry me, but it makes me suffer.

4

Young Lives

Almost every young girl dreams about having a perfect relationship with someone special. In reality it happens to very few, but it did to me. I have never regretted being with Peter. We both found someone we loved so completely that we wanted to be together all the time. We could laugh together until our stomachs hurt and tears rolled down our cheeks. We enjoyed each other's company so much that curling up on the same armchair and watching television together was just as much fun as going out to a smart party, if not more.

I have spent an enormous amount of time thinking about what brought Peter and me together and why we felt as if we were two parts of a whole. One reason is that we were a Peter Pan couple, neither quite of the world of grown-ups nor of children. He admitted as much in one of the columns he wrote for the *Daily Mail* in 1977 called 'Peter Cook's Monday Morning Feeling': 'I attempted to never grow up but found that nature had a nasty way of intervening. Only years later did I discover that La Sexburga' – one of the affectionate names he calls me – 'had been following the same set of rules.'

We were born five years apart, Peter in November 1937, me in July 1942. We both grew up on the cusp of two very different societies, the old-fashioned, stiff upper lip of the 1950s, where you behaved yourself and acted with restraint, and the revolutionary freedom of the 1960s, where the order of the day was to let it all hang out.

Our backgrounds and personal circumstances were remarkably similar too, and mine helped me understand Peter at a profound level. We both had privileged upbringings, and both sets of parents were financially comfortable, although mine were wealthier than his. Our parents were also hard-working and cultured. They tried to do what they thought was best for their children, but although their intentions were good, the reality is that we were both deprived of much home contact.

Peter was born into a family who felt it was their overriding duty to work for the British Empire and spent most of their lives abroad. Family concerns came a poor second. When Peter's father, Alec, was young and single, he took up the post as a colonial district officer in Nigeria and was only allowed a four-month break in England every two years. It was during one of these breaks that he met Margaret Mayo, a lively, academically brilliant daughter of a solicitor from Eastbourne. She was a natural intellectual and created quite a reputation at the local St Winifred's School for Girls. She wanted to go to university, but her parents couldn't afford to send her. Instead, when she left school, she became a governess to a wealthy Jewish family in Prague for a short while.

Alec and Margaret married in June 1936 and she dutifully accompanied him back to Nigeria. It was considered a serious health risk to have a baby in Nigeria, so when Margaret was heavily pregnant, she returned to England alone to give birth. Peter was a bonny eight pounds twelve ounces and Margaret was instantly devoted to him. Alec had to stay in Nigeria until his leave was due, so he first saw baby Peter when he was three months old.

At the time it was felt that, particularly for health reasons, Nigeria was an unsuitable place to bring up children, so four months later Margaret was faced with the impossible and agonising choice of staying in England without her husband to be with Peter or leaving Peter behind to be with her husband. Margaret's sense of duty prevailed over her profound maternal love and Peter was left in the care of his maternal grandmother, known as Granny Mayo, a gentle but frail woman who suffered badly from rheumatism. Peter didn't see his mother again until he was two. It took him a week to accept her.

Short meetings followed by long separations became the pattern of their relationship. It is hard to imagine how difficult it must have been for a little boy to make sense of the contradiction that his mother loved him but was rarely there. Or so it must have seemed. I believe that Peter's profound loneliness, his sense of being abandoned and distrust of women can easily be traced to what he experienced as a child. It was a loving but unfortunate upbringing, and it must have been incomprehensible to him and turned his emotions upside down when he tried to fathom out why his mother would up and leave him as soon as he got used to her.

It can't have helped Peter that his elderly grandmother didn't know any other small children he could play with, and instead of interacting with young families with children of his own age, he spent much of his time with a much older person.

Margaret was unable to return for five years during the Second World War, a vital time in Peter's life and emotional development, but managed to get to England in time to give birth to a daughter, Sarah, in January 1945. She and Peter both developed the same wit and quick repartee, and she could be just as intimidating. Alec returned to England briefly to join his wife at the end of the war. Peter was seven before he met him for the first time that he could properly remember. Both his parents went back abroad again after his father's short leave.

I too was a very lonely child whose mother, when it came down to it, also put her husband's needs above those of her child. My father, Julian, was, like Peter's, tremendously loyal to his employers, in his case to the detriment of his health. He joined Lloyd's Underwriters Co. in 1925, and two years later was appointed to the staff of A. L. Sturge, a successful underwriting company, where he became a senior partner.

He met my mother at a weekend house party in Dorset in 1940. He was a captain in the Rifle Brigade but was invalided out following an accident in which he broke his right hip. He then served as a private in the Home Guard. His hip was pinned during what was, in those days, a serious operation and left him with one leg shorter than the other. It gave him a limp and in later life caused him considerable pain.

My mother, Mary, who was known as Molly, was a widow in her late twenties when she met my father. Her first husband was a wealthy Frenchman living in England. They married in 1934 but he died of malaria in 1939 while serving in the armed forces in Africa, leaving her with a young son, Paul Gourju. My father was six foot two inches, good-looking with blond curly hair and thought to have excellent prospects. My mother was a foot shorter, and her hair was a deep auburn.

They married in 1941, and I was born a year later, on 4 July, by Caesarean section. My father chose the day for the operation because it was American Independence Day and he was fascinated by the American Civil War. My half-brother, Paul, was five when I was born.

My father underwrote the railways in America and often went there when I was small for business and to lecture on underwriting and insurance. My mother would go with him. I was very affected by her being away such a lot, just as Peter was by his mother's absences. I desperately missed her, cried a great deal and felt totally bereft. My maternal grandmother, Eva Mearns, used to try to console me by rocking me in her arms and pretending to play the piano on my back. It was a good way of trying to distract me, but these things run deep and stay with you at some level all your life.

When my father was home, he worked all hours. In addition he and my mother would be out entertaining clients or giving dinner parties at our homes in London and in the countryside. So, like Peter, I was left for long periods with my grandmother, who came to live with us permanently when I was ten. She was a warm woman with a great sense of humour. I called her 'Potts' and got on with her extremely well, far better than I did with my mother, with whom I had an uneasy relationship. My mother was a woman who wasn't frightened of anybody or anything, but although she was very confident socially, she could also be aggressive, pushy and argumentative, as her first meeting with Peter, many years later, demonstrates. She also dominated my father. He gave me unconditional love, whereas my mother's was conditional on being successful, and for many years I felt I always had to please her.

The first home I remember was Marwell, a large Edwardian detached house in eight acres in Westerham, Kent. It had seven bedrooms and an enormous ballroom, large enough for an orchestra, where I used to have my birthday parties. As a child, I had no comparisons and at the time didn't realise how unusual this was. There was a cottage in the grounds for the cook. I also had a nanny.

I spent a lot of time on my own because by the time I was five Paul was at boarding school. He later went on to Stowe public school. When he was at home, he didn't want a sissy girl running around with him. From a very early age I'd hide in our large garden and make up an imaginary life for myself. I was often lonely and would watch the children from the nearby Barnardo's orphanage playing together, sometimes for hours.

Meanwhile Peter continued to have a complicated, often difficult relationship with his mother, who was a deeply religious woman and such an imposing figure that Alan Bennett recalls he was 'rather terrified' of her. Peter and I both learnt to cut ourselves off from people who hurt us like our mothers had done. In Peter's case his mother had little choice, but the hurt was still there. It was a form of self-protection. We were both emotionally damaged and dysfunctional, and instinctively recognised that in each other from the moment we met. It helped us develop mutual trust and open up totally. In his biography of Peter, Harry Thompson says Peter never confided or trusted anyone, but he did both confide in and trust me. Although there were no barriers between us, however, his feelings of loneliness remained and initially he would fill himself with drink as a way of compensating.

Peter's grandfather Edward had also drunk heavily and Peter believed he had inherited an addictive gene from him. Edward Cook worked as a traffic manager for the Federated Malay States Railway in Kuala Lumpur, but tragically shot himself in a fit of depression in 1914. He was considered the black sheep of the family and was rarely talked about.

Alec, Peter's father, whom he admired enormously, did not drink to excess. He was a man of integrity and strong moral values, which he tried to instil in his children. Peter was brought up to have impeccable manners and never to outstay his welcome. He was expected not to be boring, but to be patient with those who were.

In 1945 Alec was posted to Gibraltar to become financial secretary to the colony. His wife went with him, taking baby Sarah. Instead of leaving Peter to be comforted by Granny Mayo, he was dispatched to board at St Bede's Prep School in Eastbourne, near the cliffs at Beachy Head, where he stayed until 1951. Although it was the convention to send small boys to boarding school, it wasn't right for Peter. He cried his little heart out as he made the lonely journey to Eastbourne and what he was soon to discover was a freezing, regimented institution. He was small for his age, asthmatic and an easy prey for bullies. Although he was deeply miserable, he never complained. It wasn't something he felt he could disturb or burden his family with. His mother wrote to him once a week, but it was little compensation for not seeing her. Each term he counted the days until he could travel to Gibraltar and join his parents again.

I might have seen him when he was at St Bede's. When I was six, my parents took me to stay in a large house that belonged to my father's partner at Lloyd's. It was next door to his school, and in a rather lonesome way I used to look over the fence and watch the boys playing, just as I had the Barnardo's orphans.

Peter was academically brilliant and, as he grew older, increasingly good-looking. He told me he became the prettiest boy at the school and used it to flirt and manipulate people. He was beginning to be able to use his wit and sarcasm to keep some of the bullies at bay, or at least amused. Although Peter's wit and looks gave him an aura of confidence, it never quite masked his intense inner insecurity. This irreconcilable conflict led to many future problems in both his relationships and work.

In 1951 he moved from St Bede's to Radley College in Oxfordshire, one of Britain's top public schools. In the early 1950s the pupils' day began with a compulsory icy shower. Peter's looks, slight frame and problems with asthma meant he continued to be a target for bullies. He was utterly miserable in his first year and even resorted to banging his head on the wall because he couldn't breathe. Once again he kept his inner agony to himself and sealed off his emotions.

Brutal corporal punishment was common and Peter was regularly caned by a senior prefect. His name was Ted Dexter and he later became England's cricket captain. Pupils were forbidden to drink alcohol and on one occasion he was caught by Dexter. Peter never forgave the unfairness of being caned one year for drinking half a pint of cider at the Henley Regatta.

Peter was usually diligent in class, but dramatically lost all interest in work when, in early 1953, he heard that his father was being posted back to Nigeria to become permanent secretary of the Eastern Region, based in Enugu, and it would be almost impossible to visit him.

Meanwhile his family pattern had changed again, as his youngest sister, Elizabeth, had been born, seven years after Sarah. Margaret couldn't bear leaving her children behind again, particularly baby Elizabeth, and persuaded her husband to let her stay in England. When Peter heard she had bought a spacious cottage for £5,800 in Uplyme near Lyme Regis, he was so relieved she was staying in England that his schoolwork instantly improved.

Sadly, though, by the time his mother made the choice to live in England, the emotional damage to Peter, who was now well into his teens, had been done. Although he adored his mother with a passionate intensity, her absence when he was a child had left him with an irreparable emotional hole, a permanent hunger for the company of women and a contradictory reluctance ever to put his trust totally in one woman. Pychologists believe that a boy whose mother hasn't fulfilled her maternal role, for what ever reason, will find it particularly hard to form a permanent bond with a woman when he becomes a man and is perhaps at the root of Peter's chronic infidelity. Wendy believes Peter was a homosexual, but I have never believed that. He liked women far too much. But there was an element of the misogynist in him, as his relationships with women were very complicated. He was both fearful of and fascinated by them.

Peter's mother remained intellectually alert all her life and even in her eighties took part in regular literary group meetings, which were early versions of book clubs. What she couldn't cope with were the feelings of guilt at leaving her children for such long periods during their childhood. Peter introduced us soon after we began living together and we immediately got on well. Although I don't take astrology seriously, I find it quite interesting in terms of what it says about people's characteristics and star signs. Peter's mother and I are both born under the astrological sign of Cancer and perhaps that contributed to our positive relationship. She knew I hated being apart from Peter when he was away working and would always ring and try to visit me. We would talk about Peter's childhood and the problems of leaving her husband for long periods of time, but also about current affairs. She showed great interest in me too, but her questions were never intrusive and I always felt relaxed in her company.

Peter was never the sort of person who would conform merely for the sake of it and this was as true during his schooldays as it was for the rest of his life. Rugby was compulsory at Radley, but Peter hated playing it and would organise illicit football matches. He was so bright he didn't have to work hard to do well. Although he coasted during his early years, the combination of his mother staying in England and reaching the sixth form spurred him to work harder and he began to shine academically. He felt confident enough to turn his hand to writing comedy sketches and articles, and one of his first comic pieces was accepted by *Punch*.

By now he generally felt more comfortable in the school environment and was made a sixth-form prefect. It was part of boarding-school culture in the early and mid-1950s for prefects to be cruel to younger boys, and even to make their lives a misery. Peter had been put through several brutal initiation ceremonies and been beaten with hockey sticks when he first joined the school. One of these ceremonies involved a prefect placing a penny on his forehead, then tucking a rolled-up copy of *Country Life* into the front of his trousers. He then had to look up at the ceiling until the penny fell into the magazine, but while he gazed upwards, iced water was poured down the funnel created by the magazine. Many of the boys grasped the chance of perpetuating this nastiness on the next generation as a strange form of revenge, but Peter refused to continue what he thought was a barbaric tradition and instead behaved kindly and humanely towards the younger boys.

Radley had an excellent drama department and even ran a school drama festival. Peter had chosen not to get involved lower down the school, but once he reached the sixth form, he began to put a tremendous amount of energy into acting and developing various comic characters. He loved imitating masters and was still at Radley when he invented E. L. Wisty, one of the greatest comedy characters of all time, and who became an essential part of Peter's future success as a comedian. Peter based Wisty on the school's table butler, Mr

Boylett, who regularly pronounced on various philosophical matters. Peter imaginatively developed the character to become a bland, monotone know-all who bored members of the public on topics that included tadpoles, his letters to Buckingham Palace, his view on peace through nudism, his friend Spotty Muldoon and his plans for his and Spotty's World Domination League, which had aspirations that included getting a nuclear arm to deter with.

Perhaps the most famous Wisty sketch centred around him admitting he failed the exam to become a judge because he 'didn't have the Latin'. Instead he passed the test to become a coal miner. 'They only ask you one question,' he explains. 'They ask, "Who are you?" and I got seventy-five per cent on that.'

When Peter left school, national service was still compulsory, but he was excused because of an allergy to feathers. Instead he applied to Pembroke College, Cambridge, to read French and German. He won a scholarship to start in October 1957. He wanted to follow in his father's footsteps and go into the Foreign Office, and this was the next crucial step.

Once he'd settled at college, he joined the Pembroke Players Drama Society, but it was only in his second year that he overcame his shyness and felt confident enough to try to be part of the prestigious Footlights Club. It was a brilliant outlet for his quirky, sardonic, fast-paced humour and he soon moved onwards and upwards and in 1960 became the much coveted president of the Cambridge Footlights Revue. He was perhaps at his most original at this time and comic sketches poured seemingly effortlessly from his pen. One, called 'Polar Bores', was about an Antarctic explorer he called Scribble Gibbons and to whom Peter gave memorably pompous lines such as 'Communications were to be our only link with the outside world.'

Peter was always at his most hilarious when he could be spontaneous and he particularly loved sketches that featured boring and uninteresting facts. This proved to be a brilliantly original concept that became his passport to both his own fame and the future of British comedy.

Boylett featured in several of his favourite sketches centred on the mundane.

> BOYLETT: Did you know you've got four miles of tubing in your stomach? You see how far the food has to travel? Four miles it has to go and it takes four hours. That's a mile an hour.
> MAN: I had no idea.
> BOYLETT: That means you never get any really fresh food in your stomach. It's all at least four hours old.
> MAN: Fancy that.
> BOYLETT: No, I don't fancy that, thank you very much. I don't fancy it at all.

At Cambridge, Peter met John Bird, who became a well-known satirist. He described Peter as 'the funniest man in England', an epithet that many other talented celebrities, including Clive Anderson and Stephen Fry, have repeated over the years.

Peter's undergraduate sketches for Cambridge Footlights were so successful that many were performed by Kenneth Williams in the West End shows *Pieces of Eight* (1959) and *One Over the Eight* (1961). Peter was paid about £100 a week, a substantial sum for a student at that time.

He also applied to join Equity, the actors' union, but was initially told there was already an actor called Peter Coke on the books, plus a singer called Peter Cook. At the time there were rules against members having names that were too similar and Peter was advised to call himself something different. Peter mocked what he thought was an administrative nonsense and sent in a list of potential names that included Xavier Blancmange and Sting Thundercock. Sadly there is no record of how the staff reacted, but he achieved the desired result and was allowed to use his real name.

Peter spent his last holiday before his finals visiting his family in Libya, where his father was now working as economic adviser to the United Nations. Unfortunately Peter developed jaundice soon after he arrived. His liver was damaged, but he continued to consume large amounts of alcohol as he had begun to do at Cambridge.

He had made such a success of his acting and comic writing at university that inevitably he became increasingly torn between his academic work and performing. His dilemma swirled round in his brain. Should he follow family tradition and go in for a safe job in the Foreign Office, or risk disappointing his father and go in for a show-business career? In the end the decision was made for him. He needed a first-class degree to be accepted by the Foreign Office, but had done virtually no academic work for two years and ended up with a lower second. Although his parents didn't express any disapproval or pass judgement on his results, Peter always believed he had failed and let them down.

If that changed the direction of his life, the event that was to have the most profound effect on his future was meeting Dudley Moore. The two men were introduced to each other in 1959 by John Bassett, who was at the time assistant director of the Edinburgh Festival. He was looking for four talented young men, two from Oxford and two from Cambridge, to take part in a late-night revue. Bassett already knew Jonathan Miller, who had been to Cambridge and was now a doctor who hoped to become a neurosurgeon. He also knew Dudley, who was an organ scholar at Oxford and studying for a music degree with ambitions to become a composer. He asked each of them to suggest one person from Cambridge and another from Oxford. Jonathan suggested Peter, whom he had seen perform at Footlights, while Dudley suggested Alan Bennett, whom he thought was good at imitating grumpy vicars and was now a lecturer on medieval history.

The planned revue was to be part of the Fringe Festival, which is why, when the four men met and agreed to work together, they called themselves *Beyond the Fringe*. The meeting went well and they agreed to work together on the revue. In the end Peter wrote about two-thirds of it, while Jonathan and Alan put pen to the rest, and Dudley provided the music.

Peter was regarded as the most brilliant of the group, but at one level this was not reflected in their future careers: Alan Bennett became one of the country's foremost playwrights and a top-selling diarist, Dr Jonathan Miller combined a medical career with being a stage director, and Dudley ultimately became a movie star with Hollywood hits *10* and *Arthur*. By contrast Peter, who pronounced, 'I think I ran out of ambition at twenty-four,' never had one golden thread running through his career. Instead he had something far greater: he is acknowledged as the driving force behind the satirical comedy movement in the 1960s that changed the direction of British humour.

I wasn't as academic as Peter, but I too had a troubled time at school. I changed schools twice before I was nine and then attended Lady Eden's School in Kensington, west London. I began as a day pupil and shortly afterwards became a weekly boarder. Like Peter, I hated boarding and felt lonely. My mother, who was a terrible snob, chose the school because at the time it was one of the most socially up-market schools in the country. It was run by Lady Eden, who was both an accomplished teacher and the sister-in-law of Prime Minister Sir Anthony Eden. At school we had to curtsy to everyone we met, and when my mother entertained my father's American business contacts, I automatically shook their hand and curtsied to them. Everyone thought it was really cute, but I became increasingly self-conscious until in the end I'd hide on our flat roof to avoid meeting guests and my father would have to plead with me to come down.

I was also always expected to change for dinner, even if no guests were coming. I was crazy about horses at the time and wanted to stay in my jodhpurs rather than the girlie dresses my mother insisted I wore. In contrast my mother always dressed beautifully and, as was normal in her social group, had lots of expensive jewellery and fur coats. My father came from a respected old Devon family, and his grandfather was a master mariner who had been declared lost at sea in 1884. I adored my father. He was a brilliant but gentle academic with a whimsical nature and loved anything to do with boats and water. He used to quote me French poetry and say night-time prayers with me as I knelt down by the side of the bed.

He was also very supportive. As a small child I'd had ballet lessons, but when I was ten I gave them up, took up riding instead and my parents bought me a pony. I quickly became very good at jumping, entered lots of gymkhanas and won many cups. My mother didn't often come to watch me, but my father always did when he could. He'd help me feed the pony or put on the bridle and was wonderfully encouraging.

My parents had by this time sold Marwell and moved to a flat in a modern block in Exhibition Road, south-west

London, to make commuting easier for my father. The long journey to work from Kent was getting him down and causing problems with his leg. In its place they bought a fifteenth-century mansion, the Mill House, in Worplesdon, Surrey, where my mother hoped my increasingly unwell father would be able to relax at weekends. It was a fabulous house, set in a ten-acre garden within a thirty-acre farm. It had a swimming pool, tennis court and lots of space for my black New Forest pony, Puck. There were also three cottages, one each for the gardener, farm manager and cook.

I found it hard to keep changing schools and as a result was horribly shy. When my weekend at home was coming to an end, I would often hide because I didn't want to go back to school. I also suffered from acute homesickness. In those days you couldn't ring your parents for comfort and I often felt choked with emotion. Eventually I developed a coping strategy. Every morning I would think through in minute detail what my parents might be doing. It took a long time, and if I was interrupted by a teacher telling me to pay attention before I had reached a suitable stopping point, I would get very upset and have to start at the beginning again. When I felt particularly awful, I'd do the same in the afternoon or evening. As a result I was regularly accused of daydreaming and didn't do well in class.

After Lady Eden's I went briefly to a boarding school in Surrey, but shortly afterwards it was closed down and sold to convert into flats. I subsequently moved on to Oak Hall in Haslemere, Surrey. Again, I hated it, partly because it was so regimented. They were very strict about the uniform and, like many schools of the 1950s, made all the pupils wear two pairs of knickers at all times. One was warm and woolly, the other much thinner. Matron used to stand at the door as we arrived for breakfast and lift up our gymslips to check we were wearing both pairs. Matron also washed our hair once a fortnight, and we all had to wear the same headband to try to make our hairstyles look similar. I'd had my long curly hair cut before I joined the school. It was very badly done and stuck out all over the place, which, combined with the headband, made me think I looked like one of the Marx brothers.

I enjoyed English literature, history and art, but felt not being academic disappointed my parents. Winning first prize in the school gymkhana didn't seem to count for them. When I was fifteen, I was told I wasn't doing well enough to move up to the next class and had to re-sit the year. I felt so humiliated that I wrote to my mother telling her I had to leave.

She listened to my plea and in 1957 sent me to a crammer for a year. When I left at sixteen, she gave me three choices – to take a typing course, find a job or get married. My mother thought I would have trouble learning to type. Harvey Nichols turned me down for a job, so the third option became the most likely. From then on my mother concentrated on my coming out as a deb and, she hoped, meeting a suitable husband. I had already incurred her wrath and caused her enormous worry when at fourteen I had been caught talking to a local farm boy, whom I'd met when out on my pony. She insisted my father beat me with the back of a hairbrush on my bare bottom to impress on me that this type of behaviour wouldn't be tolerated.

To make sure I was kept on track, at age sixteen she sent me to the Monkey Club in London, a famous finishing school for girls from wealthy families. I hated it. I was a weekly boarder and younger than most of the other girls. The school's main aim seemed to be to keep us in at night in case we got pregnant, so all the rooms were locked at nine. My only excitement was when a young man called Nigel

Taylor, who had once come to my parents' home in the country, used to park his car under my bedroom window and toot his horn. I would lean out and talk to him for a brief spell, but not for long in case I was caught. I also went for a term to St Martin's School of Art.

Sharing the experience of a British boarding school with its institutionalised and regimented way of life formed a strong bond between Peter and me. We had both learnt to cope emotionally for ourselves from a very early age.

I was eleven when I first became aware that my father drank too much, although I didn't really understand the full implications of the word 'alcoholic'. My mother asked me to find where he had hidden the gin bottle and, in the way that a child can absorb things subconsciously, I knew he had put one in a dustbin and went straight to it. My parents would argue over drink – my mother of course had a terrible temper – and my father often complained that his gin tasted as if it had been watered down. My mother also drank too much and particularly liked gin, wine and whisky. I remember telling her that whisky was very bad for her and asking her to stop, but she took no notice. That really upset me. I somehow knew that too much whisky in particular was responsible for her terrible headaches and made her extremely grumpy.

She drove when she was drunk too, as many people did in those days. Sometimes she would ask me to open the gate at the end of our driveway and I would run towards it in front of the car. She would drive fast behind me and occasionally I'd have to jump on the gate as she shot through it, to avoid being hit. My heart was in my mouth and it made me very anxious. The pain I felt from watching my parents, whom I loved deeply, drink too much made me not want to drink myself.

My father also had two nervous breakdowns while I was young. The first occurred when I was at Lady Eden's School. The second was during my time as a deb. He was under huge pressure at work, deciding where to invest vast amounts of money, and had become worn down by the hard graft of life in the City. When he recovered from the first breakdown, he went away on a banana boat to the Caribbean to convalesce for a few weeks with a colleague from Lloyd's. My mother was very upset to be left behind and made me sleep in the same bed as her. Seeing them go through this difficult experience taught me the value of putting on a good front for the world.

The drunkenness and nervous breakdowns were in sharp contrast to my otherwise very conventional upbringing. The way both Peter and I were brought up left us with some rather old-fashioned aspects to our characters. Peter was originally of an era when gentlemen behaved like gentlemen and ladies behaved like ladies. When I first met Peter, there was a part of him that was almost Victorian. He was quite plump, dressed in tweed suits, had very proper views and expected to tell me what to do. I, in turn, was brought up to expect a man to look after and care for me, and in return I would obey him. It didn't add up to the Peter he became, but that is how he started. I think the explosion of self-indulgence in the 1960s triggered something in Peter that might not have happened at an earlier time, when people were more likely to keep a lid on their behaviour. Instead he began to act in a way that was to become the opposite of what he originally believed in and against all his inherent values. Whereas most people start to rebel in their teens, Peter remained fairly conventional until his late twenties. Once the rebellion began, it was almost as though he didn't know how to calm it down and bring himself back into normal society.

He lacked both judgement and boundaries. Once he opened one Pandora's box, he couldn't stop himself from opening many others. Perhaps having absent parents when he was small meant he didn't have enough opportunity to learn from them by example. As a result, he started to hate himself and tragically the more he hated himself, the more he gave in to his addictions. It became a terrible vicious circle.

I, however, was to begin my lesser rebellion before I became a deb.

5

A Deb, a Model and an Actress

My adolescence begins at fifteen with a traumatic experience
when my mother gives my pony away to the Elphinstones,
the Queen's cousins. She says if I keep on riding, I'll get a
large backside. I am initially angry and upset, but I don't feel
like that for long. Her action triggers my transition from
being a child to becoming a young woman and I am helped
by two momentous events. One is when my grandmother
Potts takes me to see Brigitte Bardot in the film *The Light
Across the Street* in 1959. I've never seen anyone like Bardot
and am mesmerised. My grandmother says, 'She is what you
should look like,' and I think, Yes, I want to be beautiful and
glamorous. The second is in January 1960, when my mother
arranges for me to visit Virginia Lyon. She later becomes the
Countess of Warwick and a friend of Princess Margaret.
Virginia is eighteen, two years older than me, and has been
deb of the year. My mother explains our visit by echoing the
words my grandmother used about Brigitte Bardot: 'She is
what you should look like.'

It's their way of grooming me for when I come out as a
debutante in a year or so. Debs are young girls from suppos-
edly upper-class or well-to-do families who are presented to
court as a way of introducing them into society. This is
followed by a season packed full of parties where they can
seek out a suitable husband.

My mother wants me to learn from Virginia how to dress and put on make-up. Virginia's father is a wealthy stockbroker and we are invited round to their grand house in Surrey. The two sets of parents have cocktails downstairs, while Virginia and I talk in her bedroom.

She is very beautiful with a mane of red hair. I assume it's natural, but she tells me she has it coloured at René's, a famous hairdresser of the time. She also has lots of wonderful and stylish French clothes. Just before we leave, my mother buys some of her clothes for me and Virginia secretly gives me her hairdresser's phone number. I ring to make an appointment and go along without telling my mother.

I ask René to dye my hair the same colour as Virginia's and explain that I am still at school and don't have any money of my own, but that I shall be a deb soon and that it is important that I look good. I am not really into the deb scene, but it is something my mother wants me to do. When he has finished, he asks for my address and sends the bill to my mother. I love my hair, but my mother almost goes up in smoke when she sees me, and then again when she gets the bill, but there is nothing she can really do because she has already told me she thinks Virginia is wonderful.

Brigitte Bardot and Virginia become my inspirations. I decide I am too plump and must lose some weight. I stop eating bread and creamy foods and my figure improves enormously. I also grow my hair and try to straighten it using large rollers to get the same tousled, just-got-out-of-bed look that Bardot has.

My mother is keen for me to have a suitable wardrobe for my year as a deb, believing it will help me meet the right young man. She takes me to a dressmaker and we pick out clothes from magazines to make up the complete wardrobe for a respectable young lady. The fashion at the time is for daughters to follow the look of their mothers, so it's quite common to see young teenage girls wearing well-tailored tweeds, wool stockings and sensible shoes. She also buys me two fur coats. One is mink, the other rabbit, and both have my initials sewn on the lining. I have countless pairs of shoes with kitten heels, lots of white gloves and the obligatory string of pearls.

Part of our family routine is that my mother organises a weekly dinner party in our London flat. She hires a cook, discusses the menu in great detail, then orders the food from Harrods. I am expected to meet guests when they arrive, make small talk and then disappear. Even though I am now seventeen, I am not allowed to join them for the meal. Instead I have leftovers later in the evening. It makes me feel inferior and I develop a grim, antisocial take on dinner parties.

Fortunately, once I am a deb, I begin to go out regularly with my parents. My mother particularly loves revues and in 1959, when I am seventeen, she takes me to see lots of shows, including *Pieces of Eight*, which Peter has written for Kenneth Williams to perform. His name on the programme doesn't yet hold much significance for me.

In 1960 Virginia asks me to do a charity fashion show to be held at St Swithun's School in Winchester. I am thrilled and take along black tights and a black leotard to model a feather boa. We do a run-through before lunch and I am sitting in the dressing room on my own about to change back into my skirt and jumper when the *Daily Express* photographer Harry Benson comes in and asks me to pose for him. He enquires why I haven't gone to the pub with the other girls and I explain I can't because I am under age. He offers to buy me a sandwich and orange juice if I let him take my picture. I agree and the next day the *Express* prints a large photograph of me in my fishnet stockings under the headline 'Sensational Girl in Unexpected Setting'. Their report says that it's not often that the photographer is 'stopped in his tracks quite so abruptly' and asks readers to take a look 'at the beauty he found in, of all places, a girls' school'. I'm described as a 'dark, glowing beauty' with red hair, vivid green eyes and 34-23-34 statistics. It says I am the star of the show and mentions that I am soon to be a deb.

My parents are horrified by the photograph, and my father goes round the City trying to buy up every copy of the newspaper he can find so people won't see me. The mother of my friend Judith Stevens, with whom I was going to have a joint coming-out dance, rings my mother to say she doesn't approve of the publicity I've had and thinks it better if Judith and I have separate dances. I don't mind.

At five foot four inches, I am too short to be a fashion model, but after my picture appears in the *Express*, I am offered all sorts of modelling jobs in advertising. Soon I am the face for both Bacardi rum and Fry's chocolate. My name is even mentioned in an advertisement for Varaflame ciga-rette-lighters.

I am quite artistic and can see that now I have grown my hair and lost weight, I could totally change my look by wearing more informal clothes. I notice too that young men are beginning to respond to me. There is a new kind of woman developing around me, one who has a freer, more childlike look, and I think it would suit me.

My season as a debutante has just begun when one morning I have a phone call from well-known theatrical agents William Morris who ask me to go on their books. So at the same time that I am going to endless cocktail parties and balls, I am also travelling to auditions for film parts. I can't believe it. It is every young girl's dream to become an actress and model, and my chance has come about as the result of just one photograph.

I am now being photographed wherever I go and learn how to stand and pose. When I go to watch tennis at Wimbledon, I count thirty-nine cameramen surrounding me. The pictures show a very different Judy from the plain, horsey Judy I still sometimes feel inside. I am even being called 'the girl who is exploding the bubbles in the pink-champagne world'.

Lots of well-known people want to meet me. Billy Wallace, a celebrated and well-known charmer who was recently unofficially engaged to Princess Margaret, invites me to dinner. I am also invited to lunch at the Ambassadors, a private club off Park Lane, to join a party that includes the actress and incredible sex symbol Jayne Mansfield. It turns out that she and her then husband, Mickey Hargitay, a former Mr Universe, want to talk to a deb. It's an amazing experience for a seventeen-year-old. Jayne is extraordinary – a larger-than-life character with masses of peroxide hair and a voluptuous figure like something out of a Disney cartoon.

I am also invited out by top broadcaster Alan Whicker. He has been interviewing several debs and invites me to a dinner dance. I like him as a person, but he is fifteen years older than me and we don't go out again.

The *Express* announces I am 'Deb of the Year' for 1960 and the other papers follow suit. I, together with lots of other girls, am presented at Queen Charlotte's Ball, held at the Grosvenor House Hotel in Park Lane, but to a duchess rather than the Queen, who officially abolished the ceremony in 1958. My dress is white taffeta, off the shoulder and full-skirted. I also wear white gloves. Debs wear white because they are supposed to be virgins. I certainly am. I haven't even had a proper boyfriend.

Our mantelpiece at home is groaning with invitations and I could go to a ball every night for four months, but I pick and choose the best ones. I decide it all depends on the boys. You can usually tell if a dance will be good by the kind of man invited. Many of the so-called 'debs' delights' are anything but. First, there are the scroungers, who blatantly come to all the parties just for the food and drink. Then there are the fortune-hunters, who seem to treat the whole season as a kind of marriage market. I've even seen them signal to each other over the heads of girls while they're dancing – a kind of tic-tac talk as if to say, 'Hey, look how much I've got.' Thirdly, there are the publicity-chasers. They like to be seen with girls who have been mentioned in the papers. The absolute eligibles are those with either pots of money or a title, and they go to very few parties. Their mere presence will, however, make a dance a success.

My coming-out ball takes place on 4 July 1960, my eighteenth birthday, in a marquee on the lawn of our family home, the Mill House, in the Surrey countryside. We are mobbed by photographers. I have about two hundred guests and wear a pink satin dress with diamanté straps, which I have designed myself. Lance Perceval does the cabaret; he later goes on to appear in *That Was the Week That Was*. Our lawns are floodlit; we have a band and serve endless quantities of champagne. My father disappears at about three o'clock in the morning and my mother is so worried she calls both the fire brigade and the police. The house swarms with officers looking for him, and one of them eventually discovers him drunk under a pile of potatoes in one of the outhouses. It is the start of his second nervous breakdown. Both my parents have wanted to give me this party, and my mother has obviously enjoyed socialising, but I haven't. I think it is a waste of money and can only add to my father's stress, but I try to put a good face on it.

Tragically this time my father doesn't fully recover. He remains quite vulnerable and unable to handle stress or deal with the affairs of everyday life. It is left to my mother to make sure the house is run properly and all their financial investments are taken care of.

Going to so many parties brings me out of myself and I stop feeling quite so self-conscious. I also start to have boyfriends. One is John Wells. He is a teacher at Eton, dashing, good-looking and 'with it'. I think the pupils are lucky to have him. We don't stay together for long, but soon after we meet, he leaves Eton, becomes a satirist and will later co-write *Private Eye*'s 'Dear Bill' letters. He also portrays Margaret Thatcher's husband Denis on stage and television.

The best party I am invited to by far is the one given by Paul Getty, who is then the richest man in the world. It is held at his home in Sutton Place and I go with my half-brother, Paul. When we reach the wrought-iron gates, we are checked in against a long guest list and I am given a rose. The house itself is like a medieval palace and the scent of the thousands of flowers that decorate it fill the air. Lady Rose McLaren, who did the rose arch for Princess Margaret's wedding, has arranged them in displays of white and gold.

There are about twelve hundred guests; among them nine are dukes and two hundred peers. We are told to help ourselves from the buffet. It includes stuffed peacocks and boars' heads, but I consume caviar, lobster, smoked salmon and strawberries. There are two dance floors, one beside the swimming pool, and at least three bands.

Later in the evening I wander outside into the vast floodlit grounds with six fountains, which are lit up by orange and green lights. There is a Persian tent where burning incense drowns even the scent of the blooms. Here, a fortune-teller dressed in Persian costume consults the stars for any guest who asks. I decide not to. At midnight there is an amazing fireworks display. We stay until morning and the whole experience is out of this world.

Shortly afterwards I am offered my first acting part. It is a walk-on role, playing a bride in the 1960 film *Piccadilly Third Stop*. Next I am also offered the chance of joining the chorus of Peter Meyer's revue *The Lord Chamberlain Regrets*, which stars Ronnie Stevens, Millicent Martin and Joan Sims. Gaye Brown is assistant stage manager, but of course I have no idea what her future role will be in my life. My mother is both horrified and exhilarated by the whirl-wind around me, but comes on the provincial tour for the first couple of weeks as my chaperone until I settle in.

The tour becomes my introduction to a totally different world. I find show-business people so refreshing compared to the people I've grown up with, and love their different way of looking at things. I no longer feel I have to be on my best behaviour all the time; I can just be me. The people I now mix with are a lot older than me and have had a wealth of experience. I glean a great deal from them and am thrilled to be on such an interesting learning curve. The world of celebrity in the 1960s was very different to how it has become. Famous people were those who had worked hard for a long time to establish themselves, rather than today, when people have been around for merely fifteen minutes.

I initially share a hotel room with my mother while on tour, and at about 11 p.m., after the show, we usually go back to our hotel and eat ham or prawn sandwiches and I drink a glass of milk or a cup of Ovaltine.

After a couple of weeks, once my mother has returned

home to my father, my roommate becomes Jill Ireland, who is also in the chorus. Although she is married to actor David McCallum and has two children, while I have barely left school, we get on brilliantly. She is so beautiful and I want to know everything about her life. She is a warm and generous person, doesn't at all behave like a celebrity and even volunteers to help me learn my dance steps. She tells me she accepted the part in the chorus because she hopes she will be able to progress and star in some of the sketches. It doesn't happen. David is suddenly given the joint lead in *The Man from U.N.C.L.E.*, to co-star with Robert Vaughn, and she flies out to America shortly afterwards to give him support. *The Man from U.N.C.L.E.* becomes an incredibly successful spy series and turns David into a sex symbol. Unfortunately, though, their marriage doesn't last.

The routine for the revue is that our mornings are spent rehearsing, we perform in the evening, and our afternoons are for socialising. Some afternoons are particularly special. My favourite is when Joan Sims gathers all the cast together in her room and tells us gossipy stories about the theatre and her past life. She drinks like a fish, but I adore her. She is a wonderful character, and so funny.

I also spend a rather strange afternoon with Millicent Martin and her husband, Ronnie Carroll. They invite me to their hotel room, and when I arrive, I find them on the bed. They pat the space between them. I lie there and we chat all afternoon. The conversation is full of double entendres. I have no idea if it's their way of asking for a threesome, but I am still very young and just keep batting their comments away. Perhaps it's why I'm being called 'Untouchable Huxtable'.

Ronnie Stevens, another member of the cast, likes to try to shock me too. When I rush to my allotted dressing room to do a quick change, I find pictures of nude men posted on the walls. I also have itching powder put down my clothes, which means sometimes having to go onstage and try not to scratch. I discover he is the culprit, but I take it in good spirit.

We are all very excited when, in August 1961, the revue finally comes to the Savile Theatre in London's West End, but we don't play to packed houses. It seems our type of revue has already become old-fashioned. A new show called *Beyond the Fringe*, a British comedy stage revue, opened on 10 May, a few months earlier, at the Fortune Theatre and this is what everyone wants to see. It is quite different to the normal British revue as there is no bright scenery, rows of dancing girls or all-join-in songs. Instead four young men in jackets and pullovers break new comic ground with a show that is bursting with biting satire.

The revue has been to Edinburgh and toured the provinces, where the response was lukewarm, but when it opens in London, it is an overnight sensation. Not only does it become the forerunner to the popular TV show *That Was the Week That Was* and the memorable *Monty Python's Flying Circus*, its powerful impact reaches much further and British comedy is never quite the same again.

Everyone who is anyone wants to see the show and it runs for 669 performances. I am taken by my parents, though in the end my father has to be persuaded to come because he has heard that Peter Cook is impersonating Harold Macmillan. It is the first time in living memory that a current prime minister has been directly mimicked and mocked onstage and my father doesn't approve. The Macmillan sketch is the highlight of the revue and its impact is so powerful and compulsive that it is the decisive moment when what became known as the satire movement takes off. It also does much to overturn Macmillan's 'Supermac' image of the 'Never had it so good' days and instead presents him as a poseur. Peter even makes him incapable of pronouncing 'the Conservative Party' properly.

In one part of the show we hear Macmillan address a public meeting with the words 'We shall receive four minutes' warning of any impending nuclear attack. Some people may say, "Oh, my goodness, that's not a very long time," but I would remind those doubters in this great country of ours that some people can run a mile in four minutes.' Macmillan is also quoted reporting on a summit meeting with President John F. Kennedy, 'We talked of many things, including Great Britain's position in the world as some kind of honest broker. I agreed with him when he said no nation could be more honest, and he agreed with me when I chaffed him and said no nation could be broker.'

We have seats in the front stalls and my father is outraged by Peter's performance. He wants us all to leave in the interval and I have to work hard to convince him to stay.

Macmillan himself comes to see the revue, no doubt to show he is a man with a sense of humour, but his smile freezes when he sees Peter stride onstage as himself. Peter points out the distinguished guest to the audience and then starts ad-libbing in character: 'When I've a spare evening, there's nothing I like better than to wander over to a theatre and sit there listening to a group of sappy, urgent, vibrant young satirists with a stupid great grin spread all over my silly old face.' There is no sound of laughter from the audience, merely an embarrassed silence, but Peter is triumphant.

Peter has written most of the other sketches too, including the hilarious and inimitable 'One Leg Too Few', in which he plays a theatrical producer auditioning a one-legged Dudley, by the name of Mr Spiggott, for the part of Tarzan. As the audition progresses, the producer tells Spiggott he has a very nice right leg, which would be ideal for the part, then adds, 'I've got nothing against your right leg. The trouble is, neither have you.' It becomes one of the most famous sketches in comedy history. Dudley bounces up and down on one leg throughout the sketch, and I find him very funny and also love his music. He later tells me that earning £100 a week in *Beyond the Fringe* was more than his parents managed to save in twenty years.

I find Peter hilariously funny and can't take my eyes off him. We sit so close to the stage that I can see his flashing eyes and how intelligent he looks. He is audacious too, saying in a slightly patronising tone, 'Let us remember that wealth and luxury do not necessarily bring happiness. I speak from personal experience.' He somehow challenges the audience to watch him even when the others are speaking. I think he is incredibly dishy and I like the poetic way he moves. I would love to meet him, but now is obviously not the time, as I know he is going out with Wendy Snowden, his girlfriend from Cambridge.

I am feeling increasingly confident as my season as a deb continues and meet Terence Stamp just as it finishes. It is just before he makes his amazing film debut starring in *Billy Budd*, released in 1962, and he is very hot property. We go out for a short while, but it's very chaste. I think he fancies me, but I'm much too virginal for it to go far. I know I can't sleep with anybody unless I tell my mother. His attitude quickly turns to almost brotherly affection. He takes me out for meals and sometimes I go back to his Knightsbridge flat, where he plays me the pop hit 'The Lion Sleeps Tonight'.

I do like him and want to invite him to the Mill House to meet my parents, but he is a real East End cockney boy and I know my parents will be quite unable to cope with it. They would have equal difficulty in understanding how their only daughter, who they sent to a smart finishing school and has curtsied to a duchess, is meeting a 'cor blimey' person like Terence.

He asks me to help him move from his Knightsbridge flat to one in nearby Pimlico, which he's going to share with Michael Caine, another up-and-coming actor. I do and he then invites me to dinner a couple of days later. When I turn up, however, Michael opens the door and, to my dismay, tells me in his cockney accent that Terence has gone out with Jean Shrimpton. She is a stunning model and everyone is talking about her. I know I don't stand a chance. Michael sees my distress and asks me out to dinner to cheer me up. He is a shoulder for me to cry on and we become friends.

Marvellous things are happening around me. I love the way the social barriers are starting to crumble and you can meet and become friends with people from a totally different class.

6

Out with the Stars

The Establishment club opens in the autumn of 1961 in the heart of Soho and I can't wait to go there. Its name is deliberately ironic: there is little conventional about it as it quickly becomes known as London's first satirical club. Peter and I have yet to meet, but I am told it is his idea, along with Nick Luard, who has become his business partner. It's located in Greek Street and is apparently modelled on the political cabarets of Berlin in the 1930s.

All types of comedians are already performing at the club and it has revived the career of Frankie Howerd, a stand-up comic whose fortunes had stalled. Other comics, including Lenny Bruce, who is American, and Barry Humphries, who performs as a Melbourne housewife called Edna Everage, will be making their British debut at the club.

The Establishment is packed every night, everyone is talking about it, and it quickly becomes the place to go. I am still performing in *The Lord Chamberlain Regrets* but one chilly autumn evening I go along after the show with my friend Gaye Brown. I arrive just after 11 p.m. and have not the slightest idea that this is the place where I shall meet both my husbands-to-be.

The premises used to house a strip-tease show, but you would never guess it now. It is unlike any nightclub I've seen. Nightclubs in the early 1960s are usually plush and ornate with thick carpets and chandeliers, but the Establishment is a minimalist's dream of wood, glass and steel. I am immediately impressed. There is a bar in the basement where Dudley Moore and his jazz trio play. There is also an area by the side of the bar where you can dance.

The designer of the club is Sean Kenny, who has designed the set for *Beyond the Fringe* and for Lionel Bart's hit musical *Oliver!*, which is loosely based on *Oliver Twist* by Charles Dickens. Critics have paid him a great compliment by saying that you come out of the theatre humming his sets. He is now working on his next show, *Blitz*, which will open in a few months' time. It's Sean I have come to be introduced to, and Gaye and I climb the stairs to the first floor, where he has his studio and likes to hold court.

I see him through a haze of cigarette smoke. The atmosphere is electric. There are lots of people talking and Miles Davis, the charismatic black jazz trumpeter, is blaring out of the sound system. Sean looks arresting and I study him carefully. He is broad but only about the same height as me, and his hair is almost white blond. He looks highly intelligent and very Irish.

He says hello, smiles and we chat a little. He wastes no time in inviting me to come backstage with him at the theatre where he will later be assembling the set for *Blitz*. He and his team will be working all night and I agree to join them. I've recently turned nineteen and want to live my own life. I know my mother won't approve, but although, like most girls of my age, I still live at home, I know I can creep into our flat in Knightsbridge without my mother hearing.

Sean, who is ten years older than me, is an architect and civil engineer as well as a designer. When we arrive at the theatre, the set is incredible and so realistic of how London suffered during the Second World War that once the show is

up and running, the fire brigade keep getting calls from
anxious members of the audience thinking the set has
genuinely caught fire. Sean shows me how it all works and I
can see he is a genius.

We become good friends. He is an Irish Catholic and I love
the fact he is older and knows so much more than I do. He
takes me backstage at the hit musical *Oliver!* too, and introduces me to many of his friends, including actor Peter
O'Toole, writer Edna O'Brien and Barbara Hulanicki, who
owns Biba, the trendiest fashion name going.

I tell my mother about Sean and she invites him down to
the Mill House to meet him. He charms my parents just as he
has charmed me. My parents waste no time in asking what
his intentions are towards me, and although we haven't
known each other long, he tells them he is single and serious
about me. Soon afterwards, he invites me to join him, his
close friend Lionel Bart and Judy Garland for a weekend in
Liverpool. Liverpool is the city everyone is talking about
because a new group called the Beatles are playing nightly at
the Cavern Club I ask my mother if I can go. To my surprise
and delight she gives me permission, but tells me she wants
to know when Sean and I sleep together. It's not the normal
request a mother would make, but I am so programmed to
obey her that I agree.

I feel particularly excited to have the chance to meet Judy
Garland. She and Lionel are very close and she always sees
him when she is in town. Judy plays the great star offstage
as well as on, and even if I didn't know how famous she is, I
could tell by her flamboyant gestures and powerful aura of
being someone special. Even so, I find her very easy to get
on with. She has a loving, open personality and I want to
put my arms round her and give her a hug. At night in Liverpool, we troop to the Cavern to watch the Beatles perform.

The Cavern itself is a former wine cellar and consists of three tunnels connected by archways that you reach via eighteen very narrow steps. It is an extraordinary place and very hot and sweaty.

The Beatles first performed here in February 1961, shortly after they returned from Hamburg, and very quickly began drawing in the crowds. Once we hear them sing, we understand why. They are brilliant and so exhilarating we all agree they will go far. Afterwards we come back to our hotel. Lionel has taken a suite and Sean and I go upstairs to join him. Everyone but me starts drinking. There's a piano in his sitting room, so Lionel starts playing and Judy sings songs from her vast repertoire. She doesn't want to go to bed and we stay up all night listening to her.

Shortly after we get back to London, I change agents and am invited by my new agent, John Mather, from MCA, to a party in Cadogan Square. Warren Beatty is there. He is twenty-four, six foot one, sensationally good-looking and testosterone on legs. It's no surprise that, following his successful film appearing opposite Natalie Wood in the 1961 film *Splendor in the Grass*, he's become the latest American heartthrob. I've read that he is seeing Joan Collins, but she isn't with him. He keeps staring at me, but I try to look as if I don't notice. He prowls around the room, making it obvious he is the number-one man and is going to take his pick of anyone he chooses. I stand rather hesitantly by my agent all evening. I can tell Warren likes me, but I am seeing Sean, and although our relationship is in its early stages, I sense Warren spells trouble.

At about 11 p.m. I decide to leave and go downstairs to the cloakroom, which is entirely mirrored. I collect my coat, and when I turn round, Warren is right behind me. We are standing very close to each other and without a word he tilts my head back and starts kissing me. I am unsure whether or not I should close my eyes. Initially I do, but then I open them to look at him. He is not looking at me at all but is staring at himself in the mirror, observing himself kissing me. I pull away and tell him I must go home. He comes with me and watches as I climb into my sports car. He waves as I drive off and shouts, 'I'll call you.' I don't think any more of it but within seconds of arriving home the phone rings. It's Warren. He tells me he has got my phone number from John Mather. We talk until 3 a.m. and he's as familiar as if he's known me for ages.

He calls again the next evening and wants to see me. I feel flattered, but I can tell he is the sort of man who will go after almost any pretty girl he sees. I don't want to get involved with him, partly because of Sean and partly because of his growing reputation.

Within weeks of meeting Sean, my revue closes and he invites me to go with him and Kevin McClory to Paris. He wants to see the shows at the famous Moulin Rouge and the Crazy Horse to get ideas for one he has been commissioned to put on in Las Vegas. Kevin is a well-known Irish screen-writer and producer. In 1965 he goes on to produce the James Bond hit *Thunderball*, the film that becomes the template for all the big Bond movies and the only one not produced by Broccoli and Saltzman.

My mother agrees to this trip too and I immediately love Paris. We see the shows, and then one evening at about 2 a.m. the three of us go to a club on the Left Bank. Sean and Kevin are dressed up in tuxedos, and I am wearing a short, sexy silver crochet dress. As we arrive, they say that neither of them will under any circumstances dance but that I should feel free to if I wish. Kevin also tells me, cryptically, that everything is not what it seems. I don't understand what either of them means but they don't explain any further.

We take our seats by the dance floor. Wonderful smoky samba music is playing, and the club is full of great-looking men. Quite quickly a tall, dark young man with slender hips and broad shoulders comes over. He is in his early twenties and dressed in a tuxedo, black trousers and white shirt with a stiff collar and black bow tie. He asks me, in French, to dance. He looks sexy, my heart starts thumping, and I think, Wow! I turn to Sean, whose eyes are out on stalks, then shake my head to decline. Kevin just grins. The young man asks me again, and although I feel embarrassed, I agree to dance. He immediately holds me so close that you couldn't have got a piece of cotton between us. After several dances he asks me if I will go back to the hotel with him. I decline, explaining I am with my boyfriend. He looks disappointed and stares at me intensely. I stare back and suddenly realise, to my alarm, that 'he' is in fact a 'she'. I make my excuses and rejoin Sean and Kevin at our table.

Sean looks very uncomfortable, but Kevin is grinning from ear to ear and admits they both knew it is a lesbian club but thought it would be fun. I don't take offence – they have just behaved like two naughty schoolboys. I have never experienced a lesbian club before and she is the best-looking man I have ever seen. In fact, I still find it hard to believe she is really a woman.

Shortly afterwards Sean invites me to join him on his work trip to Las Vegas. I discuss it with my mother and to my surprise, she again encourages me to go, saying travel and meeting people are very important and seeing Las Vegas is the opportunity of a lifetime. She knows I spend a couple of nights a week at Sean's flat but is confident I am not sleeping with him, because I haven't told her otherwise, so doesn't believe the trip is wrong. I am amazed at how forward-thinking she is.

Sean and I stay in Las Vegas for about five weeks. His show is staged in a casino and includes lots of nude girls gyrating on a small stage that rises almost magically out of the main stage. I spent a lot of time watching Sean work and talking to the showgirls. One of them, Joan Palethorpe, was also in *The Lord Chamberlain Regrets* and I can't quite believe that now here she is in Vegas performing without any clothes on.

At night Sean often goes out with some of the showgirls. He works until 3 a.m. and then likes to have fun to help him unwind. I think it best that I don't ask him any questions. I know I can't stop him seeing other women even if I want to. We are sharing a bed and are very affectionate with each other but we don't actually have sex. Although I am nineteen, I am much less mature than girls of the same age today. I'd describe myself as a child-woman with the emotional age of a fifteen-year-old, and I know he doesn't want to sleep with me yet anyway because I am a virgin. Even the thought of sex scares me. I know how easy it is to get pregnant, and I don't want that. Our relationship is more like brother and sister, and I am happy enough that Sean wants me around. I feel cherished by him, and he introduces me to everyone, including the crew on the show, who look after me, invite me over to their homes and treat me like one of the family. Just being there is quite an experience for a young girl.

Once we are back in London, Sean starts working on the design for Michael Tippett's opera *King Priam*, which will tour Britain before being premiered at London's Covent Garden Opera House. When he isn't working, he goes to Ireland – his family live in Tipperary – or stays with me and my parents, either at our London flat or the Mill House. We always sleep in separate bedrooms, but my mother obviously thinks we have a serious relationship and asks me again to tell her when I do eventually sleep with him. He loves the Mill House and feels so at home that he takes our dog, Nicely, Nicely Jones, a Dalmatian-Labrador cross out for rides in his jeep to Chichester Festival Theatre, where he is also working on a play.

When his designs for *King Priam* are nearly complete, Sean asks me to go with him on the pre-Covent Garden tour, saying he wants to stay with me in a hotel on our own. I understand exactly what he means and know what will happen. I am so naïve and nervous that I don't do anything in advance about contraception. Sean takes precautions the first night, but not subsequently.

While we are away, to my horror and dismay I discover a letter in his jacket pocket that refers to a wife and three children, and assume he has lied to me and my parents. I don't know what to do or how to ask Sean about it. Instead I keep the letter and show it to my mother when we come home. She says, 'Don't be silly, darling. There must be some mistake. Of course he isn't married.'

I eventually pluck up the courage to ask him myself and he tries to drown me in Irish charm. He completely denies being married and says it's all my imagination. I am not convinced, and when he is out, I drive round to the address mentioned in the letter and sit and wait. Eventually I see a woman and three small children, one of whom looks almost newborn, coming out of the house. It's absolute proof that he's lied, but when I confront him again, he still denies it. It is only when I describe the children to him that he finally admits the truth. He says he and his wife, Jan, got married when he was very young, have grown apart and are divorcing.

I tell my parents and they invite him over for dinner to challenge him. Sean is so charmingly apologetic that once again he wins them round. It is obvious that my mother needs to believe him because there have been pictures of us together in the papers and she will feel terrible in the eyes of her friends if our relationship falls apart. She is like many society mothers in the early 1960s and feels it is more important for her to save face than consider her daughter's ultimate welfare. It hits me with considerable force that from now on I somehow have to make our relationship work. In any case I don't have the willpower to break it off.

I am going to lots of auditions and doing advertising work but when I am not working, I go to the Establishment to be with Sean, who spends most of his life there. The buzz is fantastic. I get to know when Dudley is at the club as there is always a group of girls huddling around him while he plays.

The Establishment also played a role in the success of *Private Eye*. Launched in 1961, initially it was just full of jokes and rather like a school magazine, but it quickly latched on to the satirical mood of the moment and started criticising the establishment and incompetent or corrupt public figures. Peter first heard about it when Christopher Booker, Richard Ingrams and Willy Rushton showed him a dummy copy at the Establishment. He liked it immediately, and let the magazine be produced in the waiters' changing rooms while it searched for a permanent office in Soho. He also came up with an idea for the cover that everyone thought was brilliant. He had seen an American magazine cover of the newly elected US president John F. Kennedy with a word bubble that read, 'I got my job through the *New York Times*,' and thought that a photograph and similar word bubble would work very well on the front of *Private Eye*. It first appeared on issue 3, which was dated 30 November 1961 and sold as a Christmas issue. It has been so successful that it is still used today.

After about six months Peter and Nick Luard bought a

controlling seventy-five per cent share in the *Eye* for £1,500. Peter initially tried to organise regular meetings between the *Eye* staff and the comedians who were doing cabaret turns at the Establishment. He thought they could spark ideas off each other and form a kind of 'school of satire'. It didn't work as the writers and performers just didn't get on. Instead the *Eye* moved down the road and into a small first-floor office at 22 Greek Street. From then on it started to take off and the circulation quickly grew to reach about 50,000. Peter's fantastic creativity and dazzling humour acted like an adrenaline injection for the magazine. He suggested ideas for both one-off stories and longer running series, including the Memoirs of Rhandi Phur, an imaginary Hindu mystic.

He also encouraged the *Eye* to take on investigations over as wide an area as possible and to include business, the arts and particularly politics, as he believed that there were what he described as 'a lot of crooks about'. The *Eye* played a part in drawing attention to the story that became known as the Profumo Affair and led to the resignation of Secretary of State for War, John Profumo in June 1963. He admitted he lied to Parliament about his relationship with a twenty-one-year-old call girl called Christine Keeler, who also had relations with an attaché at the Russian embassy. The affair helped bring down the Macmillan government.

One night in the summer of 1962 I turn up to the Establishment as usual, totally unaware that I am about to meet the love of my life. I am wearing a pillar-box-red dress with a swirling skirt that I wore on a recent appearance on *Juke Box Jury*, a popular TV programme in which panellists give their views on newly released pop records. I chose to wear something bright even though the programme itself was broadcast in black and white because it made me feel confident.

When I arrive, the atmosphere is full of excitement and I'm told with some reverence that, 'Peter Cook is here.' He's come to the club after his performance in *Beyond the Fringe*. Then I see him. He is wearing a suit and looks very dapper as he mills around on the dance floor. His girlfriend, Wendy, is chatting to a group of people at the bar. He sees me and comes straight over and asks me to dance. At the end of the dance he goes back to Wendy, but I make a mental note that he has picked me out. I then go upstairs to Sean's studio.

In 1962 Sean has work to do in New York and I go with him. Peter and the cast of *Beyond the Fringe* are there too. We don't meet, but they are the toast of the town. *Beyond the Fringe* has already been to Washington, Boston and Toronto, and has just received its official premiere at the John Golden Theatre in New York. The critics are raving about it. The *New York Times* calls it 'immense' and 'hilarious' and 'a brilliant satirical revue'.

All sorts of celebrities go to the show, including Lauren Bacall, Noël Coward and Bette Davis. Peter is the man of the moment, and in February 1963 he meets Jackie Kennedy at a dinner given by Vice-President Lyndon Johnson. Three days later John F. Kennedy, the president himself, who missed the show when it was in Washington, travels to New York to see it. It is the time of the Cuban Missile Crisis, a military confrontation between America, Russia and Cuba that many feared could lead to the Third World War. The atmosphere is so tense that the theatre is thoroughly searched before the president arrives and a special red phone is installed in the back in case he needs to launch a nuclear attack during the show.

While Peter is in New York, he buys a dilapidated night-club called El Morocco at 154 East 54th Street. It is transformed into Strollers Theatre Club, which Peter hopes will

(*Above*) My parents' wedding on 4 March 1941, at a church in Pont Street, London.

(*Left*) Me, aged 4.

(*Above*) Me (aged 6) and my father, with our dogs Sally and Susan, in Marwell, Kent.

(*Left*) This photo of me was taken in 1962 by a brilliant German photographer in his studios in Chesterfield Gardens.

Sean and I in the sitting room of 14 Cheyne Row, soon after we were married.

Strutting our stuff in front of St James' Palace as a publicity shot for *The Touchables*. We were full of hope and excitement. (*Left to right*) Marilyn Richard, Esther Anderson, me, David Antony, Kathy Simmonds.

(*Above left*) Peter and me by my mother's swimming pool at Claremont Court, Jersey, in July 1967. I'd just been swimming underwater and look a little water-logged!

(*Above right*) My mother and Peter with his golfing trophy at Claremont Court. My mother had entered him in a tournament. He won it and she was over the moon!

On the set of *Bedazzled*. (*Left to right*) Raquel Welch, Dudley, Peter and Stanley Donen, the director.

be the American version of the Establishment and indeed becomes tremendously successful for a while.

His timing is terrible, though, as unbeknown to him the Establishment in London is in terminal trouble. The word is that Nick Luard has got into a terrible mess. The creditors meet in September 1963 while Peter is still abroad and he hears by phone that the club has failed. It is £75,000 in debt and goes into voluntary liquidation. Peter pays £10,000 and narrowly escapes going bankrupt. He does, however, seize the opportunity to buy all Luard's shares in *Private Eye*.

Since I started sleeping with Sean, our relationship has changed. He is a dynamic man and sometimes we have enormous fun, but at other times he is selfish and cruel. I don't live with him, as single girls are still expected to stay at home until they marry, but from time to time I stay at his Pimlico flat and he still occasionally stays at my family flat in Exhibition Road or at the Mill House. I learn to live never knowing what his moods will be like from one day to the next. It is made worse because he, like my parents, drinks too much. He starts going on drunken binges that last three days at a time, which I find very difficult to cope with.

The saving grace is that when Sean isn't drunk he can be sweet and caring. He often brings me breakfast in bed, which consists of freshly squeezed orange juice and toasted soda bread with honey. He is hands-on in the kitchen and even helps me embroider a waistcoat that I later wear to go to America to promote *The Touchables*.

Unfortunately, his benign state rarely lasts more than two weeks. Then his face changes, he starts looking agitated, and I know he will soon go off again. It's almost like watching the weather change and knowing a storm will follow. Sometimes when I casually ask, 'What's happening tonight?' he replies, 'I might drop off for a drink with a friend,' and I know I won't see him for days.

These binges don't happen often when we first get together, though it might seem strange why I put up with them at all. It's hard to explain, other than to say I am the product of an old-fashioned public-school education and I do what I am told. It also takes me a long time to get away from my mother telling me what to do. It is a combination that inhibits and suppresses me. My mother is very ambitious for me and I feel I have to please her. Being seen with a successful man, which Sean undoubtedly is, is part of this and takes precedence over what happens to me behind closed doors.

One of Sean's regular drinking partners is the sensationalist painter Francis Bacon. They usually start their binges at Muriel's, a drinking bar in Soho, named after its lesbian owner and popular with gay men, though I don't think Sean is gay. I don't know how much time he spends there, but he obviously gets in fights somewhere as he often comes back covered in blood. I am really scared, but I don't dare tell a soul in case I make him angry. He never offers an explanation. If he doesn't go to Muriel's, Sean spends time in the Irish Club or drives round in a Rolls-Royce owned by Andrew Loog Oldham, the manager of the Rolling Stones.

He never contacts me during his three-day binges and I am left to worry about what sort of state he'll come back in. Sometimes he is so violently drunk and out of his head on drugs that he doesn't know who I am. It's terrifying.

In the late autumn of 1963 I hear that Wendy is pregnant and that Peter has married her. Their first daughter, Lucy, arrives in May 1964, and Daisy follows in September 1965.

Fortunately, I am very busy professionally. I fit it in between travelling with Sean and it helps take my mind off his erratic behaviour. In 1964 I am offered two separate small parts in the second 1964 to 1968 ITV series *Danger Man* that stars Patrick McGoohan as secret agent John Drake. The first series was shown from 1960 to 1962, was incredibly popular and became the forerunner for the spy boom and James Bond movies. Drake is unlike Bond partly because Patrick, a practising Catholic, refuses to let him get involved in any sexual adventures. The series also tries to be realistic so there isn't always a happy ending. I also appear as a computer centre girl in *Licensed to Kill* in 1965, an imitation James Bond film starring Tom Adams as British secret agent Tom Vine.

In addition I have a small part in the film *Those Magnificent Men in Their Flying Machines* (1965). It stars Sarah Miles, Terry-Thomas, Benny Hill and James Fox, who is charming, funny and a terrific actor. I play a young girl and have to run down the beach in a woolly, clingy, very unpleasant 1920s swimming costume. Although it is a tiny role, there is a lot of interest in me and I am photographed a great deal. When I get the film part I decide to stop dyeing my hair red and instead have lots of blonde highlights on my natural light brown hair. One evening, about two years into our relationship, Sean comes home drunk and wanting sex. I don't and try to push him away, but he persuades me, not terribly romantically. A few weeks later I discover that I am pregnant. I tell Sean and he immediately says I have to have an abortion. Although his divorce will soon be through, he doesn't want another child. I am devastated because I really want the baby. I force myself to weigh up the pros and cons carefully to see if I can continue with the pregnancy. On the one hand, I feel that even if Sean leaves me, I have the physical and emotional energy to cope on my own. On the other, I am not earning enough money to be able to support myself and a child. Most important of all, I can't face telling my mother I'm having an illegitimate child.

I reluctantly go with Sean to Dr Gerry Slattery, who is his doctor and friend. Gerry, a handsome, funny and caring Irishman, tries to persuade Sean to let me keep my baby, but Sean won't hear of it and threatens to leave me. I then have to see three psychiatrists in order to have a legal termination. It costs £300, which Sean pays. I feel defeated and am overwhelmed with despair. I don't tell my mother, but a few weeks after the abortion she tells me she knows what I've done. I don't say a word in response, but she can read my face like a book and must have made an educated guess. Fortunately she doesn't tell my father, who would be broken-hearted.

It changes everything and from then on my relationship with Sean rapidly goes downhill. One night he comes home so drunk he once again doesn't know who I am. He even calls me by a man's name, before grabbing me and throwing me down the stairs. They are concrete stairs with metal rails and I cut my head badly. I struggle up, and although it is 2 a.m., I ring for a taxi and go to my parents' London flat. I am in shock and my long blonde hair is caked with blood. My mother calls the family doctor and he comes round and treats my wounds. He also gives me a tetanus injection and prescribes antibiotics.

My mother is furious with Sean and, it seems, with me. She tells me I am now used goods and that nobody will want me. I feel ashamed and so ugly. The 1960s sexual revolution and subsequent emancipation of women is all about women taking control of their lives, but I, like many others, don't bring my problems out in the open and talk them through, even with close friends. What has happened is so shocking I know I must keep it to myself. To all intents and purposes, I am an only child and feel I have to deal with things on my own. Instead I keep telling myself, I've got to make it right. I've got to make it work. I've got to be seen by the world to be coping. As a result I put up with things I shouldn't.

The next day I try to talk to Sean about his violent attack. He says he can't remember anything about it, but apologises and says he didn't mean to hit me. I don't realise this is what most violent men say to the women they assault. To get me round and help me feel better, he keeps telling me we'll get married soon, that I can have a baby girl and that everything will be OK. I nod but know that he has killed something inside me, both literally and psychologically, and I vow never to have a child with him.

My parents no longer want me to be with Sean and suggest I go abroad with them to get away. I know I should leave him, but, like many battered women, I don't have the strength or courage to go. It makes my relationship with my mother very uncomfortable. I try not to see him every night, but when he senses I am drawing away from him, he gets extremely jealous and is then at his most dangerous. I am scared not only of what he can do to me, but also what he can do to himself. One day when he is in a good mood he buys me the E-type Jaguar, perhaps to make up for his violence and forcing me to have an abortion.

After five turbulent years together Sean tells me he is desperate to marry me. I don't want to marry him because the relationship isn't right. It is something I need to talk through, but I don't have any intimate friends left as I now only associate with Sean's friends. In the end I decide to confide in my grandmother and ask her what I should do, particularly now I am twenty-three, an age when most girls get married. She knows I want to escape from home and tells me she understands I am in a no-win situation.

I keep thinking about it and finally decide to marry Sean, but for all the wrong reasons – I am frightened of him and feel trapped because photographs of us together are constantly in the papers. He is thrilled, but I feel I have regressed back to that cowering little girl at school.

Sean fixes the date for 20 April 1966 and arranges everything, apart from my outfit. I am a tiny size zero and choose a pretty off-white crochet dress, which I wear under a white fur coat. My white Chanel shoes have black toecaps and kitten heels. I don't have any flowers and leave my long blonde hair to hang free. I am so worn down by our relationship that it is almost as if I am sleepwalking into marriage. We go to Chelsea Register Office on the King's Road. A press photographer turns up. Comedian John Wells is best man, there are no other guests, and I can't remember who else is witness and signs the forms. I don't tell my parents until afterwards and they are understandably very unhappy with me.

Following the ceremony we have a meal in an Italian restaurant in Soho. The next day our picture is in the papers and my mother feels that at least something has been resolved.

Sean has arranged for us to spend our honeymoon with Kevin McClory and his wife, Bobo Sigrist, heiress to the Hawker Siddeley aircraft fortune, in the Bahamas. At Heathrow Airport, we hear the Beatles' hit record 'I Wanna Hold Your Hand' being played through the loudspeakers. Sean takes my hand and I begin to hope that everything will be OK. I tell myself that although there is so much that is dramatic and sad about our relationship, in between it can still be exciting.

Once we land, we take a boat from the mainland to what is now called Paradise Island and is where Kevin and Bobo have their mansion. We arrive at Kevin's own private landing stage and walk up to the house. I gasp when I see it. It has an infinity pool and its own beach of soft white sand, plus stables and horses. We stay a week relaxing on the beach. We then travel to Nassau and spend a second week in Kevin's apartment there. We go to the local carnival, which is huge fun, and Sean is kind and loving throughout.

On our return, Sean rents 14 Cheyne Row for us to live in. It is in a very smart part of London and like a doll's house with underground tunnels that were used by priests in times of persecution. Sean fills the house with some beautiful old pieces of furniture, including an old pine sideboard and desk, Victorian lamps and lots of mirrors he's used in his theatrical shows.

The house is round the corner from where Mick Jagger and Marianne Faithfull live. I met Marianne at Lionel Bart's house, when she had just left her convent school and was young and innocent-looking with a peaches-and-cream complexion. I have also got to know Lionel. His home was once a convent and looks amazing with its galleried sitting room. It's ideal for him too, as he is constantly entertaining. He likes to have open house for show-business people, and lots of us, whether on the way up or down, regularly congregate there. It's always fun, and Lionel employs loads of servants to tend to our needs.

I try to settle into married life and keep asking Sean if I can meet his three young sons, but he wants me to know as little as possible about his past life and I only see them once. I think they are beautiful.

One day Sean and I receive an invitation to dinner with Anthony Armstrong-Jones and Princess Margaret. Tony has recently been given the title Lord Snowdon, to avoid the problem of the child of a royal princess being a commoner. I

wear a very 1960s outfit of black silk shirt with voluminous
sleeves, tiny waistcoat, black sequinned hot pants, black
tights and long black suede boots. It works very well with
my long blonde hair. Despite knowing I look good, I feel
incredibly nervous as we arrive. It is a show-business evening
and there are about a hundred of us, including handsome
actor Roger Moore and his wife, Luisa. Sean knows
Snowdon well and they immediately become engrossed in
conversation about various projects they are involved with.
Princess Margaret comes over, takes Snowdon's arm, then
says hello.

After dinner she walks up to me again and asks if I want
'to tidy up'. I am taken aback and assume she is asking if I
want to help clear away the dinner plates. Rather briskly I
say, 'I am fine,' and stay where I am. She moves on and soon
afterwards I see a line of ladies following her out of the room
and realise that her comment was a euphemism for 'Do you
want to use the toilet?' I am furious with myself for missing
an opportunity to see more of their home.

After the buffet dinner we go into a long drawing room
and Princess Margaret plays the piano and sings songs
from popular American musicals. She plays well and all in
all we have a marvellous evening.

A couple of weeks later Tony invites us to Kensington
Palace again. We accept the invitation and on the evening
concerned I start getting dressed while Sean rests on the bed
in his underpants. Without any warning he suddenly leaps
up, pulls the window shutters back, opens the windows and
shouts, 'I am Batman and I can fly.' Before I can do anything
to stop him, he then leaps out of the window, lands astride a
glass roof that is linked to the studio next door and his legs
go through the glass. I rush round, knock on the neighbours'
door and find that they are having a party. I explain about

Sean and about ten men, all smartly dressed in evening clothes, rush over to where he is hanging through the roof and kindly help shoulder him down.

Sean is in shock. There is glass embedded up and down his legs, but by some large chunk of Irish luck it has missed his private parts. I meanwhile quickly phone Tony and explain why we can't come to dinner after all. I then call the family doctor, who gives Sean an injection to knock him out. I help the doctor pick out the pieces of glass from his legs as quickly as possible. He then stitches Sean up and when he's finished asks for a gin and tonic. We help Sean upstairs to the bedroom, he falls fast asleep, and when he wakes up the next morning, he can't remember a thing about what happened. I have no idea why he behaved so strangely until years later, when it dawns on me that he must have taken the hallucinogenic drug LSD. The drug culture isn't part of my social group, but I am so young and naïve that perhaps I don't know what to look out for.

When Sean finds a gap in his schedule, he decides we must have a holiday in Greece. We visit the Acropolis and then take a boat round various islands. I love looking at buildings through Sean's eyes, which are those of an architect and stage designer and he brings Greece's ancient history to life for me. Unfortunately he is also drinking masses of ouzo, the national Greek drink, and one day he is so drunk that when he sees a man sitting opposite us on the boat we are travelling on, he suddenly decides he is spoiling for a fight, jumps up and starts punching him. In fact all the man is doing is using his rosary beads. A couple of passengers separate the two of them, the poor man looks completely astonished, and I say, 'For goodness' sake, Sean, he was only saying his prayers.'

Once we are back, Sean immerses himself in designing the

set for a performance of *Gulliver's Travels* at the Mermaid Theatre in London. He is also asked to design a ride that can be set in a diamond-shaped dome for the English Pavilion at Expo 67 at the World Fair in Canada. This means he regularly has to travel between London and Canada and will have to work incredibly hard. Sometimes I travel with him and watch him work onsite. It's amazing to see how the pavilion develops.

Other times I prefer to stay in London. One spring morning in 1967 I am walking down Jermyn Street on my way back from an audition when I bump into Peter coming out of the shirt shop Turnbull and Asser. I am wearing a saffron-coloured jacket that reaches my knees, black tights and black suede boots. It's a typical swinging-London look, but smart. We have a brief conversation. Our eyes lock together and I feel he is clocking me in his brain again.

Although Sean and I have some fun moments together, in general our relationship is going from bad to worse. I physically close down, partly because I can't forgive him for making me have an abortion, partly because of the way he is treating me and also because it is the only thing I can control in our relationship. It doesn't seem to bother him and I assume he is unfaithful while he is away.

One horrific night he comes home very drunk and wanting sex. I tell him I don't and this time he forces himself on me. Marital rape has not been recognised as abuse in the 1960s, and when he is done, I feel angry, worthless and battered. He apologises the next day, we make up yet again, and everything is peaceful for a while. But I live in fear of the next time, because I know it will come.

I don't have to wait long. Weeks later he comes home blind drunk again and, without any explanation, grabs a bread knife and starts to chase me round the kitchen. I manage to run out of the house and jump into my E-type to drive to my parents' home. As I start the engine, Sean leaps on to the car bonnet. He is still holding the bread knife and tries to slash the soft roof. I go into reverse and he falls off, but gets up straight away, and I can see in the car mirror that he is not badly hurt.

I feel so diminished by his continual abusive behaviour that I stay behind when he goes to Canada in May 1967. It is then that I meet Peter and my life completely changes.

7

Work and Play

Peter and I finally move in together nearly two years after we meet, but our wonderful idyll is quickly shattered by Sean, who comes round to Ruston Mews one night when he is drunk, thumps on the door and shrieks that he is going to kill both Peter and me. The first time Peter hears him banging on the door he quakes with fear beside me in bed. It is one thing to listen to me telling him what Sean has been doing and quite another to be on the receiving end of the tirade. He is terrified and doesn't offer to go downstairs and tell him face to face to go away.

Sean bangs so loudly we think his fists will break through the door and we are so frightened we can't speak. When he eventually stops, we wait what seems like hours. We assume he's gone away, but we don't know for how long.

Peter then rings Dudley, apologises because it is 2 a.m., explains what has happened and asks him if we can drive round to his home in Hampstead and stay the night. Dudley says it will be fine, so we put jumpers over our pyjamas and climb into my car, which fortunately Sean hasn't touched. We arrive at Dudley's like two scared children seeking shelter and Dudley lets us in with a smile. Suzy, his wife, is apparently away.

The three of us sit in the kitchen and he asks what has happened. When Peter starts explaining, Dudley roars with

laughter. Peter laughs too, but not nearly so enthusiastic-
ally. After we have had a nice cup of tea, Dudley shows us
the spare bedroom and we go to sleep. It's the first time
I've been inside Dudley's Regency house and the next morning I notice that the interior is decorated in exactly the same
way as Peter's house in Church Row. He has the same
William Morris wallpaper, virtually the same antique furniture, including an antique pram, and even the same knick-
knacks. I feel like Alice in Wonderland, not quite knowing
whose house I am in. It is the first time I am aware of the
intense competition that exists between them. I have
observed it professionally, but this is different and I can
suddenly see that whatever one has in his life the other
wants too.

Luckily the nightmare thumping and screaming isn't
repeated. Sean doesn't touch my car and I don't see him
again. It's a huge relief and means both Peter and I can get on
with our work in peace.

In 1968 Peter rewrites the film script that had originally
been drafted by John Cleese and Graham Chapman for *The
Rise and Rise of Michael Rimmer*. The film is an unnerving
political and social satire, and written well before spin
doctors became part of everyday life. Peter also plays the
lead role of Rimmer, a ruthless character who marches into
the offices of an advertising agency one morning to use the
company as his first step in spin-doctoring himself to the top.
He is smartly dressed and oozes so much confidence that no
one dares question his right to be there. He tramples on or
out-manoeuvres his enemies or anyone who stands in his
way and by the end of the film has declared himself to be the
first president of Great Britain.

It is backed by David Frost's film company, Paradine
Productions, and is David's first film as a producer. David

and Peter have a rollercoaster relationship that goes back to their days at Cambridge. Peter tells me that when they were both undergraduates, David used to worship him to the extent that anything Peter said or did David would emulate a few days later – so much so that the writer Christopher Booker used to joke, 'D. Frost and leave to Cook for five minutes.'

As it happens Peter fell out with David a few years earlier, in 1962, when he heard he was to front a satirical television programme called *That Was the Week That Was*, because it was far too similar to one Peter had earlier suggested to the BBC and wanted to host himself. He is even more annoyed when it goes on to attract a colossal audience of twelve million viewers. David still tried to stay in touch, and when Peter was performing in America in the summer of 1963 with the cast of *Beyond the Fringe*, David rang up and suggested he fly out to join them all. The cast and Wendy were taking a few days' break in a rented house in Fairfield, Connecticut, and when David arrived, Peter behaved with steely politeness and suggested he might like to swim in the pool. David was too embarrassed to admit he couldn't swim, so dived in. Peter immediately realised that he was in trouble, dived in after him and saved his life. He later tells me that rescuing him is the one thing he most regrets doing in his life and calls him 'the bubonic plagiarist'.

Peter doesn't go to the press conference to promote *The Rise and Rise of Michael Rimmer*, as he is in Majorca seeing Wendy at the time, but sends a cable saying, 'Sorry not to be there, but I am a publicity-shy recluse, known to my friends as the Greta Garbo of Hampstead.'

The premiere for the film takes place in November 1970. Peter and I are living together, and I have a sand-coloured suede suit specially made for the occasion. The trousers are fringed and so tight I practically have to be sewn into them. The jacket also has fringes everywhere and is modelled on a wonderful jacket worn by Roger Daltrey from pop group The Who.

There are lots of stars from the film at the premiere, including Arthur Lowe from *Dad's Army*, who I think is the bee's knees, John Cleese, Ronald Fraser from *The Misfit* and playwright Harold Pinter, who plays an interviewer on a TV chat show. The reviews are not very good, and although the critics say there are some hilarious moments, they don't think it is strung together very well. There are also so many rumours that Rimmer is a dig at David Frost that the film company puts out a denial, which makes everyone think it must be true. At one point, for example, Rimmer is at a party at London Zoo going round saying to everyone, 'Super to see you again.' Peter jokes that it can't be David as he always says, 'Gorgeous to see you.'

Peter drives home after the premiere but is stopped by the police on suspicion of drink-driving. The following April he goes to court to face the charge of driving over the alcohol limit. He takes a doctor along to help him get off by saying he is on the tranquilliser Valium, which affects the alcohol in his bloodstream and makes him appear drunk when he isn't really. It doesn't work. He is banned for twelve months and fined £25 with £21 costs. After being told the disqualification is automatic, Peter asks with an absolutely straight face, 'Does that disqualify me from driving a power-assisted pedal cycle or a lawnmower?' He is told that it does. I don't see it as a cause for concern. It seems quite natural to celebrate after the premiere of your own film and believe Peter just had a few too many that pushed him over the limit.

One evening Peter tells me Jonathan Miller wants to know more about what he calls 'a certain side of life' and Peter suggests we take him to a Soho strip club to broaden his outlook. The first strip club in Britain was started by Paul Raymond in 1958 and was such a success that others quickly followed and they are now attracting a sophisticated clientele. At the time topless models are only allowed onstage if they remain completely motionless, so once they have removed their clothes, their act is over.

We collect Jonathan from his home in Primrose Hill and go into the club together. The girls have feathers in their hair and initially start their performance wearing lots of showy, easy-to-remove, brightly coloured clothes – they look like they could be part of the chorus line of a show. Jonathan's eyes are out on stalks as they gradually peel off one layer after another. We stay for about an hour, then go to dinner at L'Escargot, a fashionable restaurant in Greek Street. Jonathan and Peter launch into a deeply academic discussion about the pros and cons of strip clubs. Jonathan is objective, rather than personal. He reminds me of a dotty professor and I have no idea what he really thinks.

In our free time Peter and I don't just see celebrities. We like to go to the cinema or out for meals together, and Peter still goes to watch football matches and plays golf. He also talks to everyone, especially taxi drivers, and sometimes asks them back for a cup of tea. Occasionally I take a taxi home but get out at the top of our road to avoid giving away the number of our house. On several occasions the taxi driver says to me, 'Do you know who lives down there? That Peter Cook. Took him back once and he invited me in. Great bloke.'

After I have been with 20th Century Fox for two years, they decide to cancel my contract. I don't mind, as I am booked to spend July 1970 filming *Die Screaming, Marri-anne* in Portugal. It is a low-budget horror-thriller that stars Susan George and James Mason. I play Susan's elder sister, and James Mason, whose name curiously doesn't appear in the credits, plays my father. I don't want to leave Peter in London, because I love him very much and don't want us to be apart so ask Pete Walker, who is the director, if Peter can come on location to Albufeira with me. Pete is so thrilled with the idea he offers to pay Peter's bed and board even though he has nothing to do with the film.

We stay in a beautiful house on a private estate and Peter seems very happy. He even gets up early to drive me up into the hills on the days I am filming. During the day, while I am working, he takes lots of photographs, which is something he hasn't done since the summer before he started university, when he spent several weeks at West Bay in Dorset snapping holidaymakers and was so charming to everyone he earned about £20 a week.

Peter regularly joins us all for lunch. He enjoys gossip-ing and everyone gravitates towards him. I am thrilled to have him with me, and the cast enjoy having someone amusing to entertain them. Peter is pleased that I helped arrange for his expenses to be paid. Although he earns well, he is generally quite careful with his money, except when he is gambling.

He makes friends with Christopher Sandford, one of the actors in the film, who has also appeared in *Coronation Street*. They enjoy each other's sense of humour, and in the evening after filming the three of us try to find restaurants that are off the beaten track. In some ways being in Portugal is like being on holiday, except we have to leave the restau-rants early when I have a 5.30 a.m. call.

One of our funniest days takes place when we have to

film a riding scene with James Mason, who can't in fact
ride. The director gets round it by taking some initial shots
of him sitting on a real horse. James subsequently pretends
to ride a life-size model of a horse by going up and down
in the saddle on the spot. Christopher and I then gallop on
real horses into the shot, and the three of us have to look
as though we are trotting along together, when in fact we
are stationary. Peter is in fits of laughter and I try hard
not to giggle while the cameras are rolling. Although I have
great fun making the film, it is badly received by the
critics.

Now we are living together, Peter wants me to meet his
parents. They live in Milford-on-Sea, an unspoilt village near
Lymington, Hampshire, with stunning views. We drive down
and spend a very easy day together. Margaret, his mother,
has an intelligent face, an easy smile and treats me with
warmth and kindness. It is the start of a very happy relationship between us. Peter's father, Alec, is tall and slim with
huge grey-blue eyes, slightly protruding ears and a distinguished head of white hair. When he fixes me with his gaze,
he reminds me of a startled, elegant owl who has just landed
on his perch. I also meet Peter's sisters, Sarah and Elizabeth,
known as Liz, who are equally very friendly to me.

In January 1971 Peter, Dudley and I go on a short trip to
Sydney to do some pre-publicity for *Behind the Fridge*, their
six-month-long tour round Australia and, hopefully, New
Zealand later in the year. It's perfect timing as we shall be out
of the country when Peter's divorce becomes absolute. We
are over the moon when it does, because it is what we have
both been waiting for, but we still can't do what we really
want, which is to get married, because my divorce isn't
through. Peter does the next best thing and gives an interview saying he wants to marry me but I have no idea when I

shall be free because Sean is not replying to any of my solicitor's letters.

The lack of success of *The Rise and Rise of Michael Rimmer* prompts Peter to go back to working on television, but he says he doesn't want to stand still creatively and would like to try something completely different. He is also infuriated that David Frost is being called 'the king of the chat show' because of his success on *The Frost Report*. Peter knows he is funnier and quicker-witted than David, and decides that if David can host a chat show, so can he. He contacts the BBC and tells them his plans. They are delighted to give him a chat show and immediately commission a series of twelve to be called *Where Do I Sit?* without even asking him to do a pilot programme.

The initial show is broadcast on 11 February 1971 on BBC2 and Peter's first guest is the humorist S. J. Perelman. Perelman may have written extremely funny books, but in person he is not at all amusing. His responses to Peter are almost monosyllabic and it's obvious that Peter can't cope. He hasn't been told he needs to do a lot of research into his guests, and in any case his strength is instant repartee.

He also decides to sing a pop song in each show, and on this first programme does an impression of singer Johnny Cash. It's awful, so it's no surprise that his reviews are terrible. Chris Dunkley in *The Times* says, 'The whole thing reeked of an old boys' get-together.' He calls the show 'dismally embarrassing' and Peter's interview 'pathetic', adding this is 'mainly because Peter Cook seemingly will persist in the belief that his ad-lib material is better than the rehearsed sections. Unfortunately the precise opposite is generally true.'

Peter is obviously nervous about how the next show will be received and perhaps drinks too much before going on air.

The programme includes a sketch in which he and Spike Milligan are dressed as tramps and includes the following exchange:

> PETER: I'm God.
> SPIKE: 'Oh, Christ. Oh, dear. I'm sorry. He's your son, isn't he?'

This causes an intense reaction from Mary Whitehouse, a woman who has appointed herself moral guardian of the nation. She complains in the press about Peter pretending to be God and claims it is blasphemy. Peter responds by saying that her objections are 'too farcical for words' and asks how anyone could take his sketch seriously when he is wearing old shorts and a steel helmet, and is obviously portraying an idiot.

It is by now clear that doing a chat show is not Peter's forte, and the twelve-week series is dropped after three. A young, almost unknown, journalist called Michael Parkinson is hired to replace Peter. Peter copes with the humiliation and disappointment by drinking. I am angry that he is drinking so much but when I ask him why he tells me it's only because he can't sleep and feels stressed. I believe him and assume he is in control and that if I keep talking to him about it, he will see reason and cut down.

Meanwhile I have been growing increasingly unwell. I have had pains in my stomach and pelvis area for several months but have done nothing about them because I assume they are stress-related. When they don't go, I decide I must have cancer, but am too scared to find out and believe I am going to die. My stomach becomes extremely swollen, and I lose weight. I can't bear to be touched and have absolutely no strength. Peter understands completely, and at night we lie very close to each other but not quite touching. He is anxious about me and keeps bringing me bowls of soup in bed. When I refuse, he offers me sips of brandy instead. Although I am essentially a non-drinker, I take them to try to ease the pain.

He becomes progressively frantic with worry and eventually phones my mother, who flies over from Jersey to see me. She insists I see a doctor immediately and it is quickly arranged for me to have tests at the Edward VII Hospital. I get to the hospital, but walk out when no one is looking because I am terrified of anyone finding out what's wrong. At home, I continue to feel increasingly ill and shortly afterwards, in May 1971, I collapse. Peter takes me to Coniston Nursing Home in Ealing, west London.

Peter again calls my mother and she recommends Tom Lewis, a gynaecologist. He comes to see me, takes one look and says that I have peritonitis. This is a serious inflammatory pelvic disease and in my case the result of the IUD contraceptive coil I had inserted for a short time following my abortion, which had pierced my womb. I lapse into unconsciousness, am taken to intensive care and hooked up to all sorts of drips and tubes. I remember knowing that I can't feel my body any more and can choose whether I live or die. Part of me feels it's easier to slip away and leave the pain behind. Everything is so calm and peaceful that I want to let go. Instead I begin to come round. I open my eyes and see a tree through the hospital window. It is a life force and I hear someone in my head say that it is not my time yet.

I gradually come round, and when I fully wake up two days later, I see Peter sitting beside me reading what I assume to be a racing paper. I like it because it is so normal. I can feel my body turning over like a turbine and coming to life again.

I believe that Tom Lewis's prompt diagnosis and treatment has saved my life.

Peter is with me every day, but the doctors tell my mother, who has again come over from Jersey, not to visit me in hospital as it will be too upsetting for both of us. She would have been frantic and I need to stay calm. After a week I go home with some painkillers and antibiotics. I am very happy to be back, but I have no strength and am told I mustn't drive. My weight has plummeted to just five stone, two and a half stone less than normal, and I keep fainting. I can't bear anyone, including Peter, touching my skin.

I also feel very frightened. Getting work depends on me looking good and being healthy, and I worry I'll never work again. My mother goes back to Jersey and Peter keeps her informed of my progress by telephone. Peter looks after me as best he can. While I am still in bed, he tells me that if I want something, I should bang on our wooden floor and I usually do so by throwing a shoe across the room. Peter occasionally doesn't hear because he is too absorbed in watching the racing on television, but it doesn't happen often.

He regularly goes to Highgate Village to buy me tasty things to eat, like tins of special soup and unusual bread. Sometimes he makes me scrambled egg or I have a tin of rice pudding. Some people fuss too much when you are ill and make you feel worse, but Peter gives me just the right amount of attention, and is incredibly gentle.

Once I start putting on weight and feel stronger, he takes me on short outings, usually to Ladbrokes to place bets. I put on an old T-shirt and sweater, and he drives me there – having now got his licence back – and then either perches me on a chair, which is not particularly comfortable, or leaves me in the car while he puts on his bets. Doing something so

mundane together makes me laugh and I feel like I'm returning to normal life.

He never complains about the strain that me being ill
places on him, even though it is such a busy time. Peter is still
writing sketches for *Behind the Fridge*. Once I feel a little
better, I start sitting with Peter and Dudley as their audience
again.

When they are working well together, the repartee is
almost seamless. They feed off each other with one funny
line after another. They even respond to each other's wit in
the same way, throwing their heads backwards and roaring
with laughter.

They are developing a rich cast of characters, from an
eccentric university professor and a student to a minicab
driver and a member of the House of Lords. Their accents
are priceless and they can slip seemingly effortlessly from
toff to working-class yob. What is particularly brilliant is
that each character has an unexpected aspect to his personality. The upper-class gentleman can be gauche and awkward,
while the working-class lad can have an unusual insight and
depth of knowledge in one area of life.

It is something they originally immortalised in the classic Dud and Pete art-gallery sketch. Pete tells Dud that the
sign of a good Rubens nude is when the bottom follows
you around the room. They subsequently discuss the cartoons of Leonardo da Vinci. Leonardo da Vinci's cartoons
are of course drawings and not meant to be funny, but by
playing with the word 'cartoon' Dud and Pete masterfully
highlight the pomposity and pretentiousness of many in the
art world.

PETE: I can't see the bloody joke.
DUD (with enormous self importance): The sense of

humour must have changed over the years. When they
first came out, I bet everyone was killing themselves.

When Peter stops work, we spend all our time together
and never get bored with each other's company. I feel he
really loves me and that we are reaching a very deep place
together. It is a place beyond words, perhaps the result of me
nearly dying and Peter knowing exactly how to handle that.
He doesn't reveal his own anxiety and enables me to find
peace with him. I don't feel embarrassed or awkward that he
has seen me at my worst. Peter is born under the star sign of
Scorpio and has an instinctive and deep spiritual knowledge
of human nature. He is so special.

Now Peter is divorced, the family home has to be sold. It
goes on the market for £45,000. It seems a lot for the early
1970s, but in 2007 a house in Church Row was valued at
about £4 million. Wendy comes back from Majorca to live in
the house to help sell the property. The proceeds will initially
go to Peter and then be divided between them so they can
both buy a new home. Lucy and Daisy will live with Wendy.

Wendy sees lots of properties but doesn't like anything
and decides the only place she wants to live is Kenwood
Cottage, even though she hasn't seen it. It has only been
Peter's and my home for a year, but she no doubt rationalises
that if Peter likes it, it must be good.

Things are really awkward when September 1971 comes
round, as the Australian tour of *Behind the Fridge* is just
about to start. Peter doesn't want Wendy to know he is going
to Australia, but won't tell me why. Instead he behaves as he
always does when he refuses to think about the consequences of his actions. He draws the shutters down inside
himself and won't discuss it. Wendy is bound to find out
where he is once we get there, but I don't feel it is my busi-

ness to interfere. The only explanation Peter offers is that he can't face the showdown he knows it will trigger.

With only a few weeks to go he decides that the best solution is for Wendy to have her way and move into our home. Peter desperately wants her to find somewhere before we leave so that Church Row can be sold. He also wants the children's schools sorted out so we can all get on with our lives, and Wendy can't do that until she knows where she is going to live. We agree that Wendy can move into Kenwood Cottage and we'll look for another house for ourselves when we come back.

Peter is very keen on the Australia trip. It is a really big tour to take on, but it is the ideal way to make enough money so that he doesn't need to worry about his finances for a while. To help prepare themselves, he and Dudley go to Champneys health farm for a week to lose some weight and get into top form. Peter wants me to join them, but I can only go for a day as I have no one to look after the cats. Peter and Dudley are cock-a-hoop to be spending a few days away together and talk nonstop, crack jokes and ooze an irresistible combination of high energy and charm. Peter and Dudley set off together in Dudley's Maserati and I follow in my car.

When we arrive, we see Maggie Smith, the actress, waiting in reception and looking both beautiful and haughty. I spend the afternoon with Peter and leave thinking both of them are much too attractive to be left alone. Peter rings me every day, usually after he has a treatment, to tell me all about it. He is loving and sounds as if he is behaving himself. He describes how there is a choice of restaurant, one for those who want to restrict what they eat and a normal one. Dudley is being very good and keeping strictly to the diet menu, but Peter is eating and drinking whatever he wants.

I have a medical check-up and the doctor tells me I'm strong enough to travel to Australia with Peter and Dudley, and adds that the sun will do me good. We are all hugely relieved. I don't know what would have happened if I had to stay behind. The doctor also puts me on the pill as he says it would be dangerous for me to get pregnant so soon after my illness. I start taking it, but I don't like it. It frees me from the worry of getting pregnant, but it also dampens my sex drive.

The build-up to the tour is very hectic and quite stressful. Although Peter and Dudley are well known in London, and to a certain extent in America, they are an unknown quantity in Australia, and worry about how they will be received. Now Wendy has agreed to move into our home, we have to empty it of our possessions. I want to take everything out and not leave a trace of Peter or me behind, so we pile everything into Ruston Mews, which quickly becomes packed with our stuff.

When we move into Ruston Mews, it is so overcrowded with furniture that we can hardly squeeze in the door. We have several armchairs, two beds, mirrors and at least two of everything else crammed into a two-up, two-down property. Every time we want to move from one room to another, we have to climb over piles of our possessions. We could have put things in storage, but it would have been too much of a kerfuffle with so little time to spare. Fortunately one of the bedrooms has a large built-in double wardrobe, which we cram full of our things. As a rule I am quite meticulous about the home, and Peter prefers things to be tidy too. The only way he can really work is in an ordered environment, but we know it is only temporary and we will find somewhere spacious and uncluttered when we come back from the tour.

As the date to leave approaches, Peter becomes increasingly nervous, particularly about leaving the children. It will be the first time he has been away from them for so long, and six months is an eternity in a child's life. He still doesn't want Wendy to find out where he is going.

My priority is making sure I keep Dudley and Peter as cool and calm as possible before we go. They get very keyed up when they are working. They are interdependent, can read each other's thoughts and love getting into their own little world. They are also completely fascinated by what the other is doing every minute they are not together. By now the whole show is in their heads and the tension is growing.

Dudley is particularly anxious. His marriage to Suzy has broken down. He has moved out of the marital home and into a small flat and is worried about who will look after his Persian cats. I thought he was happy with Suzy, but perhaps because of his upbringing and the fact that he wants constant stimulation and likes to do new things and meet different people all the time, he is fundamentally too restless. I wonder if he is the sort of man who will ever be able to settle with one woman.

I have to prepare myself for the long trip too and it doesn't help when my agent, I am now with Jean Diamond from London Management, tells me that if I go off for six months with Peter, my acting and modelling career are effectively over. The truth is, I don't have an option. Peter left his wife for me and nursed me through a difficult illness, and I love him and want to be with him. If he went to Australia on his own, I know it would be the end of our relationship. In an ideal world I'd like a career that would let me earn my own money and be with Peter, but I know I have to choose and I choose Peter. Just before we leave I put my cats into a cattery. It's heartbreaking and I feel I am parting with my babies.

The September weather in London is autumnal, but it will be hot in Australia, so I pack light things and roll them up small so that I don't have to take too much luggage. Luckily Peter and Dudley's costumes for the show largely consist of a suit and raincoat. It is going to be hard work, and performing is only a part of what Peter and Dudley will have to do. To get bums on seats, they also have to sell themselves and the show. It will mean being available all the time, giving interviews and being friendly to everyone. It's demanding and takes a lot of energy. It will even be hard work for me because I have to be around to back up Peter, and to a lesser extent Dudley, in whatever he wants to do. I have become their muse, and they both like me to be there when they need to spark off each other and vie for attention.

There is a very long flight to Sydney ahead of us, but luckily we have seats in first class. Sitting behind us is an oriental prince and his entourage. After several hours we all feel bored. There are only so many films you can watch, so many meals you can eat and so many books you can read. At one point Dudley starts throwing flannels at us. The first one lands on Peter's head. Peter picks it up and tries to throw it back, but instead it flies backwards and lands on the prince's face.

There is a terrible silence and several bodyguards rush over to the prince to investigate. Dudley is laughing hysterically as he gets out of his seat and goes up to the prince. The bodyguards try to stop him, but he does a lot of bowing and fawning and explains that neither he nor Peter mean any harm. Dudley offers the prince another flannel and asks if he would care to join in the game by throwing it at us. He declines but is not angry and we end up having a drink together.

We start to get excited and nervous as we come in to land. We are going to be besieged by reporters and Peter and Dudley must immediately take advantage of the opportunity to push the show. They will also be meeting Colin McLennan, the tour's promoter, for talks about extending the tour to New Zealand.

Shortly before we arrive, we freshen up and change. Dudley and Peter put on clean shirts. I put on shorts and a little silk top. We don't know what will be waiting for us.

8

Australia, Here We Come

As soon as we land in Canberra, we are surrounded by journalists. Peter and Dudley take it all in their stride and are calm, confident and very funny as they give one interview after another. I sit quietly by their side. Photographers take pictures of me and then ask who I am. Peter says I am his travelling companion. It's a description that clearly works, as they don't probe any further. After the interviews we are taken to our hotel. It's like a drab motel from a B-movie and Peter and I have the tiniest double room. It's also baking hot. We are experiencing culture shock and feel we have been washed up on a desert island.

The show opens in Canberra to rave reviews and is an instant success. It is a huge relief, as Peter and Dudley haven't been sure how their humour will be received. Canberra is the first leg of our Australian journey. From here it will be Melbourne, Sydney and Perth.

Colin McLennan turns out to be a terrific promoter and organises masses of press, and we quickly establish a routine. Peter and Dudley give interviews most mornings, and the three of us then have lunch together. Sometimes we are joined by a journalist or someone involved in producing the show. If they don't have more interviews to do, Peter and Dudley rest in the early afternoon – it's too hot to do much else. They have a light meal before going to the theatre. After the performance we come back to our hotel, and Dudley and Peter go over the show and make notes of what did and didn't work. They then alter or sharpen up the script, depending on the reaction of that evening's audience. It is all so hectic that it is difficult for Peter and Dudley to find anywhere to get away from everything and be quiet. They are either in a hotel room or out front dealing with people.

Peter is positive about the show, but gets anxious each week or two when we have to change theatres. It's a bit like moving house, except Peter and Dudley need to become familiar with their surroundings very quickly and make sure they know where everything is, right down to the smallest item of make-up in the dressing room, so they feel confident onstage.

There are regularly unexpected problems too. When we arrive at one old-fashioned theatre, we discover that none of the lights work. It is complete chaos while the production team fumble around in the dark until eventually an electrician manages to sort it out. Another underlying anxiety is that as there are only two of them in the show and obviously no understudies, neither of them can take a day off if they fall ill.

Dudley is thriving, and appears to be taking his separation from Suzy in his stride. It's a pity their marriage didn't work. It seems that Suzy didn't want to become an appendage to Dudley and began to feel lost, while Dudley was finding it increasingly hard to express his feelings to her. Instead he retreated into long painful silences. Fortunately they still manage to have an amicable divorce and stay friends. Peter, meanwhile, is missing his children dreadfully and tries not to think too much about them.

The three of us spend so much time together and are so close we become a support system for each other. We don't even have to talk to understand what each of us feels. I know instantly from looking at both of them what sort of mood they are in.

Peter and Dudley are extremely close, and all Peter has to do is mention Lucy and Daisy for Dudley to know immediately how anxious and concerned he is and respond by being very caring. Their mutual dependency and intuition of each other's needs and moods is both touching and powerful to watch.

As we tour, I devote my time and energy to Peter and make sure I am always there for him. He demands a lot from me both physically and emotionally, and I have little space for anything else. He likes me to go with him to the theatre almost every evening, and I wait in the dressing room, stand at the side of the stage or out front and watch him. Peter looks at me repeatedly when he performs, often just for a fraction of a second, as if to say, 'What did you think of that?' I try to show by the tiniest gestures and expressions that I love and support him and appreciate how much he has to do.

From Canberra we move on to Melbourne, where the show opens on 2 October 1971. Just before Peter goes onstage, though, a cable arrives from Wendy. I believe she was told where Peter was by journalists. I know he didn't tell her. She informs Peter that Daisy, who is now six years old, is having a really bad asthma attack and is going to hospital. Peter is devastated. He has been trying not to think about the distance and how long he is leaving his children. Now he is overwhelmed with worry and guilt about Daisy and how much he misses her and Lucy.

However, he is so suspicious that, instead of ringing Wendy direct, he writes a subtle letter to his parents to try and check that what she said was true. He says that she might be trying to wind him up, and hopes that if anything was badly wrong with Daisy, they would know. He also asks them to ring Wendy to make sure, and then sends love from us both.

He tells Dudley about the cable, then has a few drinks to help him cope with his anxiety. Drinking has become Peter's way of getting rid of any kind of pain, much of which has complex roots and goes back to his feelings of being abandoned as a child. I sense his darkness and know that this is an occasion when nothing I say can comfort him. His mood lingers for several days, and when he is not working, he is very quiet and I stay equally quiet with him.

Meanwhile the show is a sell-out wherever we go, which is wonderful. The tour becomes an awakening for Dudley, as he begins to see clearly for the first time how attractive he is to women and how funny they find him. It all begins one morning when Peter and I are relaxing by the hotel pool in our swimwear. Dudley joins us dressed in jeans and wearing his specially made boots. Peter, who has just been for a swim, looks Dudley up and down and asks why he is 'booted and suited', adding that he looks ridiculous and should put on some swimming trunks.

It's obvious to me why Dudley wants to stay dressed and I worry that Peter's remark will upset him, but Dudley admits straight away that he doesn't like taking his boots off because of his club foot. It is the first and only time he ever talks about his foot to either of us.

Dudley had a difficult childhood. He was born in April 1935 into a working-class family in London's East End. His father, John, worked as an electrician for British Rail, but neither he nor Dudley's mother, Ada, showed him much warmth or affection. One reason is because Dudley was born with both his feet turning inwards. His mother was so repelled that he was not physically perfect that when he was handed to her, she apparently said, 'He is not mine. I don't want him. Take him away.' Her much-loved brother had died and she had hoped Dudley would be an unblemished replacement for him: a 'cripple' wasn't acceptable.

Dudley's right foot corrected itself, but he spent many months in hospital over a seven-year period undergoing various operations on his left leg. It was a lonely as well as gruelling time, particularly as his mother hardly visited him. His hospital stays were particularly frightening during the war, as he was sometimes the only child in a ward full of wounded soldiers. Despite all the operations, he was left with a club foot and a short left leg, withered from the knee down.

At primary school he was laughed at and his leg became the subject of ridicule. Fortunately, though, his musical talent was discovered and nurtured at his secondary school, Dagenham County High. He was originally rather studious, but decided to work less and, like Peter, crack jokes to deflect the constant bullying. He continued playing the piano, mainly because he found it extremely easy. From school he won a scholarship to the Guildhall School of Music and then a further scholarship to Magdalen College, Oxford. He specialised in affectionate but irreverent parodies of composers from Beethoven to Schumann.

Dudley admitted he never got over his mother's early rejection and both his parents' emotional distance and spent years seeing psychiatrists and in psychotherapy. He liked to joke, 'I have had a midlife crisis since I was two weeks old. I went right from a midwife to a midlife crisis.' He told me a very poignant memory of being in hospital one Christmas and a nurse offering to give him a good-night kiss. He said he was so deprived of love that 'This was my first taste of real, unqualified, uncomplicated affection, and in many ways my entire life is based on searching for and recapturing that moment.'

Gradually, over the weeks and months that we are in Australia, Dudley becomes less self-conscious and eventually starts walking around hotel swimming pools barefoot and wearing swimming trunks. The transformation doesn't stop there. He also loses weight, and his increasing confidence in himself is special to see. He has had beautiful girlfriends in the past. One was the model Celia Hammond, whom he met at the Establishment, and of course Suzy Kendall is also shapely and good-looking, but Dudley has until very recently thought it a fluke that he has had relationships with attractive women.

Now, endless numbers of women are making it obvious that they want to be with him and Peter and I enjoy analysing why. Dudley is extremely interested in other people's problems and happily spends hours listening to women telling him all their anxieties. It is something that many women like and appreciate. Dudley also wants to know every detail of a woman's life and, because he's been in psychoanalysis himself, is an expert at drawing out all the facts, which he does with charm and humour. In addition he is very knowledgeable about food and wine and a delightful companion to talk to over dinner. His club foot also makes him seem vulnerable. It brings out a mothering instinct in women and stops any potential girlfriend from feeling inhibited by being with a powerful and successful man. What's more, of course, he plays the piano divinely.

As a result of the female attention and putting more effort into looking attractive, Dudley becomes a dangerous predator. He reminds me of when I was a deb and my friends and I would tell each other not to go out with a particular man because he was NSIT, 'Not Safe in Taxis'. Dudley is now one of those men. In fact both he and Peter make love to a woman with their minds as well as their bodies and it is an irresistible combination.

The three of us enjoy each other's company immensely, and although we spend all day together, we sometimes go out again after the show. Dudley soon starts bringing various girlfriends along to join us. A young Australian reporter called Lyndall Hobbs catches his eye and becomes a fixture. Lots of other girls turn up at the stage door wanting to meet him, and if he likes one, he often invites her to join us. The key thing that the three of us know and accept, almost without saying, is that anybody Dudley turns up with also has to get on with Peter and me.

Dudley never asks us what we think of any of his girl-friends, but Peter and I always give him our comments regardless. We try to tell Dudley when whoever he is dat-ing isn't around, but if Peter really thinks she doesn't fit in, he will make it quite difficult for her when she is with us. She can't, for example, be argumentative or tricky, because it could affect their performance that night. This is understandable: the show depends on both of them get-ting on well, which includes approval of Dudley's girl-friends.

I have become aware that there is a growing frisson between Dudley and me, which gives an edge to our rela-tionship and makes him want to compete with Peter for my attention, to make me laugh more and prove how clever he is. Peter obviously has more confidence because I am with him, and this makes him equally competitive in return.

After we have been away for about a month, Dudley has so many women after him that one day I decide to play a trick on him. I phone room service in our hotel just before I go to bed and order ten full English breakfasts to be sent up to his room the following morning with the instructions that they are to be delivered separately, one after the other. I tell Peter and he thinks it is very funny. In fact it's a stupid thing to do. Our suite is next door to Dudley's and we are woken the following morning by repeated knocking at his door as room service delivers breakfast after breakfast. We can even hear the waiter say several times, 'Mr Moore, sir, here is the English breakfast you ordered.'

Almost immediately after the tenth is delivered, Dudley pounds on our door and demands, 'Who has done this?' Peter looks completely innocent. I own up, then shoot into the bathroom to hide because both Peter and Dudley are looking at me po-faced. When I come out, I look at Peter and plead with my eyes for him to back me up. Instead he takes Dudley's side and tells me I have been very stupid and doesn't know why on earth I did it.

I turn to Dudley and joke, 'I thought you were having a lot of guests, Dudley,' but neither he nor Peter laugh. Dudley isn't someone you can push around and he is absolutely furious with me. For the following few days they both punish me by not talking to me and Peter keeps looking at me as if I am an idiot. It's like being with two ghastly school-boys and makes me realise that at one level they both feel they own me.

I learn from it and I know that I must be very careful of how I treat Dudley. Upsetting Dudley will upset Peter, who, as I have now seen, will take his side rather than mine. Equally, if I annoy Peter it will upset Dudley. It's a privileged but difficult position to be in. In one way I feel honoured that I am totally integrated into their unique partnership. But it is also a minefield.

As the show continues, Peter's drinking escalates. He has

started to drink over lunch, especially when he is being interviewed. He also has wine with his light meal before the show, which Dudley doesn't dream of doing. After the show he drinks nonstop until he falls asleep. It is having a cumulative effect on both his health and our relationship. We no longer have sex very often because he is too drunk. I find his drinking very difficult to cope with, but I have no idea what to do and try to stay optimistic that it will somehow sort itself out.

Fortunately he is still very professional onstage and I hope that audiences don't notice that he is often far from sober. I love Peter and am very worried about him, but I don't feel I can talk about him with anyone. If you live with a famous person, it is both difficult and unwise to confide in other people. Particularly, as in Peter's case, when it is about something as professionally damaging as excessive drinking. If the press get hold of the story, it could not only affect his career but also have repercussions for Dudley. I don't even have the kind of relationship with my mother that makes me want to talk to her about what is happening, and in any case she is too far away.

One of the reasons why I don't challenge Peter directly about his excessive drinking is because I am acutely aware that nearly every woman who comes into contact with him fancies him. They gather round and want to get to know him, and I worry that any one of them could seize the opportunity to get closer to Peter and then try to take him away from me. I gradually realise that the only person I can trust and who will totally understand is Dudley, because without saying as much we have shared the secret about Peter's drinking for years. He also loves Peter and they are the closest men in each other's lives.

During the tour I come to know Dudley intimately, even down to the small but important act of giving him space.

Space is at a premium on a long tour and Dudley sometimes desperately needs to be alone. He has an artistic tempera- ment and goes quiet and becomes reclusive when he feels low. He talks a lot about being depressed and tells me it is one reason why he has put himself in analysis. I also know he is worried about Peter and, like me, has no one with whom he can share his anxieties. We turn to each other and become a sort of mutual release valve for our concerns.

It helps keep us sane and at first neither of us feels guilty, but it becomes an intimacy that is increasingly difficult to keep within strict boundaries. Instead it develops into some- thing quite intoxicating and pushes Dudley and me even closer together. Not only are we physically close nearly every waking moment, we now spend a considerable amount of time talking about Peter. As Dudley and I become more inti- mate emotionally, his relationship with Peter becomes increasingly tetchy. I feel sad that their special bond is becoming damaged, but hope they will get back to how they once were together.

The way our relationship is ripening becomes obvious to both of us when we reach Sydney, the third stop on our tour. We have had to rough it in some of the hotels we have stayed in, but our hotel in Sydney is beautiful and we have magnifi- cent suites with wonderful views over the harbour. We discover that the Australian cricket team is also staying at the hotel. Peter is delighted to meet them and joins them several times for a drink. Peter has by now discovered Australian wine. He loves the taste and is drinking it in copious amounts. After a show he usually downs a bottle and a half of wine.

Each day Dudley can't wait to ask how much Peter has been drinking, what he's been doing and what his mood is like. He also rings our suite every afternoon to ask about him, despite the fact that we have been together an hour or so earlier. It is a little obsessive, but I don't challenge him. If I tell him Peter has fallen into a drunken sleep, which is happening increasingly frequently, he sounds pleased to talk to me. He tells me what he is doing, which is usually lying on his bed listening to classical music. Sometimes he comes to our suite and we talk in the sitting room, occasionally glancing at Peter, who has passed out on the bed. Dudley looks at me as if to say, 'Why are you with him when he's drunk and you could be with me and I'm sober?' Now and then we hug in the doorway. It is comforting at first and then becomes more meaningful.

I know he is wooing me, but it is too dangerous for me to respond. The truth is, I find him so attractive that I have come to love him. It wouldn't take much for our relationship to go a stage further, but not only would it be disloyal to Peter, it would also put me in an impossible position. Equally I can't snub Dudley by telling him to cool it, because if Peter notices a change for the worse in our relationship, he might get cross. I need to be charming to both of them and try to keep everything on an even keel, but it is increasingly difficult. It is a welcome relief whenever Dudley finds a girlfriend, as he is less intense with me, but the girlfriends come and go while I am a fixture in his life.

Dudley writes me notes telling me he's sitting in the whirlpool in the honeymoon suite and wishing I was with him. He slides them under the door of our suite when he thinks Peter is asleep. It is dangerous, and if anyone else finds them, there will be terrible trouble. I destroy them, but not before I send him one back saying I am thinking of him too. Flirting with Dudley is light relief from dealing with Peter's drinking, and when we see each other, our eyes lock as we share our secret.

One of the reasons Dudley flirts with me is because he wants anything Peter has. I have seen how he has copied Peter's décor in his home and now he wants to have the person Peter loves. I realise it is why Peter has warned me that Dudley is devious. What could be more devious than working with and loving someone and all the while waiting for an opportunity to whip his girlfriend away and make love to her, knowing you are stealing everything he cares about? At the same time, though, it is part of Dudley's make-up and adds to his appeal.

Although Dudley charms me and I enjoy his company, especially when he plays the piano, I know he likes to control any situation he is in. It is while we are in Sydney that we deliberately touch each other for the first time as we pass in the hotel corridor. It is a fleeting moment and somehow more powerful than our friendly hugs, but I tell myself I am not going to overstep the mark. Part of the eroticism between us is what we can't do.

Peter's alcohol intake increases as we move venues. He now drinks every day from lunchtime until well into the night, and the effects are cumulative. Dudley and I believe that by reasoning with Peter we can help him understand what he is doing and convince him to stop. Neither of us has any idea that he is in fact already an alcoholic and beyond being able to listen to reason.

I wait until Peter is relatively sober, then tell him he drinks too much. He makes all the right noises, says he will cut back and doesn't drink for a day or two. This happens repeatedly, and when it does, Dudley and I feel relieved and tell each other that it's all under control and he only needed a shove in the right direction. Of course, it never lasts, making Dudley exasperated and unable to understand why Peter doesn't realise how being drunk is affecting his performance. He tries to be tolerant, but he is a perfectionist and Peter's conduct is corroding both their professional and personal relationship. Sadly Peter can't or won't see it. To make matters worse Peter is also taking slimming pills that act as uppers. They make him hyper, stop him appearing drunk and help him get through a show. He also takes Valium to bring him down and sleeping pills because he has trouble sleeping.

I notice there is a growing chasm in the way they like to perform. Dudley wants to stick rigidly to their script and before each performance analyses why something is funny, then works out his comic timing precisely to make sure the audience will laugh. Peter, on the other hand, delights in ad-libbing and ignoring the script, often at Dudley's expense. Dudley can't help laughing, but he doesn't want to keep corpsing onstage, particularly as Peter stays in control of himself. He equally dislikes being manipulated by him. I notice Dudley giving Peter a stern look onstage to try to get him back to the script, but Peter likes spontaneity, and his brilliant instinctive timing means he enjoys going further and further away from what they have agreed to say, especially when he's drunk.

Luckily audiences love what they see. I laugh too, as I watch from the wings or front of house, but I am equally aware of Dudley's reaction. Some days he can take it in his stride; other days he looks as if he'd like to murder Peter. Offstage, I continue to act as the buffer between them, trying to smooth things over and keep the peace. It is an extraordinary position to be in, and the exact nature of the relationship between the three of us is increasingly intriguing newspaper reporters. Several of them are quite curious to learn more about me, which I am fine about. I'm feeling attractive again, both in my own right and because I am with two charismatic and alluring men.

When we get to Sydney, the local journalists wonder if there is anything special I'd like to see and I suggest a tour of the pubs, as it is one of the things to do in Sydney. The journalists have no idea I don't drink and escort me round all the best-known ones, while photographers take countless pictures of me holding a glass of untouched alcohol.

Fortunately Peter and I can still enjoy doing things together. Shortly after we arrive, he decides he wants radically to change the way he dresses. Because of the heat, he stops wearing his dandyish silk shirts and immaculately tailored suits. We go on shopping trips to combat outfitters, where he buys T-shirts with slogans like 'Sing Sing Jail'. It's a look he feels captures the experience of being in Australia, and I call it urban, radical chic. I don't have the money to splash out on clothes. I couldn't model or act when I was ill, and now that I'm touring with Peter the chances of me working are very slim. I worry about money, but I am too proud to ask Peter to help me out. I still don't have a clue about how much he earns, although I presume he is doing quite well. It's a no-go area, as is asking about his continual betting on the horses. Luckily practically anything suits me and I can dress quite inexpensively. I love the look of the moment, which is all big eyes and loose hair. I wear lots of false eyelashes too, with lashings of mascara, and stick gold dust, glitter and sometimes stars on my face.

In the six months we are away I only do one small commercial, for Conquista Rum. I have to drive across Sydney Bridge in a Maserati, then sit at a table with a male actor in a house designed to look like a restaurant and gaze into his eyes while we sip rum. I warn the producers that I don't drink, but I'm told sipping water won't do and I must drink the rum. The predictable result is that I get quite drunk, which is awful. I don't like the feeling of being out of control. Peter tells me I'm a very boring drunk because I want to do things like vacuuming rather than take my clothes off.

There is a short break in the tour over Christmas. Dudley flies back to the UK, but Peter and I decide to go to Fiji and then on to Bondi Beach, where we rent an apartment. We try to have fun, but it's difficult as Peter is missing his children terribly, particularly at this time of year. It is also so hot that I spend a lot of time indoors. I am quite fair-skinned and don't want to get sunburnt, whereas Peter, who is much darker-skinned, enjoys going to the beach or sitting by the pool. One day he drinks so much at lunchtime that he falls asleep by the swimming pool. When he wakes up, he obviously doesn't know where he is and walks fully clothed into the pool. Luckily, alert hotel staff come to his aid and help pull him out.

On another occasion he tells me he has met a sausage heiress on the beach. She is fifteen years old and very attractive as well as rich. I am annoyed he is flirting with a teenager. On Christmas Day we have a traditional meal in a restaurant, with lots of wine for Peter, but we both feel rather isolated.

Soon after we are back on tour, Peter negotiates a further contract to go on to New Zealand and Dudley is furious that he doesn't consult him about it. The basic deals for the tour were done in advance with each theatre, but if anything has to be re-negotiated, Peter takes charge. He refuses to have an agent; instead at various tour stops he hypes himself up and spends days re-negotiating their contract with the relevant producer. He is a tough negotiator, but working out complex agreements places enormous and needless extra stress on him. He can spend an entire day arguing with a producer about whether he will or won't do the show, in an effort to hike up the money, which I see as another aspect of his gambling addiction. He can't resist anything to do with upping the financial stakes.

It must also be extremely difficult to concentrate on performing while negotiating deals for yourself at the same time. I watch how exhausted he gets and worry when I see him downing large amounts of alcohol to calm himself both during and after the negotiations.

Our tour involves many flights and long car journeys, and Peter is brilliant at making us laugh to pass the time. On one flight Peter points out that one of our cabin-crew stewards in first class is frightfully camp. Although it is in the early hours of the morning, he is constantly arranging and rearranging various towels. Peter calls it 'Nigelling' and we have a fit of the giggles. The word sticks, and when we get home, I use it to tell Peter if I have some tidying to do: 'I am just popping upstairs to do some Nigelling, dear.'

When we have to travel long distances by car, we are given a driver and the three of us sit together in the back. Peter is usually in the middle, with me sitting on his right. To while away the time, he invents a game that eventually leads to the creation of Derek and Clive. Dudley is Derek, and Peter is Clive. Whereas Dud and Pete are two rather endearing working-class men, Derek and Clive are much coarser lads out on the street. Peter always starts with a simple idea or a funny voice. For example, when we drive past shops, Peter gives Dudley orders. 'Pop into that shop and buy your mother twelve lacy bras. Go into the hardware store and get her ten buckets and six mops. Run into the garage and get your mother twelve Mercedes and a forklift truck. Go into the undertaker's and buy your mother ten coffins.'

Dudley then tries to top it with more bizarre and outrageous demands for Peter. They gradually develop a bossy and punchy rhythm to their exchanges, around which they start to build their two characters. The initial idea is to satirise a class of people who talk obscenely and discuss unspeakable subjects like cancer in a bossy and aggressive way.

I never join in. I wouldn't have been able to compete with them and they wouldn't have wanted me to either. They are alpha males doing their thing. After several weeks Peter starts taping their increasingly belligerent conversations and the Derek and Clive scripts are born organically. Peter and Dudley later record the tapes for their own use, but recording technicians bootleg some of the recordings and they gradually became so sought after by pop groups like The Who and the Rolling Stones that Peter persuades Dudley to record them professionally.

Our stop in Auckland, New Zealand, is the penultimate leg of the tour. We arrive at our hotel at about 10.30 on a Sunday night and go up to our room. Peter immediately orders two bottles of red wine, which he drinks very quickly. It is in addition to the other alcohol he has consumed during the day and he falls into a drunken sleep. I am angry that we are wasting a rare night off and sit on the sofa in our room wondering what to do. I remember there is a grand piano in the foyer and instinctively know Dudley will be playing it. I want to spend time with him, especially now that Peter is drunk.

I ring for the lift, and as I descend, I hear Dudley playing. Then I see him. I order a glass of milk from the bar and walk towards him. There are almost no guests around, but the bar staff are still on duty and other staff are clearing up.

Dudley looks up at me and asks, 'Where's Peter?'

I reply, 'Out for the count.'

He pats the piano stool and says, 'Come and sit beside me.'

He continues to play. It's magical and gradually a few guests drift towards him. He asks what I want to hear and I ask for 'The Wedding March' by Mendelssohn, because he plays it brilliantly. Just then I notice that the light above the lift is ricocheting up and down. Dudley and I glance at each other and know without speaking that it is Peter inside. I assume he is so drunk he is having trouble pressing the right button. Eventually the lift comes down to the ground floor. The door opens and Peter stumbles out. He is wearing nothing but his underpants and looks as if he has just woken up. He walks towards us with a look of fury on his face and asks what I am doing. Dudley replies, 'She came down to get a glass of milk.'

I find it difficult not to laugh because Peter looks ludicrous and the bar staff have extraordinary expressions on their faces. Peter just says, 'Come back upstairs.' I do. He goes to sleep without another word and none of us mentions the incident again.

A few days later Dudley tells Peter he has booked a special sightseeing flight as a treat for him. It is a two-hour tour that will give him wonderful views of New Zealand. Peter is initially delighted and agrees to go. He assumes I am coming too, but Dudley has only booked one seat. It is another of his ruses to try to get me on my own. At the last moment Peter realises what is happening and immediately cancels his trip. I can tell he is absolutely livid, but again he doesn't say a word. I want to laugh because he and Dudley are again behaving like schoolboys trying to wind each other up, but I stop myself.

I sometimes wish Peter would square up to Dudley and demand to know what is going on, but he never does. I suppose you can't fight your best friend if you're onstage together every night. So even though Peter hasn't followed his father professionally, he is an instinctive diplomat and once more pulls his emotional curtains down and doesn't challenge him. It becomes an excuse for Dudley to push things further.

The three of us are invited to go white-water rafting by a group of respected local professionals who have seen the show and want to meet Dudley and Peter personally. They are all young, good-looking and obviously up-market types, and we spend a whole day together getting in and out of boats and going up and down the river. It is hair-raising fun and not just because of the rafting. Dudley is making it quite clear, by never leaving my side, that he finds me very attractive. If I sit down, he sits down; if I stand up, he does; if I take a step to the right, so does he.

Peter is extremely uptight all day, but instead of saying anything, he takes endless photographs of Dudley and me, which I suspect is partly because it gives him an opportunity to watch us closely through the camera lens. The three of us are in an extraordinary situation and have become a complicated triangle.

Peter and I at the premiere of *The Rise and Rise of Michael Rimmer*.
We had just moved into Kenwood Cottage.

(*Above left*) Our first winter at Kenwood Cottage, Highgate. Peter was
looking very moody and sexy and I couldn't resist taking a photo.

(*Above right*) Dudley working at Kenwood Cottage, getting ready for a
recording of *Not Only...But Also*.

Me and Ophelia, my beautiful Siamese cat, taken outside the garage of Kenwood Cottage.

(*Above left*) White water rafting in Auckland, New Zealand. Dudley never moved from my side, and Peter took photos, watching us through the camera lens.

(*Above right*) Peter standing in front of 24 Perrins Walk, as the proud owner. He'd just bought it.

(*Above left*) Cutting our wedding cake on 14 February, 1974 in New York. I was a bit fazed by all the press, but felt very close to Peter.

(*Above right*) Peter on the beach at Sans Souci in Ochos Rios, Jamaica, at the end of the American tour. Bliss.

Me in the sitting room at Perrins Walk in 1976, looking drawn and unhappy. It's not my favourite photo. Peter wanted me to look younger, so I am wearing a t-shirt with the number fourteen on it. I was thirty-one at the time.

I drew this picture of Peter one summer evening at Perrins Walk, copying a photograph. The intensity in his face just jumped out at me.

9

The Three Peters

The tour ends in February 1972. It's been a very successful six months, despite Peter's drinking. Peter and I return to live at Ruston Mews, while Dudley stays in New Zealand for a short jazz tour with his trio. I am delighted to be back and especially to be reunited with my cats. At first they are obviously unhappy with me, but I give them lots of love and gradually they come round.

Shortly after our return Peter arrives home with a box containing a Russian blue kitten, which he names Spiggle, from Harrods. I am surprised and delighted, particularly when he tells me that he has read about Russian blues and their temperament and thinks she will be ideal with our other two. He's right. She fits in perfectly and loves snoozing on Peter's chest.

Peter is exhausted but agrees to do a small cameo role as a BBC producer in *The Adventures of Barry McKenzie*. The lead is played by Barry Crocker, and the film tells the story of a boorish Australian during a trip to the UK. It is based on a comic strip by Barry Humphries for *Private Eye*. The idea for the strip was originally Peter's and has given the magazine a significant circulation boost. It is rather rude and Barry Humphries uses his huge vocabulary to talk, among other things, about urinating and writes in the magazine about 'pointing Percy at the porcelain' and 'shaking hands with the wife's best friend'.

Barry also has several roles in the film, including a hippie, Barry McKenzie's psychiatrist, Dr Delamphrey, and as Aunt Edna Everage, whom he later elevates to Dame Edna Everage. Dame Edna brings Humphries enormous success in the UK. The film satirises the stereotypical Australian, who is shown as being loud, drunk and unsophisticated. It is released in 1972 and panned by the critics, but audiences love it and it becomes the first Australian film to earn AU$1 million.

The film and Peter's appearance in a TV play called *Mill Hill* by John Mortimer are his only professional engagements until the London opening of *Behind the Fridge*, nine months after our return. *Mill Hill* is a weak farce in which Peter has the part of a dentist called Peter Trilby. He is having an affair with his partner's wife and keeps dashing off to see her, pretending he is going to cricket practice.

When Dudley comes back to London following his jazz tour, he rents a flat in the basement of a house in north London owned by Lysie Hastings. Lysie is his current girlfriend and was married to his best friend, George. Dudley wants us to meet her, so the four of us have dinner together. Lysie is Danish, blonde and willowy with a good sense of humour and is very easy to be with. Peter and I both like her.

Dudley continues to see his Australian girlfriend Lyndall Hobbs, so there are lots of complicated comings and goings in the basement flat. In addition he makes all sorts of arrangements for other Australian girlfriends to visit him. He is also still flirting with me. It's the ultimate bachelor existence, and his living arrangements are very tricky. His evenings are more straightforward and largely taken up playing jazz in a Knightsbridge restaurant.

Peter quickly re-establishes his day-to-day life and it is quite different to Dudley's. He spends a lot of time at *Private*

Eye's offices in Soho. He becomes the famous Lord Gnome, the magazine's spoof proprietor who is portrayed as greedy, unscrupulous and vulgar and an amalgamation of various real-life media magnates. In addition Lord Gnome writes editorials but rarely under his own name.

Peter gets on particularly well with Richard Ingrams, the magazine's editor. I met Richard at various parties well before I met Peter and am a little in awe of him. He, like Peter, can be quite sharp. Together, they are superb – fast and funny, super intelligent – and neither of them misses a trick. It is special to see, but on the whole I tend to keep away. It's Peter's world and I leave him to it.

Peter has no wish to interfere editorially, but loves coming up with ideas. The magazine was a great hit when it started, but then went into the doldrums and Peter's energy and originality have helped pull it back up again. He comes up with many of its long-running characters, including Spiggy Topes, who is leader of the popular singing group the Turds and is loosely based on John Lennon. He also suggests another successful feature called 'Mrs Wilson's Diary', which is an imaginary diary of Prime Minister Harold Wilson's wife Mary, based on the then popular BBC radio serial *Mrs Dale's Diary*. In addition he generously donates some of his own money when the *Eye*'s finances prove to be a little tight. He particularly enjoys the joke-writing sessions and is often part of a team of three or four different writers, which changes depending on who is around.

He decides when he wants to go to the *Eye* office and how long he wants to stay. There is no routine and sometimes he will go every day for days or even weeks on end. Other times he might not go for several days. Then he sometimes jokes that his greatest contribution is his idleness and says: 'Where else would they find someone like me who does nothing?'

He does, however, try not to miss the regular weekly lunch at the Coach and Horses down the road from the *Eye's* offices, where a variety of movers and shakers gather together from the theatrical, writing and political world to gossip and chat. The only problem is that he nearly always comes home very drunk. When he doesn't go to the pub, Peter 'bolsters' himself with miniature bottles of brandy in the magazine's toilet.

He also catches up with his daughters, sisters and parents. Making arrangements with Wendy to see Lucy and Daisy remains extremely complicated, as dates and timings are constantly changed, often with little or no notice. It depresses him. While we were away, he forgot how difficult it could be and it hits him hard once we are back in London. At first Wendy only lets the girls come for brief periods of a few hours at a time. They haven't seen Peter for so long that the two of them are initially quite shy, but he is very tactile with them and gives them lots of hugs and is so good at making them roar with laughter that they soon relax and it is as if he has never been away. Because we don't have much time together, we tend to take them out for a meal or go for a walk.

Slowly it becomes a little easier and Wendy allows them to make their own way to us, usually on a Sunday. I really enjoy being with them. Daisy is naughty, giggly and very quick-witted, while Lucy is quieter, more thoughtful and intro-verted.

Ruston Mews is still so full of furniture it feels very cramped and Peter decides to buy somewhere bigger. We need to move as soon as we can because he and Dudley have plenty of work to do on the script for the London run of *Behind the Fridge* and they need somewhere spacious and calm where they can write. Peter is still keen to make money out of the show, but I can tell his heart is no longer in it. I suggest we look for a property around the Portobello Road and quite by chance Peter comes across a house in nearby Denbigh Terrace that is up for sale. He loves it and takes me to see it.

It is a Victorian detached house on four floors with large square rooms and shutters at the windows. There's a small garden at the back, a roof terrace and a big basement area, which is the ideal place for the ping-pong table Dudley and Peter like to use when they take a break from writing. Luckily it is in quite good condition, as we don't have much time for refurbishing before Peter and Dudley start work in earnest. All we will have to do is put in a new bathroom and have everything painted magnolia so the rooms look clean and fresh.

A month or so after we return from the tour of Australia and New Zealand, Peter goes to Rome for an interview, for which he has to stay overnight. The car that is taking him to the airport has barely driven away when Dudley phones. He has obviously found out what time Peter is leaving and asks me to meet him that night. We can't think of where to go, so he comes round to Ruston Mews. He is gossipy and flirtatious, and as usual we talk in great depth about Peter. I need to talk about Peter too and Dudley is good at drawing me out, but I am equally able to ask him personal questions in return. We become a cross between a mutual admiration society and a private Alcoholics Anonymous support group.

Halfway through the evening he invites me round to see his basement flat. Although it is very pleasant, it is a huge contrast to the vast, exquisite Hampstead house he shared with Suzy. We spend some hours together and our conversation becomes very intimate. He tells me he has difficulty in getting a full arousal and climaxing. He believes it is linked to his physical appearance, feels it goes to the core of his being and explains how he needs both mental and physical stimulation to help him overcome it. I sympathise and his confession enables me to understand why his relationships haven't lasted. We end up cuddling and kissing, but I leave before midnight because I know Peter will be phoning me.

Dudley rings later the next morning in a very jittery state and asks if Peter is back yet and how he is. I give him strict instructions not to mention that we have met. Although Peter wants Dudley to find me attractive because I am his prize possession, I know Dudley and I have overstepped the mark. Having an in-depth conversation over several hours and then going to his flat is definitely out of bounds, let alone spending time with him alone. Peter will be very suspicious if we even mention meeting. I regret the cuddling and kissing, but I understand what made me do it. Dudley has been after me for so long. He finds it exciting to push boundaries and, as Peter has said, is also extremely devious. He knows I find him attractive and in the heat of the moment my behaviour lapsed.

As the day goes on, I feel increasingly dreadful and realise I have dipped my toe into treacherous waters. I draw back very fast. I want everything to get back on track and tell Dudley to keep his distance. I am not going to destroy Peter's life.

Peter and Dudley meet the following day to work and give press interviews to promote the London show. Dudley is quite withdrawn, probably because he knows it's too dangerous to be anything else. It marks a change in my relationship with Dudley. I know he felt sure I would fall in love with him at one point, but now he sees that my reaction is steely. I have made a mistake and want to be with Peter and I believe he wants to destroy our relationship. Even in the unlikely event that Dudley and I were to get together, I know there would be other women in his life, and he'd do what he usually does, which is to go off and play the piano somewhere, meet someone else and move on. He is just jealous of anything good that Peter has.

We move into Denbigh Terrace in the summer of 1973 and Peter and Dudley get working on the London leg of *Behind the Fridge* straight away. Their working routine echoes the one they followed in Kenwood Cottage, with me as their support and muse, sitting quietly and listening to their jokes and making them coffee. I am relieved to see that the intimacy between them is still there. They are firing off each other and seem totally in tune. When they are not together, Dudley still rings me all the time, and if Peter is out of earshot, we have a chat about him. The questions are the same as he asked in Australia – he wants to know what Peter's been drinking and even what he's wearing.

When things calm down between Dudley and myself, he comes up with what he thinks is a brilliant idea. He is spending an increasing amount of time with his psychiatrist, Dr Stephen Sebag-Montefiore, trying to come to terms with himself and his life, and suggests that Lysie, Peter and I should also go and see him and sort ourselves out. He is particularly keen for Peter to learn how to be more relaxed and less uptight, which he hopes will help him cut down on his drinking.

Although it is rather odd for all four of us to go to the same psychiatrist, Dudley doesn't take no for an answer and is so persuasive that in the end we agree. Peter thinks loosening up is 'claptrap' and only goes along with it out of curiosity and to please Dudley. Lysie and I don't take it remotely seriously. Instead we swap notes about what we are going to wear. Lysie turns up for her appointment in fishnet stockings, while I wear very short shorts for mine. Dr Sebag-Montefiore is a nice man, as well as a first-rate psychiatrist. He mentions Peter's drinking to me, but I brush away his comments and don't ask for advice.

The truth is, I don't dare ask for professional help, even though my life with Peter has become a rollercoaster of emotions and I have no idea how to cope with his drinking. Harry Thompson wrongly states in his biography of Peter that I say he suffers from manic depression, now known as bi-polar disorder. This is a serious mental illness charac-terised by severe mood swings with periods of manic highs followed by severe lows, and can be controlled but never cured. I have no medical qualifications and would never make my own diagnosis. I do know that despite Peter's moods going up and down and his suffering from regular bouts of depression, not one of the doctors he sees during our many years together offers that diagnosis.

I have often asked myself whether his depression has largely been caused by his abuse of drink and drugs, rather than a medical condition. I certainly don't know whether his depressed state when we get back from Australia is a genuine depression or a symptom of his complete mental and physi-cal exhaustion and something made worse by his drinking and drug-taking. He needs a long and complete break, but he doesn't have any time. He and Dudley have been offered a lucrative deal by Alexander Cohen, the producer, to take the show to America after the end of its London run. They are both bored with the show and even each other, but the offer is a good one, even if it will put them under continued pres-sure to keep going.

Peter deals with his depression by drinking, which must be the worst thing he can do. I try to speak to him about it, but he always denies he is a drunk and I don't realise that this is what alcoholics do. I don't even yet acknowledge in my mind that that is what he has become, just as I have always closed my mind to the extent of my parents' drinking. There are some days when he won't talk, and sometimes he is so low I don't think he could talk even if he wanted to.

He has been prescribed medication to help him cope with anxiety and insomnia, but he is abusing his pills, taking one on top of the other and too many at a time. So instead of controlling his moods, he is almost certainly exacerbating them. I now find I am living with three different Peter Cooks: the depressed drunk; the real Peter, who is an incredibly sensitive, funny and loving person; and the professional Peter Cook, which he turns on when he is performing or in company. When he is performing, adrenalin lifts his personality, he becomes a larger-than-life character and the life and soul of the party, and I sometimes think he is overloading his brain with too much stimulus.

Behind the Fridge opens at the Cambridge Theatre on 21 November 1972. It is a theatre Peter doesn't like and he sees it as a bad omen. He gets so drunk on the first night that the start is delayed for almost an hour. The audience begin a slow handclap, while backstage Joe McGrath, the director, walks Peter round and round the dressing room and gives him lots of coffee to try to sober him up.

The reviews of the show are mixed but mainly lukewarm to cold. Irving Wardle, the theatre critic of *The Times*, writes that it would have been wiser to change the show's title as it is associated with Peter and Dudley's revue in the 1960s. He adds that Peter and Dudley have lost the habit of giving offence and are 'more concerned with each other's comic personalities than with the state of the nation'.

We take comfort in that at least he agrees that the show is 'one outpost of original and intelligent fun in the West End'.

He also enjoys the show's finale, which is Pete and Dud at their best. It has a domestic setting and Pete keeps a straight face as he lectures a harassed, obviously sex-starved Dud on women's lib while Dud is doing his ironing. Feminists have been hitting the headlines by throwing away their bras, or 'bra-burning' as the press like to describe it, as a symbol of their emancipation. It makes a perfect topic for the two of them to send up.

> PETE: These women's libbers. Do you know they even regard the brassières [pronounced 'brasseeres'] as a symbol of masculine enslavement?
> DUD (looking aghast): Did we males force them into their brassières? I have been trying for years to get them out of them.

They then complain about how difficult it is to know what women of today want and Dud goes on to say, 'A man is very hard put to know where to start his sexual voyage,' to which Peter deadpans, 'Not the Northern line. You may end up in Crouch End.'

Dudley is also hilarious when he describes his wife's sad end in hospital: 'Her teeth hit the ceiling, a nurse tripped on them, propelling another nurse out of the window to fall fatally into a passing car, which went on to demolish the entire building. Suffice it to say I was the sole survivor.'

After about a month Peter and Dudley's dresser hands in her notice and I am asked to take over. It makes a lot of sense because I know the show so well from Australia and I am backstage every night anyway. The producer and Dudley hope I can be a moderating influence on Peter's drinking by measuring out exactly what he can have.

I shadow the current dresser for a couple of weeks before

she leaves and learn the layout of the theatre and where all the costumes and props are kept. Then it is my turn. Fortunately it's a smooth transition and I am pleased to be earning some money again. Each week Peter and Dudley have to do six evening shows and two matinées. Peter and I arrive about two hours before the performance, and Dudley turns up about an hour later.

I check the props and costumes, and make sure that Peter has a half-bottle of champagne in his dressing-room fridge. He likes drinking champagne and orange juice before the show and, if he can, during it as well. Dudley doesn't like him drinking at all of course, so Peter asks me to make it look as though he is just having orange juice. I mix the champagne with the orange juice in a jug, hoping that it will keep his drinking under some sort of control, but it doesn't fool Dudley and each evening he asks me how much champagne Peter has had and whether he is having it neat as well as with orange juice.

It is hectic being a dresser and I am flat out during each performance. I have to rush round the back of the stage from one side to the other to give Peter and Dudley their costumes, and some of the more complicated changes are done in a dark corner at the side of the stage with just the light of a torch to see by. At the end of the performance all their clothes have to be sent to the dry-cleaner or the washing lady.

Peter likes to play tricks and one night he takes the trousers that I have laid out for Dudley's next costume change and swaps them with a pair of his. When the time comes for me to help Dudley do a quick change, we both instantly realise what has happened. As there is about a foot height difference, Dudley can't even walk in the trousers and will look completely ridiculous onstage. I shoot back to the other side of the stage, where luckily I have put another pair of Dudley's trousers, grab them and dash back again. Dudley goes back onstage with seconds to spare.

I can tell Peter is struggling not to laugh, but I am angry because he's being funny at my expense and I am trying to be as professional as possible. I recall how cross he was when I played a practical joke on Dudley at the hotel in Australia, to tease him about how many women were after him, and am annoyed that Peter hasn't stuck to the rule he imposed on me of not playing tricks on Dudley.

Despite the cynical critics who predicted doom, the show is a hit and packed for six months. It's hard work appearing every night, and a real struggle when first one then the other gets flu. They give several interviews during the run, and one journalist suggests to Peter that it must be difficult for any double act to work together so closely for so long and wonders how they are getting on. Peter replies, 'We are still two individuals, although we know exactly what the other is thinking. We occasionally have dinner together after a show, but the truth is, we meet more socially when we are not a working partnership.'

This was once true, but now they hardly see each other outside of performing. Although they are the toast of the town and we are inundated with invitations, Dudley mainly goes off to play jazz in a restaurant after the show, and Peter and I usually come home and go to bed because there's another show to get through tomorrow.

On 7 January 1973, however, Dudley agrees to come round to us for lunch. Peter puts two bottles of red wine on the table, but although the atmosphere between us is cordial, Dudley doesn't touch a drop during the two hours he is with us. Peter finishes one bottle himself over lunch, and after Dudley has gone, he has a snooze, then downs three miniature bottles of vodka and the second bottle of wine. He says his drinking is like Dudley's depression. They both build up in a cycle and his ends in a bout of drink.

Peter's own depression is getting worse. Even the thought of going onstage makes him feel low and he says he doesn't know where he is going or what he wants to do. I know he is extremely bored, but he also desperately needs to stop drinking. One morning he tells me he has no ambition left and feels pointless. I don't know if he really means it or just believes it at that moment as a result of drinking too much. I don't know how seriously to take it and I don't dare ask him, partly because I don't want to know. He soon falls asleep. When he wakes up, he drinks two bottles of champagne and starts to cry. He says he feels like a little boy and wants to be cosseted. I hug him, but it is difficult to have an intimate relationship with someone who is a very heavy drinker. I need to believe Peter when he says he will stop drinking, and although he keeps apologising and crying, any promises he makes are quickly broken.

Peter can be desperately down at home, but if we go out, he can swap personalities and be the life and soul of the party and charm for England. There are still always women after him, and he responds by being as flirtatious and naughty as possible. He is just that sort of man and I can see how hard it is to resist him. I feel confident of his love, but I know it's important that he doesn't feel chained to me. When we go out and I sense I am in the female equivalent of shark-infested waters, I try not to react by being overly possessive. Peter's business is to make people laugh, and flirting and being charming are part of that. Many male entertainers are in similar positions and trade on their personality and sex appeal. I sometimes get jealous, but I keep it to myself. It goes with the territory and I try to deal with it positively to stop it getting the better of me. I've learnt from Peter how looking at things humorously helps lighten a load and ease a burden. There are lots of compensations too. My life with Peter is more edgy, exciting and unusual than it could ever be with anyone else.

Many glamorous female celebrities are enamoured by him and behave like bees round a honey pot. One night he is invited to have dinner with Ursula Andress, who is visiting London and has asked her agent to fix a meeting. On another occasion he dines with Raquel Welch. He is excited to see her, and before he leaves the house, he has a bath and dowses himself with Dior aftershave. I manage not to be jealous. I want him to go out and be dazzling because that is the business he is in. I couldn't bear it if he failed because I was trying to hang on to his coat tails.

Sometimes I have to be a detective and find out what Peter is up to socially. One night Helen Jay comes to see Peter in the show. She and her twin sister, Catherine, are the daughters of Labour politician Douglas Jay. They are beautiful and lively, and are said to epitomise the 1970s. She goes backstage and invites Peter, but not me, to dinner at her house. I only hear about it because she rings him at home to confirm the time. I tell Peter that I'm coming too. He says, 'Well, she asked me, but OK.'

When the date arrives, I try to look as good as possible and meet Peter in his dressing room when the show finishes. Helen is already there, looking extremely glamorous. She seems astonished to see me and even more so when I ask if she minds if I come to dinner with Peter. She answers with a curt 'OK'. Peter has recently bought me a purple Mini so I can drive him everywhere and we follow her to her home in west London. There are ten guests sitting round the dining table waiting for Peter when we arrive. There is no place setting for me and there's a real drama about trying to squeeze me in somewhere.

Part of me feels very self-conscious, but I grit my teeth and am determined to stay until the end of the evening, no matter what. After a delicious meal of soufflé followed by chicken, and then strawberries, we move to the sitting room for coffee. Most of the guests are quite tipsy. I expect they have been drinking wine for hours before Peter arrived. Peter has also been plied with wine and then strip poker is suggested. I am astonished. A hand is played and clothes start coming off while Peter and the other guests just watch. I can barely believe what I am seeing. Another poker hand is dealt and Peter takes off his shirt. He then suddenly stands up, grabs my hand and says, 'We're going,' and we leave very quickly.

When we get home, I think, How do I cope with a man so many women want to go to bed with? There isn't a simple answer, but luckily I'm good-looking and feel I can hold my own both physically and mentally. Like anyone, though, I don't want to encourage anything.

I even have trouble when I try to employ an au pair to clean. Our home is over four floors and I need some help with housework. Peter puts an advert in the local paper. We get a good response and deliberately choose a rather homely, plain-looking girl. She isn't with us for long before she breaks down in tears and tells both me and Peter that she has fallen in love with him. There's been no affair, but we still have to get rid of her and I go back to doing the cleaning myself.

I manage to cope with all his flirtations because I know his feelings for these women are transitory, whereas he needs me at a profound level. He is always telling me that I am his number one, and that is enough for me.

It's hard for me to have an independent life and I don't

have close friends any more. It suits Peter because he likes me all to himself. He certainly isn't keen when I do invite someone round. One girlfriend tells me that Peter made her feel uncomfortable and it was obvious he wanted to read the papers rather than have her there. On the rare occasions when I do go out with a friend, I have to explain to Peter where I am going and what I'm going to do and he sometimes gets jealous. Although it might seem strange, I decide it's not worth the hassle of socialising alone and it's easier to do things Peter's way. When I bump into another friend and she asks why I don't see her any more, I look up at the heavens and say it is just too difficult.

Although making an arrangement to see a friend seems a simple thing to do, in practice it is far more complicated. Peter's lifestyle is unpredictable and I don't want to make it more problematic. I never know, for example, if he is going to come back from *Private Eye* drunk or sober, or if he'll suddenly want to go out with me, and it's enough to deal with all that. Then again, the sort of topics girlfriends like to talk about – such as their intimate relationships with the men they love – are not something I can get involved in. Life isn't straightforward with Peter, and although women are now supposed to be emancipated, it hasn't permeated through to me. I live my life according to his needs and wishes, and give him far more freedom than he gives me.

Being with someone famous means lots of people talk to me because they want to get close to Peter. They find me attractive by association, irrespective of what I say or do, and Peter can get fed up if he thinks I am flirting. He doesn't say anything at the time, but tells me later.

He is so sensitive to how I react to people that he can take it to extremes. Once, when we are watching a tennis match on television during Wimbledon fortnight, I start cheering

Boris Becker and Peter says in a rather pointed way that he knows I like young tennis players. When Becker is about to serve for a new set, he yells at the television, 'A swarm of bees are about to attack you up your knickers.' It demonstrates his insecurity, but it's also his way of stopping someone winning and he does the same thing when he watches Spurs and someone from the opposing team has the ball. In fact Peter loves bees. One of his terms of affection is calling me his bee. He also calls Daisy 'Daisy Bee'.

One evening after the show we go out with Norman Rodway and T. P. McKenna, who are both Irish actors. Peter has several glasses of wine, then says he is extremely tired. Once we get home, he tells me he feels sick and I help him get to bed. He is initially very silent, then becomes affectionate and wants to make love. I say, 'Could we tomorrow?'

He replies, 'Do you think I'm pissed?' I don't answer but get out of bed. He then adds sarcastically, 'You always take the initiative, don't you.'

We don't make love that night, but I make up for it the following evening before he's had his bottle of wine.

Other times he drinks so much he can't get his trousers off and one night I watch as he hops from one side of the bedroom to the other totally unable to undress himself. I roar with laughter and he gets very cross. Of course it's not at all funny when he is so drunk he can't get a proper erection. I want to shout, 'Don't do this to me,' but I never do, because I don't like confrontation. It is especially awful because I still fancy him.

10

Endings and Beginnings

Although Peter is now basically bored with *Behind the Fridge*, he still loves immersing himself in *Private Eye*. He is proprietor and majority shareholder but doesn't make any money out of the magazine. His dividends are a free supply of newspapers and the occasional case of wine. So much of his life is transient, but *Private Eye* is always there. He knows he can turn up whenever he likes and there will always be people he knows. He loves the atmosphere, the gossip and the jokes, and it becomes a sort of home from home for him. When he gets drunk, he is not as sharp as he could be, but then he very seldom has to put pen to paper. He isn't remotely interested in turning up to board meetings or getting involved in the financial side of things.

Best of all, he enjoys talking to either John Bird or Richard Ingrams. He likes either of them to be his straight man and feed him lines, as it enables him to do what he likes best, which is to improvise. He also has an extraordinary gift for making up names and characters, and individuals like Sir Basil Nardly-Stoads, chief rammer of the Seductive Brethren, whom Peter described as a creation of utterly original genius.

I stop being Peter and Dudley's dresser in June 1972, as the original dresser returns, and I look forward to spending the summer in London. On 24 January 1973, quite out of the blue, my divorce comes through. Sean has cited my adultery with Peter, and Judge Dow, who hears the case in the family court, orders Peter to pay the costs. Peter doesn't mind and I feel exhilarated that at last Peter and I can get married.

I am on a high for the next few months, but then everything starts crashing down around me. I barely think about Sean, but nearly six months later his girlfriend, the actress Judy Geeson, rings. She tells me Sean has died suddenly and she wanted to tell me personally before I see it in the newspapers. He had what she thought was an epileptic fit and she arranged for him to be taken to hospital, but it turns out he had had a heart attack, which was quickly followed by a brain haemorrhage. Sadly the hospital couldn't save him. I am dumbfounded. It is so unexpected as he was only forty-two. Judy explains he is going to be buried in Ireland and asks if I want to go to the funeral. I say I can't. She accepts my refusal graciously and we have a friendly talk.

I think about our conversation afterwards and feel I have made the right decision. My divorce has only recently come through and Peter wouldn't want to come with me. Even if he did, I wouldn't let him. It wouldn't be fair on Judy because the spotlight would be on Peter and not on her and she doesn't need that extra pressure. Also, going on my own without Peter could have given the wrong message to the press, who might have made mischief speculating where my loyalty lay and could also have upset Judy.

My feelings are very mixed. Although I no longer love Sean, I still feel affection for him, and although at times he was awful to me, I have always wanted him to be well and happy. Peter has contradictory feelings too. Like me, he is relieved about the divorce, but is very shocked about Sean's death, because he was once a good friend. Apart from their connection at the Establishment, well before Peter and I got together, they used to write funny letters to each other, and would always joke when they met. I feel so sad that Sean has obviously brought on his early death by heavy drinking and taking drugs. It is such a waste of his life. He was an incredibly talented man. I don't at the time make any connection with Peter, as I still believe he is basically in control of his drinking.

Peter makes no effort to comfort me, but perhaps he doesn't realise I need it and it's my mistake not asking him to. In retrospect there could have been several reasons. He might have been so upset by my distress that the only way he could cope was to withdraw. Seeing me miserable made him uncomfortable. Or he may not have liked the fact that I was getting a lot of attention and sympathy from the people Sean and I used to see.

I have barely come to terms with Sean's death when, less than a month later, my mother rings to tell me that at eleven o'clock that morning my father fell down the stairs and died. His death too is totally unexpected. Although he has had many health problems in recent years, my mother has rung me so often sounding fraught and saying something awful was about to happen that I have become rather immune to her anxieties.

I felt particularly distant from both my parents while Peter and I were in Australia, but when I visited my father when we returned to the UK, I thought he was still holding his own and, despite being heavily sedated, was managing to enjoy life by doing simple things like pottering around the garden. I leave Peter in London and fly to Jersey with my half-brother, Paul. Paul has lived in the south of France since I was nineteen and we don't often meet. I can tell immediately that my mother has had several drinks to bolster herself. I suppose it is fair enough and I accept she needs them.

Although Peter is performing each night, he manages to come over for the funeral itself.

I find the whole experience totally distressing and am beside myself with grief. I stay in Jersey for five nights in all, but I can't really cope with the stress and come back home to Peter. Peter is again neither kind nor comforting, and the night I return tells me he is going out to a party. I don't understand his coldness until much later, when I wonder whether he simply felt unable to cope with me being so emotional. Sometimes when the person you love is very upset, it's so painful it's easier to pretend that nothing is happening.

My mother rings me constantly and I can tell by her voice that she is drinking too much. Perhaps it is the only way she can cope. Now she doesn't have my father to look after, she is focusing all her attention on me. I'm not happy about that, largely because she makes it clear that she no longer wants me to be with Peter and is against me marrying him. I think it is a mixture of jealousy and her love of intrigue. I later discover she is talking to one of my friends to find out more about us, and I am furious.

Peter isn't well either and keeps being sick. On the evening of 14 July 1973 he calls me from the theatre to say he has been sick yet again and this time has brought up some blood. I immediately ring Stephen Sebag-Montefiore, who comes to examine him and tells me that Peter has an inflamed liver and a viral infection. He takes some samples and we wait for the test results to come through. They show he has a mild form of hepatitis, probably caused by his excessive drinking. The doctor tells him he must rest and also stop drinking for about eighteen months. Peter agrees to stop and says he will get fit for me. Hepatitis is such a debilitating illness that he must have felt awful for some time before he owned up to having any symptoms. He doesn't seem in the least bothered about the bad state of his liver, other than wanting a lot of attention. I try to convince him to see it as a wake-up call, but he doesn't and is soon drinking again.

When the show ends its London run, Peter suggests we go on holiday and asks where I'd like to go. He tells me that Dudley and Lysie have booked a cruise around the Greek Islands. I feel so grief-stricken that I don't want to go anywhere, but I can't just think of myself. Peter is exhausted from the show and from having hepatitis. He feels the rest will do him good and restore his health before he and Dudley take the show to America. I suggest the south of France and Peter books a two-week holiday in St Tropez, which in the early 1970s is glitzy and the height of chic.

We stay in Hotel Byblos, which is situated between the Citadel Park and the central market square. Brigitte Bardot chose to stay there and helped make it famous. It is also where Mick Jagger married Bianca Pérez-Mora Macías in 1971.

Hotel Byblos is the place to be seen, tremendously glamorous and superbly run with attention paid to the smallest detail. We spend our days sitting by the pool or walking down the main street to watch the old men playing boules in the village square. There are lots of little shops around, which, when we look closely, turn out to be expensive boutiques selling tiny bikinis for huge amounts of money. Peter buys me one. It is a sort of tangerine colour, knitted and very saucy. We also enjoy sitting in various outdoor cafés and wandering around the harbour to watch the boats and the people parading up and down. St Tropez fashion is all about sex and showing off your assets and most girls wear tiny bikinis, short hot pants or flimsy dresses. I have brought lots of bikinis with me and walk up and down with the best of them.

During our second week Peter hires a car and we drive to various different beaches to sunbathe. There are a couple of topless girls around, but most of those who want to strip off go to the topless beach out of town. One day a splendid yacht arrives, and when it is moored off the beach, Charlotte Rampling appears on deck. She is a stunningly beautiful actress who has just married actor Bryan Southcombe. The two of them and their young baby, Barnaby, live in a *ménage à trois* with an Australian male model. I remember seeing her at a party Peter gave at Church Row in 1969. Wendy was in Majorca at the time and he wanted to show he could give a good party without her. Charlotte had so much to drink that she fell asleep on an armchair quite early in the evening and Peter had to arrange for her to be taken home by taxi.

In the evenings Peter and I usually have a meal by the hotel pool and afterwards go for a walk to see what is going on in the local clubs. One night we meet a couple who recognise Peter and we end up going to a club together. The evening is quite wild and ends with Peter jumping fully dressed into a swimming pool. He is fine, but I am cross because he was wearing my favourite straw hat, which is now ruined.

Late at night, in bed, Peter reads me extracts from *Wuthering Heights* by Emily Brontë. He is not drinking much at the moment and we get on so well we both begin to feel much better for our holiday. St Tropez is fun, and the heady, indulgent atmosphere gets to us.

When we return, Peter starts working on improving *Behind the Fridge* before taking it to America. Lately Dudley has sometimes been too passive and Peter too bored for them to work together effectively and they have fallen into an exhausted routine, but the thought of appearing in New York fires Peter up. The atmosphere between him and Dudley lightens, their relationship gets back on track, and

they are thrilled to be together and inspiring one another
again. All past unpleasantness seems to be forgotten and
they behave like a couple of kids excited about going to a
fantastic party. It is as if they have both been given a shot of
adrenaline. The Big Apple has a buzz, is stimulating and
much more of an adventure than London, so Peter can enjoy
stimulation to the point of overload. To avoid any connection with *Beyond the Fringe*, the revue they took to America
in the early 1960s, they change the name of the show to
Good Evening.

Peter also decides he wants to sell Denbigh Terrace and
move back to Hampstead because he loves the shops and
village environment. We put it on the market and decide that
until we find somewhere, we will temporarily move back
into Ruston Mews. I have let it on and off but at the moment
it is empty and I organise, yet again, for all our furniture and
clothes to be stored there. This time the cats go too, along
with a cat sitter, which will be so much better than putting
them into a cattery.

One evening Dudley comes round to visit. The three of us
share a joint and Dudley becomes very flirtatious and giggly.
He has a naughty twinkle in his eye as he keeps telling me
that the meek will inherit the earth. His implication is clear –
he means that Peter will not. Peter becomes incensed and
says Dudley is behaving stupidly and that I must not pass
him the joint any more. He stays in a huff for the rest of the
evening.

I start searching for a new house and see a newspaper
advert for a Queen Anne coach house in Perrins Walk, a
cobbled mews just round the corner from Peter's former
home in Church Row. It looks just what Peter wants and we
go round to see it. The house is very close to the pub and
wine shop that Peter knows so well. It is spread over three

floors and is like a small, enchanted castle with strawberry Gothic windows and an ornate skylight in the top-floor bedroom. There is also a large and very pretty garden.

Inside, it is a mess and needs a tremendous amount of work. The vendor has had it gutted it but can't afford to do any more, which is why she has put it up for sale. Peter loves it and decides to buy it. I am so pleased I have found somewhere so idyllic for him. He describes his happiness in a letter to his parents, saying that he hopes he never has to move again. He also asks them not to tell Wendy, as he thinks she will go green with envy and ask for more money.

It will be our third move in four years. Although Peter seems happy to move, he is becoming increasingly reticent with me. He and Dudley need to fly to the States to sort out things in New York before they embark on the tour and Peter suggests I stay behind to sell Denbigh Terrace and sort out the building work at Perrins Walk. I feel anxious about this plan because I know Peter very well, and although I believe him when he says he feels sad at leaving me behind, I also sense his inner excitement at the chance of spreading his wings a little. I suspect he will be up to no good in America. It's the land of fast food, fast girls and plenty of everything, and Peter loves all that.

Peter and Dudley leave for New York on 25 September. Dudley is in a particularly good mood, as he is going to meet a new girlfriend, Hollywood actress Tuesday Weld, for whom he has broken off his relationship with Lysie Hastings. Tuesday was born into a dysfunctional family and was put under such pressure to become a child model and actress that she had a nervous breakdown at the age of nine. She lost her virginity at eleven, became a heavy drinker and made a suicide attempt when she was twelve. I think she sounds a handful.

Peter is excited, but I can't bear to see him go. I love him so much that I feel physical pain at parting. It's arranged that I join him in a few weeks, but it feels like a long time. There will be temptations for Peter if he is left on his own for three seconds, let alone three weeks.

It can't be helped and I force myself to concentrate on sorting out our homes. The first would-be purchaser of Denbigh Terrace is Richard Branson, known as 'Handsome Branson', who comes to see the property with his wife, Kristen Tomassi. He tells me almost immediately that he wants to buy it and a deal is quickly done with both him and the owner of Perrins Walk.

The vendor of Perrins Walk gives me the plans of her proposed renovations, which include replumbing and rewiring the property, and I more or less follow them. Peter and I also want to put in a new staircase and bathrooms. Peter says he wants the walls magnolia and the window frames white. In addition to everything else that is going on, my mother flies in from Jersey to stay with me. She tells me again that she doesn't like Peter. It upsets me greatly, but I realise it is part of her desire to manipulate me.

Peter and Dudley fly to Boston for the out-of-town preview of *Good Evening* on 12 October. The plan is that the show will then move to New York, Washington, Detroit, Toronto, Montreal, Philadelphia, Chicago and finally Los Angeles. Peter and I speak on the phone every day about the progress at Perrins Walk. He likes to ring early morning my time, which is late at night in Boston.

One day, when my mother is staying, and Peter has rung me from Boston, he tells me that Tuesday has called the hotel where he and Dudley are staying asking to speak to Dudley and been inadvertently put through to his room. I don't take too much notice, but a couple of nights later I have an awful dream about him going to bed with Tuesday and tell him about it when he rings the following day. There is a brief silence on the line before Peter admits it is true. What I said must have thrown him completely, but he sounds so cool and in control as he goes on to insist that what happened between them is merely something he couldn't resist. He explains he started chatting to her and they ended up in bed, but it meant nothing to him. He adds that in any case Dudley wants to go out with her.

She is the first woman I know for certain Peter has had an affair with since we have been together. It is a scenario I have been dreading and hope, although not confidently, that there won't be any more. I am surprised by his honest answer and realise what happened is yet another example of how both Dudley and Peter are driven to want what the other one has. Dudley has wanted me, and now Peter wants the woman Dudley cares about. At the end of our conversation Peter tells me to come out as quickly as I can and I promise I will.

I am suddenly aware that my mother may be listening in on the other phone downstairs. I tell Peter to hold on and rush downstairs to discover she has indeed picked up the phone and has been eavesdropping on our call. I am furious. At first she refuses to put the receiver down, so I wrestle it out of her hand and tell her that she must never do that again.

My behaviour enrages her and she starts to tell me how rude I am, but I won't stand being treated like a little girl. I am not sure exactly what she has heard but tell her my conversation with Peter is private. We have a terrible row and she storms out of the house and goes back to Jersey. We don't speak for months. When I eventually calm down, I feel I overreacted and didn't take into account that she was still in a terrible state over my father's death and was drinking from first thing in the morning. Nevertheless I am also finding it hard to cope with my own sorrow. I don't condone what Peter has done, in fact I feel devastated by his behaviour. But I am so overwhelmed by what is happening in my life that I can't deal with it. I am still grieving for my father; I am trying to cope with my mother who is drinking so heavily she even concealed bottles of alcohol in her suitcase when she came to stay. I have to sort out our move and the renovations; I am also missing Peter desperately. I love him totally and want to be with him.

I make up my mind I won't let my mother or Tuesday come between Peter and me. I prefer to think of what has happened as a silly mistake. I won't give him up just because he slept with one woman. I also believe him when he says he loves me and don't feel what happened threatens our relationship. I doubt he would have told me if I hadn't mentioned my dream, and at one level I am pleased to have caught him out.

I partly blame Tuesday for Peter's infidelity, but I don't hate her. She was looking for affection and Peter was unexpectedly in her path. Bizarrely, when Sean and I were in New York, people often mistook me for her, so I know Peter would be intrigued by her elfin looks and fascinated by her personal history. I am determined to sort out the renovations on our home and get to America as quickly as possible. Luckily I am so busy with the move there isn't time to feel sorry for myself.

There is a break between the end of the show in Boston and the New York opening and I fly out to join Peter in New York on 14 October, feeling rather vulnerable, but knowing that already, even before the opening, the show is the hottest ticket in town.

New York, New York

The phone rings as I reach our hotel room in New York and Peter asks me to answer it. It is Tuesday. I mouth her name to Peter and he mouths back that I should tell her he's busy. When she realises it's me, she starts chatting away and suggests we meet. I think, Oh, no. She's just slept with Peter and now she wants us to be friends. Although I am intrigued by her reputation, I avoid committing myself.

Peter then tells me he has another confession to make. As well as having an affair with Tuesday, he has also had an affair with Lee Radziwill, the sister of Jackie Kennedy, now Jackie Onassis. Peter originally met Jackie Kennedy in September 1962, when she came to see *Beyond the Fringe* in New York, and she has recently taken Lee to Boston to see his new show. Lee is a very beautiful society woman, and Peter began an affair with her shortly after they were introduced, but he insists it is now over.

It seems that one attractive woman after another wants to be with him and I am more upset than I let on that in the space of a few weeks he's been unfaithful twice. My only consolation is that if Peter is interested in Lee, he can't be that interested in Tuesday. I long to be with Peter for ever, but I am learning that if we stay together, regardless of how pulverised I may feel inside, I have to cope with his unfaithfulness. It is just part of the man.

Good Evening opens in New York at the Plymouth Theatre on 10 November. It later transfers to the Lunt-Fontanne Theatre. It is an immediate hit with both critics and the public. One reviewer says, 'They [Dudley and Peter] are perhaps the funniest pair of comedians in the world.' Another comments, 'It will astonish me if anything else this season will supply me with equal fun.'

Peter is thrilled with the reception, particularly as the revue is very English. Although Alexander Cohen has persuaded Peter and Dudley to make several cuts to the script to make it tighter, the only concessions Peter has made for an American audience are minor – for example, using the word 'eraser' for 'rubber'.

The show includes a sketch on women's lib, another on the one-legged actor auditioning for the role of Tarzan, plus an in-depth interview by a reporter from the *Bethlehem Star* with one of the shepherds who was at the birth of Jesus.

The show is a sell-out, breaks the theatre box-office records, and Peter and Dudley become the toast of the town. They are reborn as huge stars, which is exactly what they have longed for. Countless numbers of celebrities, including Walter Matthau, Groucho Marx, Cary Grant, Charlton Heston, Tennessee Williams and Foreign Secretary Dr Henry Kissinger, not only see the show but also come backstage to meet Peter and Dudley.

The night Kissinger comes, the theatre crawls with secret service people checking everything. I am introduced to him and feel really proud to meet such a great man. I ask him why he isn't president and he says it is because he wasn't born in the States. Peter and I are also invited to countless show-business parties, and Peter and Dudley regularly hold court at Sardi's, Broadway's famous theatrical restaurant.

Peter loves the fast pace and overdrive atmosphere of New

York. He is also enjoying the generous financial rewards. He and Dudley are now earning £500 a week, which is far more than he earned when *Beyond the Fringe* was first performed in London. Peter later tells me the London show was produced with a total budget of £50 and that he was annoyed that his work eventually made £400,000 profit for its backers in England and America.

Keith Moon, the drummer in The Who, who has a wild reputation, is staying in the same hotel. He drinks and parties to excess, regularly trashes hotel rooms and seems to destroy more drum kits than most musicians have a chance to play on. It makes him just the sort of person I want Peter to stay well clear of. Unfortunately he spends a lot of time in the bar and whenever he sees Peter asks him to join him. I try to pull Peter past him very quickly, saying, 'No, we don't want to go in there,' because I suspect Keith will, at the first opportunity, encourage Peter to get up to all sorts of antics. I just about manage it.

Peter's mood blackens when he is told by a reporter that Wendy, Lucy and Daisy have been seen at Findhorn, an ecological project and spiritual community in northern Scotland, and that the children are taking part in meditation sessions. He gets agitated and contacts his solicitor, who puts a legal block on her keeping the children there. He wants them to stay in school in London so that he can see them when he is home. Wendy does so, but the effort to sort it out makes it hard for him to concentrate on work.

Alex Cohen has arranged for Peter to have a minder. He is a hip, good-looking college graduate learning about the theatre. The idea is that wherever Peter goes he goes too, to keep an eye on him, especially as I will have to return to London at some point. Alex hopes it will help Peter not get blitzed out on drink or drugs in various clubs.

I soon discover that Peter has persuaded his minder to adapt to his way of life, rather than the other way round. Peter asks him to get him some uppers, which apparently he does, and, to Peter's delight, is soon happily partying along with him. I have a furious row with his minder and tell him this is not what he is supposed to do, but in the end I don't report him to Alex. It would have been one voice against two, and if he lost his job, Peter would be furious with me.

I also know that if his minder goes, Peter will work his charm on the next minder. I don't want to be thought of as a telltale either. The key thing is that the show must go on with as little upset as possible. If I cause a ruckus, the ripples will affect Dudley. It is a difficult dilemma, as I can't bear Peter taking drugs, but at heart I know I can't cope with either the responsibility or the blame.

Although the show is incredibly popular and Peter and Dudley should be getting on well, the reverse is true and tension is growing between them. The nub of this particular disagreement is that Peter has done most of the writing for the show and wants more recognition, particularly from Dudley, and it is bugging him that he is not getting it. Dudley meanwhile is insisting on joint credit. Peter goes on and on about it and believes he is the driving force behind everything. His resentment festers like a cancer. It is like a simmering subplot that I fear will destroy both their partnership and friendship.

Dudley, on the other hand, is becoming increasingly irritated by Peter's heavy drinking. I don't think it is affecting Peter's work more than it has done in the past – he is still funny and sharp – but Dudley is furious that he continues to ad-lib throughout the revue at his expense and manipulates his timing so brilliantly that the often very sophisticated audience laughs at Dudley rather than with him. Dudley feels so powerless and humiliated that he starts treating Peter with icy hostility.

Aside from Peter's drinking, I am becoming increasingly concerned about his drug-taking, and not just when he is out partying. He is self-medicating to tailor his moods to suit himself. He is quite secretive about it all, but I know at the very least he is taking uppers in the morning to make him feel alert and tranquillisers with alcohol in the evening to calm himself down. He is also smoking marijuana with the aim, so he tells me, of helping himself unwind after the high of performing. He claims he wants to use it instead of alcohol because it is less addictive, but in practice he is having both. I don't think his body can tolerate the abuse and I am sure it is a reason for his increasingly bad temper. It makes me believe he could get addicted to anything.

Dudley is so angry and fed up with Peter's determination to dominate and control what they do that for the first time he tells Peter to his face that he's drinking too much. Peter is hurt and spitefully calls Dudley all sorts of names. It's awful to witness and I can tell that the jealousy and tension between them is smothering everything they do.

They have often disagreed in the past, but it feels different this time and I know I am witnessing the beginning of the breakdown in their relationship. Apart from when they actually perform, they sometimes don't say a word to each other for days. Even when they do speak, Dudley often goes off to a restaurant immediately after the show without telling Peter where he's going or who with.

Because they both still want to know the minutiae of each other's lives, Peter tries to second-guess where Dudley has gone and insists we chase all over the city looking in various restaurants until we find him. If we do, Peter proceeds to tell

him what he thinks of him and they argue, seemingly oblivi-
ous of anyone else.

It's always been important for Peter to feel he has a home
where he can relax and after a few weeks he rents a fabulous
apartment in New York from Tony Walton, a stage designer
who was formerly married to Julie Andrews. It has four
bedrooms and three bathrooms, and all the rooms are large
with high ceilings. The hallway has been designed as a sitting
room with parquet flooring, there is a piano in one corner,
and the walls are lined from floor to ceiling with books,
which is fabulous. There is also a wonderful view of the city.

Off the kitchen is another large room that was originally
the maid's room, but has been converted into a bedsit with
its own bathroom. Tony is renting it to Julie Christie, the
actress who is having an on-off relationship with Warren
Beatty. She uses our kitchen when we are not there and
comes and goes via the fire-escape stairs at the back of the
building, rather than the main staircase at the front.

Her film *Don't Look Now*, in which she stars with
Donald Sutherland, has just come out. It is a thriller, but the
main source of interest is the very graphic sex scene she has
with Donald Sutherland, which has put her name in front of
the public. She has become a source of gossip and several
journalists are keen to find out who she is currently dating.
Peter and I know it is a handsome young man who runs the
local grocery store and who isn't famous at all. Our cleaner,
who also cleans for Julie, passes on lots of titbits about her,
including how she makes her hair look like corkscrew curls
and sometimes sleeps all day.

Peter, Dudley and I have dinner with her one night when
we are invited to a party at Maxwell's Plum after the show. It
is the first restaurant to have a formal dining room, a bar
and a casual pavement café all under one roof and has revo-

lutionised the way New Yorkers eat and meet. It's a fantastic place with lots of stained glass and Tiffany lamps, and its regular customers include Barbra Streisand and Warren Beatty.

Julie makes an entrance by arriving last and we are all knocked sideways by her beauty and presence. She sits at one end of the table holding court, and Peter and Dudley give her their full attention. She is a man's woman and so attractive I think to myself, I hope she doesn't come out of the bedroom tonight as I wouldn't trust Peter if she does.

I haven't lived in the apartment for long when I am invited to meet some of the other female residents at one of their regular coffee mornings. The women are chic, warm and generous, and talk endlessly about what they have seen and done. They tell me they love my accent and think English people are really quaint. They also ask me a lot about Peter. I'm polite, but I'm wary of talking about him and keep making excuses why I can't come again.

Instead Peter and I go off a lot on our own. One night he suggests we go to Times Square, the glitzy centre of New York, which is always buzzing with life. I am delighted, until I discover he is taking me to a peep show and that he's been there before. It is pitch black inside and initially all I can see are pairs of staring eyes. Then I notice a nude woman standing in a glass cage on a revolving turntable. He says the last time he was here he managed to get backstage. He tried to have a conversation with her, but the bouncers threw him out. I find it all rather weird and want to go, but an hour passes before Peter agrees to leave. If he's staying, so am I, but I worry that he is discovering a really seedy side of New York life.

After a month or so I have to return to London for a few days. Peter rings me very early one morning. It is a couple of hours after his show and he sounds drunk. I casually ask, 'Where are you?' expecting him to say, 'At our apartment.' Instead he says he is missing me and he loves me. Suddenly our call is interrupted by a woman's voice on the line. She shouts, 'Get your arse out of here if you're going to call your wife on my phone.'

Peter shouts back at her, 'Get off the phone. I am talking to my wife.' He then says to me, 'Judes, what am I going to do?'

I reply, 'For goodness' sake, Peter, go back home to your apartment.' He sounds so out of it, that instead of being cross, I can't help but laugh.

Later, when I ask him what happened, he says he can't even remember how he got there and I can't help being amused again. If anything occurred, the most it would be is a one-night stand and because I don't know exactly what happened, I don't let myself think about it.

In mid-December I return to London to oversee the building work. We want to be able to move in on our return. I plan to be back in New York by Christmas and invite Gaye Brown to join us and even pay for her ticket. As bad luck would have it, I get a nasty dose of flu, am stuck in bed and cannot travel. I tell Gaye and ask her to wait a few days for me. I expect her to cancel her ticket, but to my amazement she decides to go on her own. I phone Peter to warn him, then spend a miserable Christmas Day in bed on my own with just my cats for company. I feel worse when Peter phones to tell me he and Gaye are going to the Russian Tea Room with Woody Allen. It is a great restaurant, very popular with celebrities, and I wish I was there with Peter.

I soon feel much better and on impulse have my hair cut very short before I return. I tell Peter, but he doesn't seem to mind and, when I arrive, says I look OK. I see Gaye, who has decided to stay in New York for two weeks, but I don't want to speak to her ever again. She wants us to continue as friends, but I feel her behaviour has been such a betrayal I make it clear the friendship is over.

Soon after I am back David and Angie Bowie invite us to go with them to a club, and one freezing winter's evening they pick us up after the performance in a huge black limo with darkened windows. David is wearing lots of make-up and looks very exotic, while Angie, who is tall, skinny and muscular, looks quite masculine in a trouser suit. We join them in the back of the car, and the driver covers our laps with rugs. Angie tells me she really likes my hair and suggests that I should dress like a boy too. Almost immediately I feel someone's foot rubbing up against my leg. I am sure there is deliberate footsy going on, but I am unsure whose foot it is.

When we get to the club, Peter and David start an intense conversation. Angie asks me to dance and immediately takes control. It reminds me of the time I was in the lesbian club in Paris with Sean. It's quite sexy and we carry on for a few dances. When we rejoin the men, Peter says he want to get back because he's performing the next day, so we all pile into the limo and the friendly footsy happens again. Nothing else happens, though, and we get home, thank them for a good evening and go to bed.

Despite all the ups and downs, Peter and I still love each other so much and I am thrilled when he tells me he wants to fix a date to get married. We choose Valentine's Day and Peter jokes, 'It's a date even I won't forget.' It is also a practical choice in terms of Peter's work. We have the required blood test, and discover we have been resident long enough to be able to marry in New York.

I return to London, where I have a fantastic trouser suit made for my wedding outfit by the legendary West End tailor Dougie Hayward, who has a huge number of famous clients. It is in white gabardine edged with white satin and has a tiny waistcoat that fits me like a glove. The jacket is beautifully cut, and the trousers cling in all the right places but are not so tight that they look vulgar. I use the trip to check on the building work and return to New York on 27 January 1974.

Peter tells me he is not going to drink for three days before the wedding because he wants to marry me when he is absolutely sober. I am deeply touched. It is heart-rending to see the supreme effort he makes. At the time I don't know how dangerous it can be for an alcoholic to stop drinking suddenly and how easily it could trigger an epileptic fit. Peter only has two hours free on 14 February because he is booked to do a TV interview in the afternoon and then has to perform in the evening.

Our venue is Sardi's, in the heart of New York's theatre-land. I love it not just for the food but because of all the hundreds of caricatures of famous people that line the walls. We don't invite Dudley, largely because he will want to bring Tuesday and I don't want to see Peter flirting with her on my wedding day. When Dudley finds out, he is very upset. I don't want my mother to come either, because she is so nega-tive about my relationship with Peter.

We ask Alex Cohen to be best man, and without telling us he rings many of the TV news stations and newspapers, so when we arrive at the restaurant, instead of the usual family and friends, we are greeted by a scrum of television camera-men and reporters. We aren't angry, because we understand that Alex is bound to want to use the occasion to promote the show.

Peter is wearing the navy striped suit he wears onstage. He teams it with a dark blue shirt and looks very smart. I wear my wonderful white suit and feel very nervous, mainly because our marriage means so much to Peter, who is stone-cold sober, quiet and serious.

The justice of the peace begins the proceedings and everything goes smoothly. As the ceremony finishes, we are dazzled by a bank of flash bulbs from the photographers' cameras. One of the reporters asks where we are going on honeymoon and Peter explains we aren't having one as he can't leave Dudley onstage by himself.

We cut our tiered wedding cake, eat a slice and then go straight to a TV studio for Peter's interview. Despite Peter having to work, the day is wonderfully romantic, an oasis in a troubled period of our lives. I feel relieved, happy, very protective of Peter and enormously hopeful because of the effort he's made to be sober. After the interview I ring my mother to tell her the news. Although she's upset that I haven't invited her, to my surprise she is thrilled that I am married and a respectable woman at last.

After the evening show Peter has some wine as he can't hold out any longer. We come straight home and spend our wedding night in our huge bed, but not in the usual post-wedding way. Peter surrounds himself with newspapers and the various books he is reading. He likes to read about the dark side of people's nature and what they get up to. He is fascinated by Charles Manson because he is such an extreme character. Manson lived in America and was an icon of evil. In the late 1960s he founded a hippie cult group known as the Family and manipulated its members into brutally killing others on his behalf.

We also put on the television so he can flick between chat shows, football and politics. It's the best way for him to unwind. We don't have sex, but that doesn't matter and it happens naturally the following morning. I am not in the least disappointed that our wedding has been so low key because I am so touched by the huge effort Peter has made not to drink. Our wedding is featured on the evening news, and every paper covers it the following morning.

Being married gives me confidence and I begin to toughen up a little. Peter absolutely loves us being married and keeps referring to me as 'my wife' or 'Mrs Cook'. It also gives him confidence where Dudley is concerned. He has at last won the battle for me and knows I am committed to him. As for the affairs he has had, each of us has a choice and I chose to stay with Peter because I never felt he was really in love with any of the women. It is also a case of deciding how much a relationship is worth, and for me it was worth a lot more than a few women crossing his path.

After his short abstention Peter starts drinking more than ever. One day Rita Moreno invites us to dinner. She is Puerto Rican by birth and moved to New York at the age of five. She has appeared in great films like *Singin' in the Rain* and *The King and I*, and won an Academy Award for playing Anita in the 1961 film version of Leonard Bernstein's and Stephen Sondheim's *West Side Story*. We both like her and her husband, Leonard Gordon, very much. Leonard was a doctor but has now become Rita's manager and they live close to our apartment.

During the evening Peter and I, very unusually, start to talk about his drinking. Leonard doesn't beat about the bush and tells Peter straight that he has to stop and dry out. I really like his manner. Far too many people are so charmed by Peter that they don't dare say anything. He also immediately recognises that Peter wouldn't be talking about his problem with alcohol unless he was fairly desperate. Sadly Peter can't follow his advice because he needs to stop working to dry out and he can't take the time out in the middle of a successful run.

One of the things I learn about living with Peter is how to cope with his confessions. I am pleased to hear them, but they can also be wounding. One evening he reveals that he and Dudley have shared the same prostitute. He saw her first, then Dudley went along, and he then went back 'to have a long, meaningful talk with her about Dudley'. He is full of bravado and says how funny it was and how nice she is. According to Peter, they spent a good hour talking about how Dudley performed, exactly what he did to her and what he talked about. Apparently Dudley has also enquired about him.

Initially I am so intrigued at how bizarre it is that I don't take in that they have gone to a prostitute for sex. This hits me later and I feel both shocked and terrified. I don't know quite what to say to him except to warn him to be very careful. He tries to reassure me that he hasn't had penetrative sex. I know that once Peter has broken the moral barrier of going to a prostitute, he is unlikely to stop at one and is probably now keen to explore this sleazy part of life.

In many ways Peter is a cool character and good at concealing areas of himself he doesn't want people to know about, but there is now a part of him that is becoming increasingly self-destructive. He is developing an unhealthy curiosity that is verging on the depraved. I also sense his inner turmoil and pain, and can tell he is beginning to hate himself. I tell myself that there must be a deep-seated reason, but I have no idea what it is. It marks the start of Peter delving into things that are dark and dangerous.

One night when the two of us are alone in our apartment, he suggests we play the Ouija board. I have never even seen one before, and it alarms me when soon after we begin it starts moving around and spelling out a name. Suddenly Peter shouts that we must stop immediately. We do and I wonder if he has played it before or feels frightened.

I don't want to cross a line and join him in dabbling in black magic, but it seems Peter can't help himself. The self-destructive part of him seems to force him to push boundaries and go further in everything he does. I, on the other hand, still don't realise that my tolerant, acquiescent approach to him is counterproductive. I can't help it: I love him and can't bear any confrontation.

I have to return home again to check on the work on the house. Peter doesn't want me to leave him, so I try to get everything done as quickly as possible. On my way back to the airport I suddenly double up in so much pain that I ask the taxi driver to turn round and take me to my doctor. I manage to get an immediate appointment and he diagnoses a severe infection of the fallopian tubes and tells me that my tubes are blocked. The doctor believes it has been sexually transmitted.

I have been faithful to Peter, but a terrible fear overwhelms me that Peter didn't take precautions when he went to see that prostitute. The doctor prescribes strong antibiotics and suggests I make Peter face up to what he's doing. I know it won't be easy and try to think up a clever way to say, 'You're giving this to me. Please stop,' knowing he will probably deny it.

My opportunity arises earlier than I expect. Peter rings to say he is flying over to see me. He has asked Alex Cohen if he can travel back to London for one night after the last show on Saturday and fly back sometime on Sunday because he wants to spend the night with me.

It turns out that he has come all this way because he misses me and wants to have sex, and although I don't want to, as having the infection means it is bound to hurt, I can't turn him down. He sees that I am in pain but continues because he believes he is expressing his love for me. Instead I want him to take on board the dangers of being sexually promiscuous, but when I bring the subject up, he barely talks about it, and won't even accept how it is affecting me. I stay in London for a few more days after he has returned to New York, then fly back to join him.

The whole episode makes me feel I have suddenly grown up sexually and I know I must look after myself. I have learnt about safe sex and birth control. I know from experience that IUDs don't suit everyone and can cause pain and infection, and equally that the pill, promoted as the answer to every woman's contraceptive needs, doesn't suit us all.

I arrive to find Peter and Dudley in terrific form, as *Good Evening* has just won a special Broadway Oscar for its unique contribution to theatre comedy. Shortly afterwards Peter, Dudley, Tuesday and I are invited by Lee Radziwill to a party she is giving for Jackie and Aristotle Onassis. I know most of the women guests will be amazingly attired in Chanel and Valentino cocktail dresses and that I can't compete. I decide instead to look stunning in a different way. I dress for maximum effect in very tight black trousers and a short-sleeved vintage peasant-style embroidered top that falls off my shoulders and is rather sexy.

Peter and I share a yellow cab with Dudley and Tuesday to Lee's apartment. It is the first time I go out socially with Tuesday and the irony of attending Lee Radziwill's party accompanied by Tuesday – two women with whom Peter has slept – is not lost on me. As it happens I view it very positively and can't wait to see what Lee is like. I feel reassured by the fact that I am the one Peter is proud of and wants on his arm and it is up to me to carry it off. Tuesday, Dudley and Peter sit in the back of the cab and I sit on one of the folding-down chair facing them. Almost immediately Tuesday starts playing footsy with Peter in front of me. Peter stares back at her. I suspect it is her way of telling me she has been intimate with Peter. I force myself to pretend it's not happening and look anywhere apart from their feet or their faces. Then Dudley starts playing footsy with Tuesday while looking at me. I can hardly be bothered with it, but fortunately we arrive soon afterwards.

The lift takes us right into Lee's apartment and a butler ushers us into the drawing room, where we are offered champagne. The rooms are huge, wood-panelled and reminiscent of the inside of an English country house. There are about twenty guests and Lee rushes to welcome us and is particularly all over Peter. Ari Onassis is sitting on the sofa with Peter Beard, the photographer and playboy. Ari is suffering from myasthenia gravis – a debilitating disease that weakens the muscles – and is obviously not well. His eyelids are being kept open by adhesive tape. Jackie is leaning on the mantelpiece of a carved fireplace. It is the first time I have seen her. She is wearing a simple, exquisitely cut black cocktail dress and looks stunning. Her shoes have quite low heels, no doubt because she is taller than Ari. Lee is wearing black too. She, like Jackie, is beautiful, but she seems tougher than her sister.

Peter goes over to talk to Jackie. She flirts with him and I hear her asking him for a cigarette in a breathless, soft Marilyn Monroe-esque voice. She stays in the same spot all evening, watching everything that is going on. Lee behaves quite differently and makes sure she is the life and soul of the party.

At one point Lee grasps hold of Peter's hand and asks him to dance. She starts gyrating in an exaggerated way in front of me. Peter is quite embarrassed and excuses himself. She then goes to Dudley and tries to dance with him. After a while she returns to Peter and at one point they sink to their knees, which looks rather painful, as they carry on dancing. Later Peter tells me she reminds him of a snake.

I go over to Ari and sit down next to him. He is still chatting to Peter Beard and looking at some of his photographs of beautiful girls and African wildlife. I stay quietly with them and try to avoid watching Peter and Lee on the dance floor.

Ari is very charismatic and asks if I am one of the girls in Peter and Dudley's show. I explain I am not. Despite his condition, he is quite flirtatious and asks if I'd like to give my phone number to Peter Beard. I thank him, but decline, explaining I am with Peter, but his interest is good for my morale.

Later in the evening Jackie goes over to Ari and asks, 'Hi, Senior. Shall we go home now?'

He replies, 'OK, Junior,' and off they go.

Peter knows how hot the summer is in New York and decides to leave the apartment and rent a clapboard house in Connecticut, from where he will commute to and from the theatre. He picks a modern house in Nutmeg Drive that has five bedrooms and is light, spacious and comfortable. It also has a guest suite, a huge garden and a swimming pool with a terrific barbecue.

It is bound to be very expensive, so Peter must be earning well, but I still don't ask him about money, even though I am now his wife. It is the way I have been brought up. I am equally sure that if I did, he wouldn't tell me. He keeps most financial matters very close to his chest and I doubt he even discusses them with his professional advisers.

Peter and I don't have a joint account; he just gives me a small amount of housekeeping each week. If I need anything extra – for example, if I have to buy something for Lucy and

Daisy or extra food if we have guests – I run up a small over-draft, show him my bills and he then pays me back. As I am not working, I have no income of my own, and I hate having to keep asking him for money, but that's the way he is.

At least he is renting this no-expense-spared house so the children can come stay and we can all have a fabulous summer. Daisy and Lucy join us when they break up from school. I also invite Lysie Hastings to keep me company, while Peter commutes to and from New York. I thoroughly enjoy her company and she needs cheering up after Dudley suddenly dropped her when he met Tuesday. Her divorce has also just come through, so she is feeling quite upset with life.

Lysie, who is a piano teacher, says she'd love to come but can't afford the plane fare. I tell Peter and he generously offers to pay for her and her seven-year-old son, Magnus, whom Lucy and Daisy know from Hampstead. She is such a nice person that even Peter doesn't mind her being around.

All the arrangements are made, and just before Lysie is due to travel, she rings in great excitement to say a friend has given her the phone number of a very attractive screenwriter with whom she thinks Lysie will get on. He lives in New York and she will be able to contact him because she's coming to Connecticut. She tells me he's a writer by the name of Claude Harz and I gasp in astonishment. He's Tuesday's last husband. I tell her if she stays with us, she can easily meet up with him.

She arrives with Magnus and we have a great time visiting neighbours, shopping and taking it in turns to cook. After she settles down, she rings Claude and arranges to have dinner with him. Peter's chauffeur, who takes him to and from the theatre, drives us all to the New York flat we have kept on. Lysie gets ready for her date and we all feel curious to see what Tuesday's ex is like.

Peter goes off to do the show and Magnus and I have supper together. I am babysitting so Lysie can enjoy her date without any worries. Magnus doesn't want to go to bed, so we read books and wait quietly for Lysie to come home. She returns at about 11 p.m. with Claude. Magnus and I stay discreetly in the bedroom, occasionally peeping round the door. Lysie gives Claude a drink and then sits down at the piano and plays him classical melodies.

Claude listens entranced, but after a while Magnus and I can't contain ourselves and suddenly burst out of the room to say hello. Claude is a little taken aback, but we all instantly get on so well that we invite him back with us for a weekend. In fact he stays for much longer, in what we call the honeymoon suite at the end of the house. Peter and Claude get on extremely well, and the relaxed atmosphere is exactly what he needs. Lysie is down to earth and Claude seems to be her perfect partner, which is wonderful as she was so upset by the way Dudley treated her. We have wonderful barbecues with steak and chicken and lots of salad, and we feel like an extended Swiss Family Robinson. Claude's daughter, Natasha, also comes to stay. She gets on very well with Lucy and Daisy, and we have a continuous house party all summer long. Once Dudley knows Lysie is with us, he rings wanting to speak to her and hear what she is up to, as he is very curious to know what is going on.

Peter is still drinking, but controlling it slightly better because the children are with us. He loves being with them and enjoys playing golf or very competitive Frisbee with Claude in the garden. It reminds me of how he used to play table tennis with Dudley. He is cracking endless jokes too, which eases the pressure on him, and it is wonderful to see him enjoy life outside work.

Peter is obsessed with the series of political scandals that come to be known as Watergate and which reveal the corruption and dirty tricks taking place at the White House during the presidency of Richard Nixon. Peter has a fascination for politics and what people get up to in public life and sits in the den, morning, noon and night, watching endless re-runs on the television of what's happening. He becomes totally absorbed by every aspect of Nixon's life. He thinks he is a shady character and can't see enough of him. Watching Watergate unravel has temporarily taken over from his love of football.

He is still gambling on anything and everything, however, and even puts a £350 bet that Vichy water is bubbly, not still. He also places a £1,000 bet that Nixon will sweat it out until his term ends in January 1977. He gets so worried that he might lose his money that he sends Nixon a telegram asking him not to resign. He gets a personal letter back from the president thanking him for his support and saying he is a source of strength 'in these difficult times'. Nixon resigns on 8 August 1974 and Peter loses his money.

I am happy that Peter seems happy, but one dark shadow casts a cloud over our stay when I discover a huge pile of pornographic magazines under the bed that must have taken a while to accumulate. It's not just *Playboy*; some of them are hardcore. I row with Peter about them and barely sleep that night. At one point I go into the spare bedroom and start flicking through the magazines at random, wondering what those girls have got that I haven't and trying to understand why on earth he needs to look at this awful stuff. Peter is suddenly beside me and asks what I am doing looking at them. He accuses me of being a lesbian. It's typical of him to turn a situation round on its head and blame someone else. I again ask for an explanation and he says he has liked girlie magazines since he was at school, which doesn't answer my question at all. I am disappointed in him. Pornographic magazines are so demeaning for women. It's also terrible he has them when Lucy and Daisy are staying and could find them.

On 30 November 1974 *Good Evening* sets an all-time Broadway record for a two-man production by reaching 438 performances. Both Peter and Dudley are tired and bored and want to come home, but they have agreed to go on tour. Luckily there is time for a two-month holiday first. The nightly sell-outs and rave reviews from critics have guaranteed Peter and Dudley more successful runs. I just hope their relationship holds up nearly as well.

Torn Apart

Dudley loves America and tells us he's decided to take his chance living here. The money he has earned from *Good Evening* will be a cushion while he sets himself up. His news worries Peter. If Dudley stays in the States rather than coming back to London, he knows it will be almost impossible for them to continue to write revues and TV series together, but Peter, as usual, doesn't want to confront him, says nothing and just worries instead.

The reality is that Dudley has more strings to his professional bow than Peter. He is a better actor and also enjoys playing with his jazz group, while Peter's talents focus on being a skilled writer, raconteur and comedian. Dudley hasn't set in concrete that he won't work with Peter again, but it is clear he won't come back to London and carry on as before. He feels he needs to restart his life somewhere else, and Peter understands that things are no longer going his way.

Nothing is going to change immediately, though, and we arrive in Toronto in the spring of 1975. Tuesday and Peter's minder come too. The show goes down brilliantly and I love being in such a beautiful city.

I no longer go to the theatre with Peter every night. Instead I sometimes remain in our hotel suite and watch television. Tuesday and Dudley are in the same hotel, and our suite is directly below theirs. Tuesday stays behind too and begins to ring me every night after Peter and Dudley leave for the theatre. She wants us to chat like two wives together and keeps asking me up to her suite. I make a few excuses, but the phone calls occur with increasing frequency and I begin to dread them. Eventually I agree to see her. She seems fascinated by how slim I am and invites me into the bathroom to weigh myself. She then weighs herself and compares our figures for ages in the mirror, asking if I think she should go on a diet. Her weight fluctuates a lot, and at the moment she is quite plump. We discuss the pros and cons in minute detail, but it bores me as I don't enjoy this sort of intimate girlie chat.

She also asks about the Hampstead house Dudley shared with Suzy and why I think he gave her the property when they split up. She seems very keen to have a house in London. In addition she asks lots of personal question about Peter and me. Eventually I feel so awkward that shortly afterwards I make my excuses and return to my suite.

The next night, when Peter comes back from the show, he tells me that Dudley is very annoyed with me because I am not being sociable. I tell Peter I think Dudley wants a foursome and his face is expressionless as he suggests we join him and Tuesday for a quick drink. I refuse and in the end he doesn't go either.

As a result Dudley stops talking to me and gives me filthy looks when he sees me at the theatre. Peter is cross because Dudley is upset. I understand that Dudley wants to marry Tuesday and needs me to be friendly, so I try to explain to Peter that I just didn't want to be sociable that evening. Instead of supporting me, though, he starts giving me the cold shoulder too. I am so angry that they both feel they own me and can tell me how to behave and who to be friendly with that I suddenly think, That's it. I'm going home.

I book a flight to London for the following day. I get to the airport and board the 747 feeling very determined. The doors close and the plane starts taxiing along the runway. Then a voice comes over the intercom saying, 'Is there a Mrs Cook on board?'

Puzzled, I shout, 'Yes.'

The voice replies, 'Your husband had requested that you come off the plane.'

The plane stops, the doors open, and there is Peter coming straight towards me. It is like something out of a movie. When he reaches me, he says, 'Please come back. Don't go home.'

All the passengers and crew are looking at us, and when he asks me to stay, they stand up and cheer and clap. It is obvious that they recognise Peter. I can't refuse him, and to be honest, I don't want to. I find him irresistible and am quite happy to be persuaded by him. In fact it is the best thing he could have done. I get off the plane, and we wait ages for my baggage. Then Peter takes me back to our hotel in Toronto. Mine has been an extreme course of action, and Peter's response has been equally extreme. He looks as pleased as the cat that got the cream.

When we get back to the hotel, he drinks a bottle of wine, then lies down on the bed and falls asleep. I don't mind because he looked so amazing as he boarded the plane, and his behaviour is such an outward display of love.

There is no more talk about going up to see Tuesday or spending an evening with her and Dudley or whether I am sociable or not, but to be on the safe side I go to the theatre in the evenings rather than stay in the hotel. Dudley remains cold to me, but it doesn't matter. He'll come round. Dudley and I have been getting along fine until now, and all our earlier problems have been forgotten. We are good friends and I treat him and Tuesday as if they are a married couple.

When we get to Philadelphia, Peter decides he wants to do some scriptwriting for another show. I think he is feeling competitive because Dudley has found an American agent and is being offered various acting parts. He employs a secretary, and although he comes up with a few ideas, nothing gets off the ground, partly because he is drinking too much.

The last leg of our tour is a six-week run at the Shubert Theatre in Los Angeles. Peter rents a rather grand house on Roxbury Drive, a few doors up from where Lucille Ball, the comedy actress, once lived. It's a road that tour buses constantly go up and down, which is quite amusing. Our house has five bedrooms, each with an en-suite bathroom, a big kitchen and formal dining and sitting rooms. There's also a big games room with tables for pool and table tennis, which will be wonderful when Lucy and Daisy come to stay.

The main bedroom has a huge rotating bed with various buttons to press that make it vibrate and go up, down, to the left and right. Off the bedroom is an enormous bathroom about sixteen feet by fourteen feet with a walk-in shower. There's also a stunning sculptured garden tended by a Mexican gardener, who turns the sprinklers on daily to keep the grass a rich green. A den curves itself round an enormous swimming pool, which a man comes to clean each day.

Despite our grand lifestyle, Peter doesn't like Los Angeles very much and finds the relentless blue skies and hot sun rather depressing. I'm not keen on it either. It's quite a tricky place to live, and you've got to be absolutely on top form to deal with the residents, most of whom look as if they are made out of plastic. The women in particular are relentlessly young-looking with such clouds of blonde hair, surgically altered faces and elaborate clothes that they look like expensive hookers.

During our stay Lucy and Daisy fly over to join us for ten days. The run-up to any holiday that involves the children is always full of tension. Peter makes arrangements through his solicitor, but these often change at the last moment. It always has an effect on Peter. He gets both excited and anxious, and this often prompts him to drink to excess. This time Wendy insists on sending the girls' nanny, Mary Corkram, with them. They haven't come with a nanny before, but I think Wendy is worried about life in Los Angeles and wants peace of mind.

The girls and I have a marvellous time together. We go to Disneyland, swim every day in our pool and play games. We also do a lot of shopping. Sunset Boulevard is within walking distance, but no one walks anywhere in Los Angeles. Instead the chauffeur supplied by the producer to ferry Peter to and from the theatre drives us there. I don't go to the theatre with Peter while Lucy and Daisy are staying with us because I enjoy being with them.

Peter is drinking so heavily he is now doing so in front of the children. Fortunately he also tries to be on his best behaviour and keep his moods under control. He is just as funny and loving as usual, and his drunkenness isn't obvious. It crosses my mind that perhaps he is taking more of the slimming pills that made him look less drunk. Neither girl mentions anything, so perhaps they don't notice.

I fly back to London after the school holidays and shortly afterwards Keith Moon calls me. He's working in LA, has met up with Peter and thinks he is depressed and lonely and missing me so much that he wants to organise a surprise party to cheer him up. He'd like me to be there too and offers to buy me a plane ticket so I can fly out and surprise him. His plan is to fill our swimming pool with bunny girls while Peter is onstage, which will really surprise him when he comes back. My heart sinks and I tell him I don't think it is a very good idea and I won't fly out specially. He goes ahead anyway. Peter tells me that Keith arranged a surprise party but doesn't mention bunny girls.

It is traditional in Los Angeles for members of the theatrical community to have lunch parties on Sunday. One of the first we go to is given by Mike Nichols, who directed *The Graduate*, the film that made Dustin Hoffman a star. He is married to my friend Annabel Davis-Goff, whose flat I rented when I first left Sean. They have just had a baby boy, and we have a wonderful time with them and swim in their large pool.

Our next lunch is with Tony Newley. He is a great actor and singer, and was married to actress Joan Collins, but now lives with Dareth Rich, a former airhostess who has recently become his third wife. Tony encourages all his guests to sit around his beautiful pool, which is encircled by overhanging cherry trees in full blossom. He then passes round a joint, which he insists we all smoke. I reluctantly take a puff and immediately think I am going to tip into the pool. I hang on to my chair very tightly and look round at Peter, who I notice is hanging on to his chair too. Tony, meanwhile, is running around with a camera, filming everyone. I find I can't move and stare at the pool, which looks extraordinarily large and has huge amounts of wonderful cherry blossom floating in it.

After what seems like hours I begin to be able to move again. I feel very thirsty and get some coffee and lots of water. Peter and I ask some of the other guests if they know what was in the joint and they tell us it was opium. Los Angeles is a dangerous place because you can get addicted to something without making any effort. I would never have smoked it if I'd known what it was, but it was passed around as casually as you would offer guests some canapés and no one mentioned what it contained.

Peter's day starts at around noon. He is always hung-over and immediately wants gallons of coffee. Sometimes he is quite tearful and we have endless discussions about his drinking. He likes lunch soon after he gets up. I buy fresh food for him every day and try to put on a spread that he will enjoy. The choice of food is fantastic, and I particularly love the delicious kosher meat that is available. Peter's favourites are lamb cutlets with lots of salad followed by cheese. He drinks wine as if it is water and endless vodka and beer chasers until he falls into a stupor and goes to sleep.

He likes me to wake him up around mid-afternoon, and this has become the time of day I dread most. He staggers into the shower, turns the water on full and demands sex, forcing my head on to him and insisting I do things I don't want to do. When he forcibly holds me down, I nearly choke. I can't even talk or cry out, 'I beg you, Peter, let me go.' The only saving grace is that I know he is too drunk to realise his strength and how insensitive he is being.

The reality is that he is too drunk to get a full erection, and when he can't climax, he blames all womankind for his problem, especially me. He gets quite vicious, not physically, but with words. Peter's mind is sharp and witty, and when he is drunk, it can be very cruel. His continual verbal abuse of me during our time in Los Angeles is terrible and I am petrified when he starts to shout. I don't want to eat and so rapidly lose weight.

After these appalling episodes he still expects me to prepare a light meal for him before he goes to the theatre. He is no longer in control of his drinking and drug-taking, although he thinks he is. I don't know if an audience can tell, but if you know him, you can see the signs. His voice is slightly slurred and his demeanour shaky, and that is after a cocktail of drugs to help him appear sober. He's also stopped coming straight home after the show. Instead he goes to clubs – I believe on his own – and often stays out until 4 a.m. I worry where his increasingly depraved appetite is taking him.

I am living on my nerves and feel lonely much of the time. I am fine in the house when there are people staying with us, especially if it is Lucy and Daisy, but not on my own. It is open to the road and I become increasingly afraid that someone will try to break in, so I lie awake until I hear Peter come home. He doesn't say where he has been, and he is invariably out of his head on something and is often abusive to me.

The only opportunity I have to talk to him is in the morning, when he is slightly more sober. I tell him what he has done and said the previous night and plead with him not to do it again. He always apologises, says he doesn't mean it and that he loves me and will try to drink less that day and then the tears flow. The same afternoon, though, he starts drinking again and wanting me to join him in the shower. Our days have become a terrible cycle and our relationship has hit rock bottom.

He no longer takes any exercise, and has stopped swimming in the pool or even sitting by it. Instead he spends his spare time in the den, drinking, chain-smoking, reading and watching television. Peter's impotency is not just sexual but in every aspect of his life, from dealing with his addictions to coping with Dudley's growing rejection. He is trying to drown his negative feelings in rage, but the angrier he gets, the worse he feels and the more he takes it out on me. I feel I have returned to the battered housewife I was when I was married to Sean.

I move into one of the spare bedrooms, but not entirely because of his sexual demands. Peter insists on keeping the television blaring all night and also turns on the switches for the bed so that it rotates up and down and sideways and makes it impossible to sleep.

It is such a waste of his amazing talent for him to behave in this destructive way, but I know it is partly due to anxiety. Now the tour is nearly over, he is increasingly frightened about finding other work. I also don't think he has made as much money as he hoped, and he has in addition got too used to a life of room service and being fêted.

Worst of all for Peter are Dudley's constant comments that he is going to stay in America and concentrate on a solo career. Peter dreads losing Dudley, and when he thinks about what he is going to do without him, he gets so upset he downs another bottle of wine. I try to talk about it to him, but he doesn't respond. I have to wait until he wants to open up. Occasionally he tells me how cross he is, but we have gone beyond our time in New York when we followed Dudley from restaurant to restaurant until we found him.

I have also lost Dudley as an intimate confidant and it is so difficult to find someone else to talk to that one day I gather my courage and approach the nice doctor who lives next door and ask him to see Peter. He agrees, but that is only half the battle. I now have to persuade Peter to see him. Although my life is spent trying to please Peter, I can be determined and know that this time I must do everything in my power to help him. I tell Peter every day for over a week that his drinking is very bad and finally persuade him to see our neighbour. I feel hopeful, but as soon as we arrive, Peter turns on the charm and becomes the professional Peter. He is so bright and funny that the doctor says he doesn't think his drinking is a huge problem. My heart sinks, but there is nothing I can do.

Shortly afterwards I go back to London, and while I am there, I have a smear test. The results come back abnormal, which really scares me. It reveals pre-cancerous cells and I go into the Chelsea Women's Hospital to have a cone biopsy to cut out the problem tissue. I am told I shall need to have regular six-monthly check-ups, which makes me feel very low. I hate having the anxiety hanging over me. It also puts paid to any thoughts I may have had of having a baby. Not only are my tubes blocked but now I am at risk of having cancer. Coming to terms with the fact that I shall never be a mother is very painful. I believe Peter and I would have made brilliant parents and that our child would have been so loved and wanted that he or she might have helped Peter control his drinking.

By the time I return to Peter a few weeks later, in August 1975 the tour is over and he seems to be in a better state. He wants to stay in Los Angeles or nearby for tax reasons before returning to the UK, and we agree to holiday in Jamaica. Christopher Blackwell, the founder of Island Records, has a cousin, John Pringle, who owns the Sans Souci Hotel in Ocho Rios, the first town in Jamaica to be developed specifically as a resort, and we book ourselves in.

We are away for five weeks and it unexpectedly turns out to be some of our best times together, which at one level is wonderful, but it also makes our rollercoaster relationship even more difficult to deal with.

We stay in one of the small clapboard houses, which are painted white or in pastel colours, that surround the main Sans Souci Hotel. All of them have their own gardens and back on to a private beach of soft white sand. We spend some days lying on the beach reading or listening to the local radio station, which has Peter in hysterics. He wants to take countless pictures of me in the sea, and I happily pose for him.

In the evening we change for dinner and dance to a Jamaican band on a white veranda overlooking the sea. Peter loves doing mock ballroom dancing and we tango across the dance floor, much to the amusement of the other guests and the band. Peter is agile and dances dramatically, and the dancing lessons I had before I appeared in *The Lord Chamberlain Regrets* make me a willing and able partner. Peter is given a local smoke of cannabis, and on a few nights we are so stoned we can't even find the hotel restaurant.

Once we feel more relaxed, we start exploring the island. Peter is very loving towards me and I have rarely seen him so relaxed. He is drinking much less too, just a moderate amount of wine and some local beer. It is so reassuring that when it is just the two of us, we can still have a wonderful time together, and I see yet again why I love him so much. At heart he is such a sweet man; it is just alcohol that causes all his terrible rages.

Halfway through our holiday we fly over to New York to see Dudley. Peter doesn't know for certain that Dudley won't work with him any more, and in the meantime they have agreed to make a farewell appearance on NBC's *Saturday Night Live*. It is a ninety-minute American variety show hosted by Chevy Chase, who is an Emmy Award-winning comedian, actor and writer. They perform 'One Leg Too Few', 'Frog and Peach' and do a hilarious impression of singers Sonny and Cher. Afterwards, as we fly back to Sans Souci, I wish Peter could be like this for ever.

Drink and Desperation

The effect of our wonderful holiday doesn't last long. Reality hits Peter almost as soon as he walks through the front door at Perrins Walk in the early autumn of 1975. I have managed to get all the main building work completed before we move in, but although it is homely and welcoming, and Peter is pleased to be home, he ignores his surroundings and goes straight to bed. It is hard to persuade him to talk, let alone get up. Over the next few months our life revolves entirely around his moods. Everything has crashed down around him, and although there are some days when he is sociable and funny, most of the time he is depressed and on such a short fuse that the tiniest thing makes him explode with anger. I try my best to cope with the different types of Peter, but the hardest is the one that is controlled by alcohol. I also miss not working, but at heart I no longer have the stamina to push for modelling or acting jobs. I would have liked to have been able to manage Peter and have a career, but I can't. Instead I have chosen Peter. I don't feel bitter about it. It is my choice and I believe the right one.

As the days pass, I begin to recognise different shades in his despair. Sometimes his mood is so black he doesn't want to do anything apart from drink, smoke and take pills, and several days can pass without him saying a single word. His depression drains me too. Our emotions are so interwoven that I cannot function properly when he can't.

He feels as if nothing exciting or good is ever going to happen to him again and refuses to open months of mail waiting for him or even answer the phone. Wendy wants him to spend time with the children, but he is so paralysed by depression he can't make any arrangements. When I tell him she's on the phone, he cries, 'Judes, I can't talk to anyone.' I talk to her instead and say he is going through a form of burnout after all the touring and I think he is having a break-down. She suggests he has a cup of tea and pulls himself together. It's fair enough. She cannot know the full picture of how bad he is.

Shortly after my conversation Wendy sends us a package in the post. Peter opens it. Inside is a carved African death mask. It was apparently one of their wedding presents, which, after all this time, Wendy has decided to send on to him. Peter is so superstitious that he starts shaking and won't touch it. I avoid touching it too, but pick out a note from the box. It reads, 'Whoever touches the mask will die.' Our cleaning lady comes up the stairs, sees Peter's face and says, 'Mr Cook, whatever is the matter?'

He replies, 'I can't touch it. Please get rid of it for us.' She takes the box away.

Friends expect him to be switched on too and want him to be out and about, but much of the time he can't go anywhere. I learn to be grateful when some days are dark grey rather than black. These are the times when he leaves me notes telling me he loves me.

Three weeks after we arrive home, Dudley turns up in London. He comes over to see Peter and stays all afternoon. He looks healthy, sorted and in control. He has also married Tuesday. She told him she was pregnant and intended to keep the baby and they wed in a quiet ceremony in Las Vegas at the end of the tour. Peter sits smoking and trying to keep himself together so Dudley can't work out how he really feels. I make coffee and stay out of the way. I can't hear all their conversation, but I do catch Dudley finally confirming that he is not going to work on TV or stage shows with him any more. I understand that he feels the need to stand on his own feet and that he can't take Peter's drinking, but I am angry he is hurting Peter so deeply.

To soften the blow, he says he will record the Derek and Clive dialogues and do the occasional commercial and personal appearance. When Dudley finally leaves, Peter physically crumbles in front of my eyes and changes from a dark, angry person to a weeping individual full of hopelessness. It's heartbreaking to see. Dudley has been the love of Peter's life in a work context and Peter feels rejected by him both personally and professionally. He can't bear the fact that the man he thinks should always be there for him is walking away. Dudley has been his perfect workmate, and he knows he is irreplaceable. Over the years they have formed a deep personal and professional bond, and although they have both worked separately, their emotional, creative and financial lives have depended heavily on each other. Peter is anxious about how he can earn a living without Dudley and I too feel sick with worry.

Perhaps in his heart Peter knows his drinking has caused their split, but he won't admit it. Instead he insists Dudley has betrayed him. He becomes obsessed with him from the moment he gets up until he goes to bed. For several weeks all we seem to talk about is Dudley. Peter's mood is contagious and I can feel both of us plunging down into a deep gorge that is going to be very difficult to climb out of.

Sometimes I sit on the bed in the morning and cry, and

when he asks why, I say, 'Everything in our life is so hopeless. We have lost so much,' but I avoid specifically mentioning Dudley. Although he is at the root of Peter's current unhappiness, highlighting the fact will only make him worse. He comes to sit on the bed bedside me, holds me very tight and we cry together. I know he is crying because Dudley has said he won't work with him, and I cry all the harder because he is crying.

For a week or so it becomes almost a daily routine, and at one level the tears give Peter some relief. Sometimes he complains that he feels like a workhorse and has to keep providing when in truth he wants to do nothing. Other times he admits he is frightened no one will want him to work any more. I believe Peter's breakdown is the result of a combination of factors. He hasn't earned as much money from the American tour as he had hoped, he hasn't made any plans about what to do next, and he has to face the future without Dudley. In a strange way it is as if Dudley has died for Peter and he is deeply mourning his loss as an individual as well as the life they have led. Sometimes he looks like a mortally wounded animal.

He is eating like an automaton and chain-smoking so heavily he often lights two cigarettes to smoke at the same time. Occasionally he watches television. I try to persuade him to sit on the patio in our beautiful garden, especially when the weather is good, but he refuses. I feel I am treading on eggshells all the time and have to be very careful of what I say and how.

We have stopped living a normal life. Peter sleeps until at least 1 p.m. every day and is often up most of the night. If he is disturbed in the morning before he wakes up naturally, he flies into a rage. I creep about like a mouse and use a bathroom on another floor to avoid his fury. When he wakes, our conversation is often reduced to what he wants to eat or if I am going out to the shops. The rest of the time he shouts at me, and there are weeks when he refuses to wash his hair, cut his nails, bathe or even change his clothes. I never retaliate by shouting back because I hate confrontation. I saw my parents arguing so much when I was a child that I can't stand it in my life. In any case it would be pointless. Peter is so clever with words that he could easily twist round and top anything I say. It is more worthwhile trying to calm him.

After a few weeks I feel so pulverised by his continual yelling that I move into a spare bedroom. It doesn't help. He regularly wakes up in the early hours of the morning and rampages around the house, kicking or banging on the walls or hammering on my bedroom door. Despite his fury, I cynically notice that he never smashes anything that is either valuable or antique. He doesn't actually hit me, but his constant shouting feels like mental abuse and turns me into a typical alcoholic's wife, nervy and with no self-esteem. I am not eating or sleeping properly, and my weight has now dropped to six stone. I feel too shaky to drive. I don't have the physical energy to do anything other than exist from day to day. I just about manage to get enough food in for Peter to eat and do the minimum in the house. I've become so fragile mentally that the smallest thing Peter does can make me panic. I see him eat some liqueur chocolates one day and get into a state because I think they might tip him over into complete drunkenness.

Often when he is drunk, he storms into my bedroom during the night, hate oozing from every pore, and starts arguing, going on and on about one particular thing that has annoyed him during the day. The smallest thing can trigger this rage, and I sometimes feel terrified of him. One day when I come back from shopping with some new clothes, he shouts, 'Can one eat clothes?' and remonstrates with me for buying them. Another time it's over trees for the garden. We manage to have a civilised talk about our sunken pond and how to improve it and agree to buy some trees. I am so pleased he is showing an interest in something that I go to a local garden centre and buy four palm trees. One of the employees brings them back with me, but when Peter sees them, he goes ballistic. He screams, 'What the fucking use are palm trees? Why do we need them?' His reaction is out of all proportion and it doesn't seem to bother him that he is humiliating me in front of a stranger.

He apologises afterwards and then, as he often does, writes me a whimsical poem. He leaves one on the bed for me called 'As I Was Walking Up the Stairs, I Met A Man Who Wasn't There'. In it he says he doesn't want to know my secrets and wonders if perhaps I don't even have any. He says he is 'very bright and funny' and describes me as 'very beautiful and odd', which is Peter's way of saying I am unusual. He then asks if there is anything else to us, and says he'd like to have a 'natter' about it one day. Most significant of all, he ends with the words 'I think I love you. PC.'

It becomes a pattern. He blows a fuse, then sort of says sorry. I don't know whether I should try to weather his erratic behaviour or leave him. I am caught up in such a destructive situation that it's hard to see beyond it.

In October 1975 Peter is invited on to *Russell Harty Plus* on ITV and his mood brightens at the thought of earning some money. Russell is a popular TV chat-show host and so sympathetic that Peter reacts well to him and is marvellous on the programme. Peter likes flirting with both sexes and responds to Russell with great panache, but he doesn't totally hide his general anxiety. When Russell asks, 'Have you come back to England to recharge your batteries?' Peter replies, 'If I could find them, I'd recharge them.'

His spontaneous banter is still brilliant. He tells the story of two men at a party. One says to the other, 'I am writing a book.' The other man turns to him and replies, 'Neither am I.'

This is one of many appearances Peter makes on the show. Later he issues a warning to any one-legged people who are invited on to Russell's programme, saying that the lavatory is unsuitable for them as it can only be flushed by standing on one leg and pressing the pedal on the floor with the other. He suggests it is part of Russell's determination to keep his guests off balance.

A few months pass and Peter is then invited to talk on Michael Parkinson's BBC chat show. It is recorded the week before it goes on air, and Peter gets completely drunk before watching it on television. Michael's other guest is the Spurs footballer Danny Blanchflower. Peter appears wearing a safari suit and red trainers, and slightly slurs his words. He seems rather subdued as he talks about how he hates rugby league and that he spent most of his time at school 'trying to avoid buggery'. He tells Michael his plans are for 'some more resting'.

I, meanwhile, keep trying to think up ways to get Peter to address his drinking. At various times I beg, plead, cajole, argue and fall silent. I keep suggesting things I can do, including how I look or behave, that will please him and make him love me and stop him drinking.

One day in 1976 Peter asks me to buy an iron-on number fourteen and put it on one of my long white T-shirts and he asks me to wear it when he is drunk. He wants me to look like one of the fourteen-year-olds in the teen porn magazines he reads. I feel awful and humiliated. I am thirty-four now, but I am so desperate to have some emotional contact with him and break down the barriers between us that I do as I'm told. I pose in it and let him take Polaroids of me. He directs me how to stand and instructs me to hold a feather duster. I tell myself that at least he is not shouting at me or refusing to speak.

I try another strategy by asking if I have upset him and if he is drinking because of me. He says he is and that it's all my fault. He even declares that his temper has been at its worst since he has been with me. I don't realise I am handing him an excuse on a plate. Instead I feel responsible for his rages and everything else that is going wrong in his life and making him feel wretched. It takes me a while to see that it is ugly game. If I offer to take the blame, he always accepts it. I only appreciate later how cunning alcoholics like Peter can be. My apologies let him off the hook, and instead of taking responsibility for his own actions, he passes them entirely on to me. I have no idea that however hard I try, I can't please an alcoholic.

After several months I force myself to see a solicitor as I feel I need to take some steps to protect myself from Peter's continual verbal abuse. He is recommended by an acquaintance, and although I avoid saying in advance exactly why I need him, I discover quite by chance that he specialises in problems caused by alcoholism. He is understanding and advises me to practise 'tough love'. He suggests I stop cooking for Peter, doing his washing and going to bed with him, so he realises he can't go on treating me like this. I try it for a few weeks, but it doesn't make the slightest difference. If I don't cook Peter a meal, he goes out to dinner.

I feel so desperate I impulsively go across the road to the woman who runs a leather shop. I don't know her, but she is kind-looking and when she asks in a general way how she can help, I burst into tears. She doesn't say anything, but makes me a coffee and I sit with her and cry. I know that just as I kept my parents' drinking secret I must now keep Peter's secret too. If it gets out, it will inevitably be detrimental for his career. Producers will see him as a liability and won't want to employ him, and the general public could easily reject him. I now know his situation is far from unique and that nowadays all sorts of stars announce through their publicists that they are going into a detox clinic for their drink or drug addictions, but in the mid-1970s they didn't.

I find the shopkeeper's presence so comforting that I return several times. She doesn't question or interrogate me. Instead she invites me into the backroom of her shop and, while keeping a watchful eye out for any customers, lets me talk. I am careful not to be too specific, but she seems to understand that I am in a lot of mental pain, and although it might seem odd to confide in a stranger, when you are somewhere so painful and dark, it can be better therapy to tell someone who doesn't know you than someone who does.

I don't tell anyone else what is going on in our lives. I am too proud and private, and, like Peter, do not want people to see that I can't cope. Instead I try to put a brave face on things. Probably too brave a face. Luckily deep down I retain a glimmer of optimism that doesn't let me give up. I keep nagging Peter to seek help over his drinking, and one day, completely out of the blue, he suddenly agrees he will. It is the first time he has admitted something is wrong and I am full of hope. I immediately get in touch with Richard Bell, who has been my doctor for many years. He also looks after Spike Milligan, so he understands the problems of show-business people. He sees Peter and, at the same time as avoiding using the word 'alcoholic', recommends he dries out. He suggests the easiest way is for him to stay in a small Mayfair hotel with a nurse to look after him. Peter agrees. I think it is a relief for him, and I suspect he is pleased he doesn't have to admit he is addicted to alcohol.

It is sorted very quickly. Dr Bell gives him tranquillising injections, puts him on a strict diet and recommends lots of glucose and vitamins to help detox his system and combat any withdrawal symptoms. I move to Ruston Mews for the week, as there are some household jobs I need to do. Peter's sister Liz has rented the property and the cat sitter stayed there while we were in America, but it is empty now and I want to spruce it up before selling it. I visit Peter every day and take him the papers and whatever magazines he wants.

The nurse who is looking after him is sweet-natured but physically rather large, and Peter asks me to get Dr Bell to provide someone more attractive. I do so, and when I visit Peter the following day, he has a very pretty blonde nurse looking after him. His mood has picked up considerably and midway through the week he tells me he is feeling much better and is going to take his nurse out to dinner. I can't believe that Peter feels as well as he says he does. It is only later that I discover that when alcoholics initially stop drinking, they feel so much better they believe they are ready to live a full life again and this includes alcohol.

I am suspicious about his dinner with the blonde nurse and ask a friend to come home to Perrins Walk with me. I don't explain exactly why; I just say I want to tidy up and that Peter's gone out to dinner with a nurse and I have a bad feeling about it. We arrive and I have started to feed the cats when I suddenly hear footsteps and voices outside. It is Peter and the nurse. On the spur of the moment my friend and I decide to hide. We sprint upstairs and into the third bedroom, where there is a large trunk and a vast suitcase. We each climb into one. Mine is hot and airless and extremely uncomfortable.

Peter and the nurse talk together downstairs for what seems like ages. Then I hear footsteps coming up the stairs. One set of footsteps goes into the bathroom, while another, which I recognise as Peter, goes into the bedroom. After a short time the female steps walk to join him. I hear Peter tell her that he thinks her little black lacy pants with red flowers are very saucy. It then goes quiet and I imagine they are probably having sex. Part of me is horrified by what is happening, but I can also see that it has elements of a French farce. It is ludicrous that I am hiding in my own house. Instead of thinking about what Peter is up to, I force myself to concentrate on getting my friend and I out the door as quietly and quickly as possible before Peter finds us.

A while later I hear her call him 'Mr Cook' and say 'good night' before she goes to another spare bedroom. I wait until everything is quiet and assume they are asleep. I then creep out of the trunk and help my friend out of the suitcase. We tiptoe down to the kitchen and I make a cup of coffee. Peter's behaviour is so bizarre and his moods swing so quickly. One minute he's feeling depressed and dark, and the next he's on a high and acting as though the world's a very sunny place. The three cats start running around as we drink our coffee, but then the Russian blue kitten Peter gave me jumps into a brown carrier bag, gets the loop handle caught round her neck and starts making a terrible noise.

I hear Peter's footsteps coming downstairs and him asking, 'What's that noise?' My friend and I look at each other, then rush out of the house and drive back to Ruston Mews. I don't sleep a wink and ring Peter very early the following morning. As friendly as can be, he says, 'Oh, Judes, I think we had burglars last night.' I ask why and he tells me there were signs that two people were in the house as they left two cups of coffee on the kitchen table and that the cat was running around making a dreadful racket.

I reply by describing the blonde nurse's black lacy pants, using the same words Peter said to her. He says nothing, then bursts into tears. I tell him I'm coming home and that I want him to tell the nurse to go. He apologises and I drive round. It only takes a few minutes and she is still gathering up her things when I arrive. He seems quite impressed by the fact I have caught him out, and for a short while is particularly nice to me. I, on the other hand, worry how fragile and shaky he is. He only stayed in the hotel for a few days and I think it is very early days to assume he will stop drinking. I am right and he is soon back on alcohol again. There is no point in trying to persuade him to spend more time in a hotel. I need to think of some other way.

As he feels a little brighter, Peter decides to commission a mural by Ralph Steadman for our downstairs living room. Ralph is an award-winning British cartoonist and he paints a huge mural that is about six foot long, divided by an arch in the middle and very dramatic. One side consists of a Greek column and is very phallic, which for some reason Peter says represents me. The other side is scenic with rolling greenery, which Peter says is him.

He also goes to *Private Eye* a lot. He can almost guarantee to find someone to chat and joke with, which is a consolation now that Dudley doesn't want to work with him. He still has the ability to reduce people to a state of hysterical laughter, and although he rages at home, and often comes back utterly drunk, I never hear of him losing his temper at anyone at the magazine. The year 1976 is a difficult one for *Private Eye*. The phenomenally wealthy tycoon James Goldsmith is suing the magazine for libel and it looks as if it may have to close. Richard Ingrams generally refers to Goldsmith in print as 'Sir Jams', but during his involvement in the short-lived Referendum Party he establishes, it changes to 'Sir Jams Fishpaste'.

I don't talk about it to Peter, as it is his world, but I quietly follow what is happening. Goldsmith issues over sixty libel writs in all and applies to the High Court to bring an action for criminal libel against the magazine. There are at least twelve hearings over a year, and it attracts more attention than any libel action of modern times. No one can say quite why Goldsmith is so determined to go ahead, and Peter even secretly goes to see him to try to work out why he is so angry. At one level Peter enjoys it all. He nearly always attends the *Private Eye* court cases, partly because they give him material for his humour and partly because he is fascinated by the whole process. It's a huge relief when Goldsmith eventually agrees to settle out of court for £30,000.

Peter's attitude to life stays upbeat a while longer when he turns his attention to the Derek and Clive tapes. Initially he and Dudley made them for themselves and a few friends. The original recording sessions took place in 1973 at the Bottom Line Club in Greenwich Village, New York. Peter and Dudley mainly ad-libbed from a few notes they had written down on various bits of paper, and Peter used the opportunity to be as insulting, aggressive and barmy as he liked.

Derek and Clive are angry, foul-mouthed and hateful about women and talk in a much coarser way than Pete and Dud. The tracks are wide-ranging. In one they discuss

lobsters, and both agree that the worst job they have had is
retrieving lobsters from the rear of Jayne Mansfield. Another
is about a blind man. Peter says, 'Good evening. I am blind.
And yet I am reading this message. I am reading it on the
wonderful system known as broille ... I'm sorry, I'll feel that
again.'

There is an amusing little ditty too:

> DEREK: *Oh, dear Little Flo,*
> *I love you so,*
> *Especially in your nightie*
> *When the moonlight flits*
> *Across your tits.*
> *Oh, Jesus Christ almighty.*
> CLIVE: Thank you, the Reverend Ike.

They also detail the toilet habits of the Queen Mother.

Peter drinks copious amounts while recording the tapes,
which is awful. His deep well of anger could be recycled into
something more upbeat and creative. Instead he is often
vicious and unkind to both Dudley and me, the two people
who are closest to him and love him the most. Dudley comes
right back at Peter with equally awful comments, but I don't.

The bootleg copies become so popular that in August
1976 Island Records decide to release them in an album
called *Derek and Clive Live*. Peter is thrilled that he and
Dudley have done something together again, but disappointed that it is immediately banned by the BBC because of
its use of four-letter words. Peter tells journalists that it is a
deeply philosophical record with material that comes
'straight from the top of my head'. He adds that he and
Dudley hung back from releasing it earlier because they were
worried it could ruin their image as family entertainers, but

points out that there are warnings on the record sleeve and that no one is forced to buy it.

Dudley agrees to fly over to the UK from Los Angeles to help Peter promote the album. Although it is a collection of rambling improvised dialogues, *Derek and Clive Live* becomes a huge hit and rekindles interest in both their careers.

Around this time Peter and Dudley are asked by the makers of Guinness, the popular dry stout, to front a TV advertising campaign and on 9 August 1976 go to Amsterdam for a week to make a commercial. Peter arrives back drunk and tells me he and Dudley have once again used the same prostitute. I don't know why he is bothering to confess and this time I refuse to be shocked. I tell myself Peter isn't a run-of-the-mill type of man. He is a funny, loveable, idiosyncratic rogue and it is pointless for me to throw my hands up in the air and complain. I know it is an appalling thing to do, but I can't change his behaviour, and as I have no choice, I put up with it and merely encourage him to be as careful as possible.

Peter is so pleased that he and Dudley are getting along better that on Dudley and Tuesday's first wedding anniversary, in 1976, we all go out for dinner and Peter insists on paying the £116 bill. It's a vast amount for the time and not surprisingly Dudley is amazed. Peter is careful with his money and it's not the sort of thing he normally does.

Dudley and Tuesday and their baby son, Patrick, have now moved into a rented house in Cheyne Walk, Chelsea, and I can already see cracks in their relationship. One evening they decide to have some friends round. Dudley invites his trio and they play jazz wonderfully throughout the evening. Dudley is playing the piano with his back to the French windows that open on to their beautiful garden, which slopes quite steeply downhill. Peter is in a mellow mood and for once not trying to be competitive with Dudley. Tuesday has drunk too much and keeps interrupting Dudley's playing to complain that the room is too hot, but he tells her she can't open the windows behind him as he will fall out. She ignores him, leans over and opens them, whereupon Dudley falls out and rolls over and over down the lawn. The remainder of his trio continue to play, while Peter, several other guests and I rush to the French windows. Dudley gets up, dusts himself down, climbs back up the hill, comes through the windows, sits down and starts playing again as if nothing has happened.

Once I stop laughing, I realise that Dudley is in denial about Tuesday's drinking. He keeps telling Peter that he can't stand it when Peter is attention-seeking because of his drinking and that he doesn't know when to stop, yet here is Tuesday displaying the same behaviour. She seems unable to take a back seat and let him have the spotlight, which is the key to having a successful long-term relationship with a star and particularly important with dominant men like Peter and Dudley.

Lucy and Daisy also come to stay with us for two weeks in the summer of 1976, as arranged. It is very hot and one day they ask if they can go swimming. I ring the Holiday Inn in Swiss Cottage, north London, as it has a pool and is quite close to us. I'm told it is for members only, but if they talk to Peter, they can arrange membership over the phone.

It is early afternoon, and although Peter has negotiated for hours to sort out this long stay with Wendy, he is now lying on the bed drunk and completely out of it. I shake him until he eventually opens his eyes and ask him to phone the hotel and sort it out. He can hardly register where he is, let alone what I am telling him, so I repeat several times, 'Tell them you are Peter Cook. Say I am bringing your two daughters swimming. Tell them my name is Judy.' When he eventually understands, I bring him the phone. He makes the call and is asleep again before we go out.

A day or so later the four of us fly to Jersey to spend about ten days with my mother. We lounge by the pool and eat delicious food. She behaves impeccably, which is a huge relief for me, makes us feel welcome and even invites other children round to play with Lucy and Daisy.

Peter is asked to write for the *Daily Mail*, and at the end of January 1977 the first of his weekly columns, 'Peter Cook's Monday Morning Feeling', begins. It cheers him up enormously and he employs a secretary to spend Sunday typing it out for him. He likes me to sit beside him while he dictates it to her and I become his audience again, either laughing at his work or making the occasional constructive comment. I am sure he has a hidden agenda too. It's obvious Peter's secretary finds him extremely attractive and he wants me to witness the effect he has on other women.

His column, which he continues for about a year, is half a page of jokes and quirky observation on a wide range of subjects that include politics, royalty and football. He introduces the first one with an explanation. He tells readers he is writing it on a trial basis for four weeks and that if it disappears suddenly there are three possible explanations: it was 'found to be insufferably tedious by all and sundry'; the work takes up too much time and he feels 'ill rewarded'; or finally, the option he thinks most likely, there has been 'a massive walk-out' by other writers on the paper due to the unfairness of the 'sustained brilliance' of his column.

His first column is illustrated with a photograph of himself sitting behind a desk in the middle of a field and looking rather pompous. On the desk is an unconnected telephone. He writes that he asked the features editor to select a photograph of him looking 'Byronic', but adds, 'He claims that it was a bad line and thought he'd heard me say "moronic".' Subsequently his by-line picture appears at the top right-hand corner of the column, usually of Peter but sometimes of 'Pete' wearing his cap and looking deliberately serious. The column is illustrated under the caption 'I can't draw either' with a squiggly self-portrait/doodle of Peter with a one-liner in a speech bubble.

The column is the perfect outlet for him to make repeated digs at individuals, like Sir James Goldsmith and David Frost, who have at various times and to various degrees rubbed him up the wrong way. He describes Frost as 'the ruthless Frosticle' for his 'amazing revelations' when interviewing President Richard Nixon. He says pointedly, 'As a comedian, he is a good interviewer.'

Peter likes to be self-deprecating too and in one column he writes, 'It's an awful lot of effort to look intelligent, honest, industrious and competent – as I've discovered over the years.' He even contrives to discuss Jackie Onassis's nipples. He points out that an identical picture of her appears in the *Mirror* and *Sun* but that her nipples can be seen under her top in the *Mirror* but not in the *Sun* and muses whether or not the *Mirror* painted her nipples in or the *Sun* airbrushed them out.

Another one of his items highlights the ridiculousness of banning Manchester United football team from Europe because some of their fans showed overzealous behaviour in France. He asks whether if the ban goes ahead, victims of razor attacks could sue Wilkinson Sword, or people run down by a drunken driver could collect damages from the distillery.

Peter also starts referring to me as 'La Sexburga' in his column. He loves making up names for me. Sexburga was married to Erconbert, who reigned as king of Kent from 640 to 664. She later founded a monastery in the Isle of Sheppey for nuns and then became abbess of Ely on the death of her sister Etheldreda. I am the last person to resemble a nun, but how can I refuse to be named after a pious queen? I have no idea that other newspapers will assume it is sexual. Peter later amends the name and calls me 'Judy Sexburga Cook'.

As well as starting his *Daily Mail* column in 1977, Peter and Dudley are offered starring roles in the film *The Hound of the Baskervilles*, which is very loosely based on Sir Arthur Conan Doyle's novel. Dudley is keen. He hasn't yet made it as big in Los Angeles as he had hoped and is very conscious that he has to support his wife and son. Peter is pleased to work with Dudley, but I am none too happy with the film's avant-garde director, Paul Morrissey. I sit in during his early meetings with Peter and think he is a bit wacky and not very self-disciplined, and don't think he will bring out the best in Peter. The two men get on fine as individuals, but professionally Peter needs someone who can not only inspire him but also be a strong hand on the tiller. Dudley always has been, but Paul obviously isn't. I don't think Paul's idea of using some of Dudley and Peter's old material in the film is a good one either.

Peter goes off happily enough to Dudley's home to start working on the screenplay. On one occasion, though, he comes back at 8 p.m. totally drunk. It seems that although he and Dudley are supposed to have been working, Dudley went out, leaving Peter with Tuesday, baby Patrick and Tuesday's daughter, Natasha. Peter says he has drunk lots of vodka with grapefruit juice and has enjoyed flirting with Tuesday again. He tells me he has dreamt about her and can tell by the way she looks at him that she still loves him. He says he is not taking it any further because he no longer fancies her. I am so upset I leave a note on his desk for him to see before he goes to bed.

> Darling PC,
>
> Please do not go to work with Dudley tomorrow – I couldn't stand it if you came back like you were tonight. I've cried, been lonely and miserable – you must know the answer does not lie in getting drunk with Tuesday or whoever – if Dudley was so busy seeing to the house and baby, why didn't you come back?
>
> Tuesday has told me you drink too much, so how do you think I feel knowing you have spent the best part of the working day drinking with her and her knowing that you get drunk so easily? It's now 10.30 p.m. and you are fast asleep on the floor. Oh, Peter, I feel so drained and miserable.

Filming starts in June 1977. Peter is Sherlock, and Dudley is Dr Watson. Peter jokes that Dudley is unsure how to play Watson and tells him that Dr Watson is basically a small, bumbling, ineffective fool, adding that Dudley is reluctant to play himself. Other members of the cast include Kenneth Williams, who plays Sir Henry Baskerville, Denholm Elliott, as Stapleton, and Joan Greenwood, who plays Beryl Stapleton. Spike Milligan is a policeman, and Penelope Keith is a massage-parlour receptionist.

The basic plot is that Holmes sends Watson to Baskerville Hall on his own to solve the mystery of the curse that hangs over the Baskervilles, while he takes a break touring London's seedy nightspots. Watson begins to suspect everyone he questions, including himself, until he calls for Holmes to help him out.

(*Above*) Peter's thirty-fifth birthday in Oz, with promoter Colin McLennan, Dudley and show girls on stage in *Behind the Fridge*.

(*Left*) I bought Peter a skateboard from Harrods for his fortieth birthday. He took to it like a duck to water, causing havoc around Hampstead.

Peter and I dancing at the Lyceum at the *Time Out* Christmas party in 1978.

I was very tired after moving into Mitchell Leys Farm, and said to Peter, 'Have you goated Billy in the lock house?'. As you can see, the horses are asking the same question!

Peter posing outside the chicken house at Blagdon Close with his teasing stick, ready to coax the chickens in.

Me, Sweep, Jade, Tiggy and Sadie. Peter took this photo of me. He called me 'Baroness Blagdon' in my Jamaican hat.

These two photos were taken in 1983 in a garden in Somerset, and are the last pictures taken of Peter and me whilst we were still a couple. He posed me for my picture, and it's my favourite. He then posed for me. Although he has dark glasses on, you still know it's Peter.

In my field at St George's in 1988 with Foggity, Chutzle, Elsa and Finnegan. I'm in charge with the mop!

The script is weak and full of crude British innuendo, and Paul, who is a fan of British comedy films, especially the 'Carry On' series, uses some of that material, as well as asking Peter and Dudley to re-enact tired sketches from *Beyond the Fringe*, including the funny but very well-known one-legged man.

Peter is taking so many uppers and downers and drinking so heavily that getting out of bed at 6 a.m. to be on set by 7.30 a.m. is a Herculean task. His driver tries to help by banging on the front door very loudly and, if there is no answer, rushing to the local phone box and trying to ring him from there. I am no help, as Peter keeps me up so late at night that I have usually just fallen into a deep sleep. Peter eventually stumbles off with a bottle of red wine. He insists the car windows are kept closed and smokes nonstop to create the nearest thing to a fog in the car, which he calls 'a fug-up'.

When he arrives home in the evening, he talks ceaselessly. He doesn't just go through what he's done that day, but also tells me endless Kenneth Williams-type jokes, as though he is performing in front of a huge audience. I try to calm him down but without success. He also rarely touches the food I have prepared for him, even though it's something easy to eat like macaroni cheese or chicken and mashed potatoes. Some evenings he seems quite manic and drinks red wine until he passes out in the early hours of the morning. He is so hard to live with that I suggest he stays in a hotel, but he refuses. The film, full of coarse language and camp innuendo, comes out the following year, 1978, and is a flop. The *Time Out* film guide states: 'Every single gag and every single comedy role is mistimed, misplayed or simply misconceived.' One evening I ask Peter what he would cast Dudley as if they had free choice in making a film together. He replies without offering any explanation, 'A murderer,' which is an extraordinary thing to say.

In 1977 Peter also joins forces with Dudley again to make a second album of their Derek and Clive tapes, called *Derek and Clive Come Again*. This one is recorded in Virgin's west London studios, which are owned by Richard Branson, and takes place in front of a guest audience mainly made up of Richard's friends. Peter and Dudley discuss the availability of food inside an intimate part of actress Joan Crawford, and at one point are thrown a blow-up doll. Peter takes it and starts slapping it around and gets quite nasty, saying this is what you should do to women to keep them under control. I look at Dudley, who seems as shocked as I am.

They also compete over who has more cancer. Peter goes on and on about it, which is horrendous as Dudley's father has cancer.

> *My old man's a dustman. He's got cancer too.*
> *Silly fucking arsehole, he's got it up the flue.*
> *He's got so much fucking cancer it drives him fucking mad.*
> *He says, 'I've got fucking cancer,' and he's my fucking dad.*
> *Oh, what a fucking boring cunt, he goes on and on all day.*
> *He's got this fucking cancer and he's too gone on the way.*

In addition a four-letter word is repeated 174 times in sixty minutes. The audience laugh, but I don't know whether it is because they are embarrassed, shocked or have had a few drinks and think it is actually funny. Apart from the cancer sketch and the blow-up doll, both of which I hate, I do find many of the sketches funny, even if they are vulgar.

The record is launched at Virgin Records at Marble Arch, central London, in the summer of 1977, and is immediately banned by Boots, EMI and WHSmith. Virgin representatives refuse to be defeated and instead go round individual record shops to sell the album. Sales worth £100,000 are achieved within months, and astonishingly it reaches number twelve in the charts.

Peter deals with the criticism about the language and content of the album in his *Daily Mail* column. He says he believes he was drugged by an employee of the 'notorious' Virgin Record Company, while Dudley 'claims to have no memory of having made the record at all. The last thing he [Dudley] remembers is that somebody handed him a Walnut Whirl.' There is so much ongoing controversy over the album that a petrol-pump attendant is fired from his job after it was discovered that he owned a copy.

The real drama is that the distribution of the record goes haywire and in November 1977 over seven hundred children whose parents have ordered a tape recording of the classic children's novel *Black Beauty* for Christmas from Kay's, a mail-order firm in Worcester, receive in error a copy of *Derek and Clive Come Again*. Apparently the company that records *Black Beauty* and Peter and Dudley's tape use the same processing company.

When Dudley returns to the States, he is offered a part in a film called *Foul Play*. He plays a would-be swinger who is picked up by Goldie Hawn in a singles bar. He only has a cameo role, but he is touching as well as funny and the film is his first cinematic hit.

Life with Peter is never the same two days running and he surprises me one day by sending me one of his tender notes. He writes how much he loves me, and says that if he added together all his feelings for his family (and in typical Peter fashion includes for good measure visitors and bank managers) it wouldn't even amount to even a part of how much he cares for me. He calls me a wicked bad possum and hopes his love rises up through the ceiling to reach me on the floor above. He then signs it 'Rook the Greek'.

He manages to cut down on his drinking. We start getting on better again and decide to throw a fortieth birthday party for him in November 1977. We hire caterers, who prepare a main course of rice, beef stroganoff and green beans, followed by raspberries and cream and a wonderful huge, square, dark-chocolate birthday cake for dessert. At one end of our sitting room, we make a bar by covering a large table with a white tablecloth. A barman pours champagne, wine and spirits for our guests, and we have a variety of fruit drinks for Peter.

It is autumn and too chilly to go outdoors; instead we have the garden floodlit. We have about fifty guests, who include our neighbours, Peter's sisters, some friends and a sprinkling of celebrities, including Barry Humphries. Peter is a brilliant host. He goes round chatting to everyone and, crucially, doesn't get drunk. At one point in the evening everyone sings 'Happy Birthday' and he blows out forty pink candles on his cake.

My birthday present to him is a large skateboard from Harrods. I also get smaller ones for Lucy, Daisy and myself. It will help get Peter fit and give all of us some fun. Peter loves it and we skateboard through the streets and round the local graveyard. He calls himself 'Son of Skate' in his column and tells readers he can sometimes be seen wearing dark glasses, a blond wig and a Californian helmet. He describes me as skating 'with infinite delicacy and balance', but says that he 'floundered along doing an elaborate parody of Jacques Tati playing tennis'.

The third and last Derek and Clive album, called *Derek and Clive Ad Nauseum*, is released by Virgin in 1978. If the other two were close to the edge, *Ad Nauseum* is savage, bleak and horribly obscene. It is really over the top. Peter has gone too far and is overindulging the darker side of himself, one that I think he should keep under wraps.

He is also horribly vicious to Dudley, which is his way of getting his own back for Dudley deciding not to work on shows or TV with him. At times he makes no attempt to be funny and is just obscene.

> CLIVE: There was a conference held recently where representations were made on behalf of all the countries in the world, and the motion put forward was that you, Derek, should be wiped out completely. Not humanely, but torn limb from fucking limb, tooth by tooth, and the last thing to be left was to be your nose, and on your nose they were going to put a whole load of kerosene and set fire to it. That's the only thing the world is united on – the thought of seeing you burnt to fucking death and extinct.
> DEREK: If that would bring the world together, mate, I'm quite willing to sacrifice myself.
> CLIVE: Well, why don't you do it now?
> DEREK: If that's going to bring world peace.
> CLIVE: It won't bring world peace, it'll just bring one laugh. That's all you're worth, one fucking laugh!

Some of the recording sessions of *Derek and Clive Ad Nauseum* are filmed to make a documentary called *Derek and Clive Get the Horn*. Peter is keen for it to be released, but Dudley, who understandably hates it, is not. It all becomes rather complicated. The British Board of Film Censors won't give it a certificate, but Peter works round this by releasing the film on home video. Dudley then blocks its release in America. Meanwhile the UK videos are seized by the Greater Manchester Police under obscenity laws and distribution is held up. The video company then goes bankrupt and it is only finally released in 1993. It marks another heavy blow to their already cracked working relationship.

Richard Branson throws a party for us while we are at the studios recording *Derek and Clive Ad Nauseum*, and at one point various joints are passed round. I don't smoke any of them, but just as I pass one to Peter, the front door opens and several police officers appear. They ask us what we are smoking and go round interrogating everyone. I glance at Dudley, who has quickly slipped a joint into his pocket. I can tell he is as terrified as I am. Cannabis is illegal, and being found in possession of even a small amount can result in serious consequences. Peter remains unperturbed and lights up a normal cigarette. Just as suddenly the door opens again and in comes Richard. He is laughing his head off. It is one of his pranks. We are so relieved we forget to be cross with him. Richard has filmed everything and will later release his footage as *Derek and Clive Get the Horn*.

After the final album Peter has second thoughts about its content. He worries that a new generation are only identifying him with Derek and Clive, and admits in an interview that he is concerned about what people think. 'I don't want to be disliked,' he says. 'It's just that sometimes I put my foot in it. I make light-hearted and ironic comments and they get taken for more savage attacks than I had in mind. It's upsetting.' The point is, of course, that he gets nastier when he's had too much to drink.

Shortly afterwards we go down to Richard's country house, Kidlington Manor, in Oxfordshire. Peter is recording an album called *Consequences* with Kevin Godley and Lol

Creme, who have recently broken away from the pop group 10cc. It will be a triple LP set with contributions from Peter. I have the role of Lulu, a French trophy wife, and speak with a French accent. It is only a tiny part, but I am pleased that Peter wants me involved.

Kidlington Manor is a beautiful house filled with antiques, and Richard encourages pop stars to stay there and use the recording studio next door. Staff are on duty twenty-four hours a day, and there is always a big communal dinner in the evening for whoever is around. The recording itself is a disaster, as Lol and Kevin are stoned most of the time, while Peter is drunk. They are out of sync time-wise too. Peter somehow gets up, showered and is in the studio ready to record by 8 a.m., whereas Lol and Kevin stay up half the night and stagger down for breakfast about noon, which is when Peter starts drinking. Although *Consequences* later gets cult status, at the time not surprisingly it is a commercial and critical flop. Peter remains loyal, and when a hostile Dutch journalist criticises it, Peter asks what he does with his free time. The journalist says, 'Nothing,' and Peter replies, 'Well, fuck off home and do it.' His bolshiness makes me laugh.

One evening while we are still staying at Kidlington Manor, I have to get back to London. Peter needs to stay longer, so I ask one of the staff to book me a car for 10 p.m. I'm waiting in the hall at the appropriate time when Richard appears and offers me a lift. He has apparently heard I am leaving. I thank him, grab my things and off we go. Unbeknown to me, he has an elaborate plan that initially seems like another of his stunts.

Richard is usually driven everywhere by his driver, but our journey begins with Richard taking his driver to the casualty department of the local hospital to see if he has appendicitis.

While we wait for him to have various tests, Richard chats me up and when the driver is, as expected, given the all-clear, he insists on driving him home first. It's a complicated way for him to keep the car without the driver knowing what he is up to. He then persuades me to come back to his house-boat in west London for a coffee. I am a sucker for attractive, dynamic men and he is such a charismatic, crazy character that I agree. We have a one-night stand, but I don't tell Peter. He would be devastated. In any event, telling him would only be an ego trip for me.

Although Peter can feel very negative about himself, many both famous and up-and-coming celebrities hold him in great respect and court his favour, and although he sometimes wants to be a recluse, he can also be gregarious. I can never anticipate who he is going to be from one day to the next. On one of Peter's better days Malcolm McLaren rings and asks to pop round. He is the partner of designer Vivienne Westwood, who specialises in anti-fashion, and he wants to talk to Peter about a new group he is managing called the Sex Pistols. He stays for tea and plays Peter some Sex Pistols music. Peter likes the sound of the group and tells Malcolm he thinks they have possibilities. I can't make head or tail of the music, but I like Malcolm. He is a bouncy, up-for-it character with bright red hair, and his group soon kick-starts the punk movement in the UK.

Meanwhile Peter's eating has become very erratic and I fear he is developing yet another addiction. Watching Peter eat when we go to our local restaurant Villa Bianca is rather like I imagine watching Henry VIII would have been. He has a gargantuan appetite and orders huge platefuls of food, which he washes down with vast quantities of red wine.

If he fancies chocolate, he can buy six large bars and eat one after the other. He is becoming so bloated and overweight that he barely resembles the man I fell in love with. He's also stopped trying to control his drinking when we go out. One evening we are invited to dinner by petite pop singer Lynsey de Paul. Many years ago she had a relationship with Dudley and now lives in a beautiful house in Highgate, north London. There are eight guests, including Lionel Blair, the dancer and TV presenter. During the evening Peter drinks himself into oblivion and suddenly slips off the dining-room chair and passes out on the floor. It is the first time he's behaved like this in public and everyone is very embarrassed. I feel so humiliated that I wish the ground would open and swallow me up. It's ghastly to see the man I love crumble publicly in front of relative strangers. One of the guests cries, 'Oh, my God, what's happened? Let's help him get him up.'

I reply, 'No, leave him,' because it's the best thing to do. I tell everyone he will come round in about half an hour and until then we should ignore him and carry on talking.

I'm right. He wakes up about thirty minutes later and shouts, 'Where am I? What the fuck am I doing here?'

Everyone laughs and Lionel Blair helps me get him up. Peter remembers where he is and of all things asks for another drink. Then he starts challenging various guests, asking, 'What the fuck are you doing?' which is embarrassingly unsociable. We all try to make polite conversation, while Peter tells us what we can do with ourselves. By the time we get home he is in a foul drunken rage and wants me to get him more drink and food.

He falls down regularly at home and is often too drunk to get up by himself. One cold winter night when he tumbles down the stairs yet again and I need all my strength to haul him to his feet, I decide I've had enough. I know he doesn't stand a chance of beating his addictions unless he admits he needs help, so I tell him if it happens again, I'm not going to help him get up unless he admits he's an alcoholic and agrees to see Dr Sidney Gottlieb. He falls down again shortly afterwards and I stick to my word. He tries to persuade me to give him a hand, but when I refuse, he finally admits he needs help and agrees to see Sidney. There is another ray of light, but will it be successful this time?

Drying Out

Peter and Sidney have a strange relationship. They spend a great deal of time together, particularly when they watch football, but I never think Peter relaxes in his company. I don't understand why. Sidney is concerned about Peter's drinking, but in the past there has been little he could do as Peter wouldn't cooperate, but now there is a chance. It is a major breakthrough and I feel hopeful again. Sidney repeats that he must dry out, and Peter says this time he will do so at home. Sidney prescribes a sodium amytal injection, a strong drug to make him sleep at night, as a short-term measure to help him cope with any withdrawal symptoms.

It is only effective for three nights and then Peter rings Sidney to ask for a higher dose. Sidney explains he is on the maximum amount. Peter gets frantic and worries that he is already addicted to it. I confide in Sidney that I no longer know where I am with Peter. One minute he's sober and loving, kind and funny; the next he is drinking and very angry. I tell him about Peter wanting sex but not being able to achieve it and that he is reading pornographic magazines and watching hardcore blue movies. Sidney listens then asks if I have any particular passions in my life. I tell him I love horses and he suggests I focus on riding as therapy. It's a good idea and I contact some stables in Wimbledon.

He also sends an Indian male nurse to look after Peter,

who tells me he has worked for families who own large houses for many years. One of the first things he does is empty the fridge. He explains he doesn't want too much food around as it will prevent Peter's drugs from having their full effect. He tells Peter to go to bed and make himself comfortable, and then injects him with sodium amytal.

Afterwards the nurse comes down to join me in the sitting room. 'Mrs Cook,' he begins, 'please don't worry, but I am going to take my trousers off. Nursing is a twenty-four-hour job and very tiring.' He proceeds to do so in front of me, sits down in his underpants and carries on talking as if nothing untoward has happened. 'I know how troublesome these situations are between husband and wife,' he continues, 'so I am going to lie on my bed in my underpants and wait while you have a bath. Then when you are in bed, I will bring you some cocoa and give you a neck massage so you sleep well.'

I am completely astonished, but I thank him and politely refuse.

The next morning he gets Peter up and tells him to have a bath. I hear muffled sounds from the bathroom before Peter shouts, 'For God's sake, fuck off.' He then goes back to bed.

While the nurse is tidying the bathroom, I rush into the bedroom and climb in bed with Peter. Peter stares at me through his sedated haze. I say we have to get rid of the nurse and explain his odd behaviour. Before I've finished, the nurse appears in the doorway, asks what I am doing in Peter's bed and insists I get out and let him rest. I grasp Peter's hand tightly and reply, 'I need to be with my husband, and he wants me beside him, even if he is resting.'

Despite Peter's drugged state, he heaves himself up on his elbows and asks the nurse to go out and buy him some magazines. It's a brilliant ploy to get him out of the house, and as soon as he's gone, I tell Peter to ring Sidney and get rid of him.

Sidney arrives within minutes, and when the nurse comes back with the magazines, we quickly dispense with his services. Sidney tells Peter he feels he is personally too close to him to help any more, but he knows drying out at home won't work. He recommends Max Glatt, a specialist in alcohol and drug addiction. At the first appointment Peter again turns on the charm and makes both Max and me laugh.

Fortunately Max has too much experience to be side-tracked by a few jokes. He understands how bad Peter is and books him in to Galsworthy House, an addiction clinic in Kingston, Surrey, for two weeks. While he is in the clinic, I buy a horse for £600, which I hope Peter will pay for. I keep her at a livery yard in Boreham Wood, Hertfordshire, and spend most days riding and looking after her. She has to be mucked out, fed and stabled, and it is such a relief to think about something other than alcohol and Peter. Having my own horse is a new start, and for the first time I feel I have a family of my own to care for.

Although riding gives me some release, I still sometimes feel too shaky to drive and when I do a doctor friend kindly takes me to and from the clinic. He reassures me that it is normal for a woman who is a partner of a drug addict or alcoholic to feel as wretched as I do.

I ring Peter every morning to check what newspapers and magazines he wants and then take them to him. He is gradually detoxing and is so quiet and withdrawn when I visit that he seems in shock. He is surprised that I am wearing jodhpurs, and when I tell him I now have my own horse, he accepts it graciously. I explain I have taken out a small overdraft and he agrees to reimburse me. It is the way we have always sorted out financial matters.

Once Peter has dried out, Max asks him if he will join the clinic's Alcoholics Anonymous programme and he agrees. He goes to the first group meeting and luckily immediately clicks with the participants. No one has to give their real or full name, and although they obviously know who Peter is, they never publicly acknowledge it.

They are a witty and intelligent group and Peter is amazed to meet a set of people with whom he instinctively feels comfortable. His whole life has been built around show business and it is refreshing to suddenly find a selection of people from all different walks of life, including a company director, a doctor, an antique dealer and an artistic director, to whom he can relate.

I make about four good friends in Peter's AA group. I also go to some of the Al Anon meetings that are specifically for friends and family of alcoholics. It was formed in 1951 by Lois Wilson, the wife of Alcoholics Anonymous co-founder Bill Wilson. It is important that I am involved, and it is a huge relief to have others in a similar situation to talk to. We also swap suggestions for helpful books to read.They are a delightful bunch and so easy to get along with. I relax with them, and it is the first time in ages that I feel comfortable in a social situation. We seem to have an instinctive uncondi- tional friendship. We trust each other, and no one is trying to encourage anyone to have a drink. Most significantly of all I begin to take one day at a time. I also learn to stop judging myself, accept what I have done and let it rest. I am even encouraged to no longer say to myself, If only I had done this, he might not have done that. I take all the advice on board and find that it has a huge impact on me. Gradually it changes the way I think and behave. It is a life-saver, and even today is still the way I live my life.

Peter is such an acute observer of people and situations

that at first I suspect he might send the whole thing up, but to my delight he totally enters the spirit of it. He feels humbled by the meetings and by being with like-minded souls who are going through the same addiction problems he is.

If any of his show-business connections saw how modestly and normally he behaves in an AA meeting, their jaws would drop. Peter is assigned someone to ring if he feels desperate to have a drink at any time, including during the night. The individual knows how he feels because he has been there too, but is now further on the road to recovery. He can talk until the yearning goes and for as long as he needs.

Peter continues going to the group when he gets home. Several of the recovering alcoholics have become such good friends that, after the official meetings, they regularly come back to our house for coffee, tea or orange juice. It is wonderful that Peter now has a social life with people who don't drink, as it stops him feeling under pressure. Sometimes they stay up half the night giggling and reminiscing about all the ghastly things they've done when drunk, while I make endless pots of tea. Peter being Peter holds forth a bit, but only as someone within the circle. Many of them are strong characters in their own right, with heart-rending or funny stories to tell that match every one of Peter's. It's a real leveller and I am now seeing a side to Peter that has been hidden for years, the one that I fell totally in love with when we first met, and I gradually feel I am getting my Peter back.

For many years his confidence has been almost entirely fuelled by increasingly high levels of drink and drugs, but AA is giving him a chance to show his real self, and his false bravado is replaced by something more gentle and natural. I am sure that his feeling of being abandoned when he was small when his adored mother left him for long periods has emotionally damaged him and made him vulnerable. He has blocked it for years, but he is opening up in these AA meetings. Finding a new group of people also helps him cope with not being with Dudley. Another world is available to him, and he doesn't need him as much.

Part of the recovery process involves Peter relearning how to look after himself. He is encouraged to eat healthy food, keep regular hours, get up at a sensible time and develop a workable routine. This in turn helps build discipline and avoid stress. He is also encouraged to take one day at a time. It's basic stuff that someone who is healthy would take for granted, but Peter needs to rediscover how to appreciate life, and he now has the opportunity to do so with the comfort of others around him. I can see it is giving him hope where there has been none and is helping him to trust again.

I get up and speak at the meetings I attend too. Normally I'd find this very difficult, but the friendly atmosphere makes it much easier. Once, I am asked if there is anything I will miss about Peter's drinking and I say, 'The sight of him trying to get out of his trousers when he is drunk.'

Several months later Peter is still on the wagon and becomes a leading light in AA. He is now in a position where he can help others and is around day and night for other alcoholics to talk to when they feel desperate. He willingly chats for hours about any subject they want and is so gentle, sympathetic and funny that it confirms what I felt when I had peritonitis and he cared for me – that he has a natural healing streak and is kind to those in worse situations than himself. He is delightful when there is no drink around.

There is, however, a downside. Although he has stopped drinking, he is still taking a cocktail of drugs to control his moods. His weight is ricocheting too. Some days he puts himself on what he calls a 'death diet', which consists of vast amounts of black coffee and a daily steak. During these times he will also play a lot of tennis and golf. Then he can suddenly switch, give up the diet, eat vast amounts and stop exercising. He is basically quite a vain man, so likes to be skinny and putting on weight makes him unhappy.

He is still going to *Private Eye*, but less regularly, as his life now revolves around a regime of not getting too hungry or tired and avoiding anything that could tip him back into drinking. At home, he is sometimes quiet and looks so vulnerable that I often feel overcome with emotion. He wants me to be affectionate too, but his libido has gone right down, which makes him fear he is getting older.

One day Peter and I are invited for tea by Alan Bennett. Alan has become a very distinguished playwright and lives opposite Jonathan Miller in a large house in Primrose Hill, north-west London. To reach his front door, we have to pass a dilapidated caravan, which is lived in by an elderly bag lady called Miss Shepherd. Apparently she turned up at Alan's house one day in the early 1970s and parked her caravan in his small front garden. Barnet Council had forbidden her permanent parking in the streets and Alan decided to let her stay. Miss Shepherd stays in Alan's drive-way for more than fifteen years and he writes a hilarious short story about her.

She is a shrivelled old woman and has become a human guard dog. As we approach the house, she pulls back her curtain, stares at us, grunts and waves her arms rather threateningly. There is a terrible stench as we pass the caravan, so we don't dawdle. Her van is overstuffed with decades' worth of old clothes and kitchen utensils still in their original packaging.

Alan's house, by contrast, is comfortable and full of books. It is the first time I have met him. He has corn-coloured hair and a twinkly, flirtatious manner. I think he is a very attractive man. He makes me feel really welcome and behaves like a mother hen, offering us tea and scones. He tells us that he is so annoyed about not hearing from his boyfriend in New York that he has sent him a letter, or rather a blank piece of paper, with nothing on it.

Peter stays on the wagon for a year, but at the beginning of 1979 he starts drinking again and stops going to the AA meetings. There isn't a trigger I can pinpoint; it could have been something or nothing. I wrack my brains to try to work out what in particular makes him feel bad, but sometimes I think his mood plummets regardless of what is going on, and it is merely made worse by an event or incident.

It twists me inside out, and I feel actual pain that he is deliberately destroying himself when I know he is a wonderful man. I want to shake him and say, 'How can you do this, not only to yourself but to me?' He is supposed to be on a drug called Antabuse, which makes you violently ill if you drink, but he pretends he is taking it when he is not. His AA pals come to see him and try to persuade him to come back to the meetings. He agrees to go along and pretends he isn't drinking. I know the truth and so do they, but none of us challenge Peter. We all know he has to want to stop himself. Instead we phone each other without him knowing and share our experiences. Peter's mindset is described by AA members as 'stinking thinking', which is lying about your drinking. The important thing is that no one gives up on him. Members of AA are like a loving family. They stay with you through thick and thin and make friendships for life.

It is about this time that I am involved in a car crash. I am driving our Mercedes 350SLC home from Richmond, Surrey, one evening when a car smashes into me. I don't go to hospital, but visit my doctor the next day. He tells me I have a whiplash injury. Although I feel lucky, as it could have been much worse if I hadn't been in such a strongly built car, I am shocked and in pain. Sadly Peter isn't sympathetic.

As a result of him drinking again, all too soon the abuse returns and he is back thumping on my door during the night and demanding sex, even though we both know he can't get an erection. I can just about cope with his changes of mood, but I can't stand any more of his aggression and begin to feel so battered mentally that in desperation I seek the help of a solicitor. I need legal advice about what I can do to stop his behaviour.

The lawyer suggests I apply for an injunction on the grounds of mental cruelty to prohibit Peter coming into the spare bedroom. It's dramatic and in theory not at all what I want to do, but I feel I have no option. I go to court, my appeal is heard, and I am granted the injunction on 24 March 1979. It gives me the power to apply to the court to have Peter evicted from his house for my mental peace of mind and protection. If he behaves badly, I'm told to ring the police and they will arrest him. I return from court with the order, which is served on Peter, who, ironically, has just come back completely sober from *Private Eye*.

At that moment the phone rings. Peter picks it up and a reporter from the *Sun* tells him what is in the court order before he has a chance to read it for himself. One of the court clerks must have leaked it to the paper. I can't believe such a thing can happen, as the court heard everything in secret because of its sensitive nature. At first Peter goes black with anger and shock that I have done such a thing, let alone that it has been leaked. He stares at me barely able to speak and just asks, 'Why?' I plead with him to imagine what it's taken me to go to such desperate measures. I think he understands, but he won't admit it.

The following day the story is in all the papers, and the press camp outside our house. They stay put for about a week. Peter goes to *Private Eye*, but I can't face walking through the army of journalists and feel like a prisoner in my own home. To make matters worse, my solicitor's secretary rings to inform me that he won't be able to continue representing me for some time as he is an alcoholic and has gone into a nursing home to dry out. I can barely credit it. The whole process has been so traumatic that I don't have either the physical or mental strength to start again with another lawyer and decide not to take the injunction further. A few days later Peter gets a letter from the judge who heard my plea. It confirms that someone from the court leaked the details of the injunction and informs him that he has the right to sue the court. I pluck up the courage to ask Peter if he wants a divorce. He says, 'No.' He then offers to buy me another horse, which is his way of apologising.

After this traumatic experience our life together gradually calms down. I think I have really shocked him, and he becomes so benign that to my amazement he agrees to come to a yoga class. It is held in Hampstead, close to where we live, and when we arrive, we find actress Ava Gardner standing on her head in a corner. She explains the position helps clear her sinuses. The actress Susan Penhaligon is also a regular. I think Peter fancies her, but he comes twice and then gives up. I go regularly and really enjoy it.

Dudley, meanwhile, is still chasing Hollywood stardom. In 1979 he is living partly in London and partly in Los Angeles as he pursues various parts. He also continues his intense introspection in both countries, but it is a group therapy meeting in the States that changes his life. One of those present is film director Blake Edwards, who is married to Julie Andrews. Blake is making a film called *10* with

George Segal, an actor at the height of his fame. Segal apparently was not happy about script changes and so he pulled out. Blake desperately needs a replacement and, to Dudley's surprise and delight, offers him the part.

The film is the story of George Webber, a successful forty-two-year-old musician who is going through a midlife crisis. He has a regular girlfriend, Samantha, played by Julie Andrews, but dreams of being with the perfect woman and starts rating all women on a scale of one to ten. He then sees Jenny, played by newcomer Bo Derek, who is all curves and tightly plaited blonde hair. He becomes obsessed with her beauty and rates her as an eleven. Apart from when Dudley appears stark naked in an orgy scene with countless full-breasted nude girls, much of the rest of the film is about him trying to get her into his bed. He eventually does, to the accompaniment of Ravel's 'Bolero', but despite the musical background, he ends up feeling disillusioned.

When I first see the film, I can't believe that the Dudley I know is up there selling himself. I don't see his character, George Webber; to me it is pure, unadulterated Dudley. It is Dudley with his hang-ups, Dudley watching girls and Dudley desperately searching for the perfect woman, who will understand and unconditionally love him. I think, How is he getting away with it? And what a fantastic chance to exploit himself and make money out of it.

Peter and I talk about the film and both agree that Dudley is playing the role in the identical way he sent Peter up backstage on tour when Peter had drunk too much. He used to mimic and mock him by slurring his words in a certain way and we are both sure he has merely honed his performance for his role of George Webber and that basically he is still having a go at Peter, but this time on the big screen. The film catapults Dudley into superstardom, and at forty-three he becomes a millionaire sex symbol, or, as he is often called because of his height, 'a sex thimble'. The film is released in 1979 and is a huge hit worldwide, making 1,000 per cent profit on its $6 million production costs. It is also a cinematic trend-setter. The Hollywood Women's Press Club award Dudley their coveted Golden Apple Award for 'Male Discovery of the Year'. The runner-up is Richard Gere.

Reporters seize on the opportunity to ask Peter about Dudley, and Peter in turn uses the opportunity to make several digs. 'He has always been a power-crazed egomaniac, a kind of Hitler without charm,' he says. 'But seriously, what has happened is no surprise to me. He always wanted to be an enormous star ... I am not envious. Dudley also has an intensive desire to know who he is and what he is and so on. This has been going on ever since I've known him through group therapy and psychotherapy. What he's looking for probably isn't worth bothering about. I definitely have no desire to know myself by being alone.'

I know not to take Peter seriously. He would never take a back seat and praise Dudley unreservedly, and Dudley would have fallen down the nearest drain from shock if he had. He gives as hard as he gets. It is what they have built their relationship and joint careers on.

As Dudley achieves superstardom in Hollywood, Peter's career undergoes a certain renaissance with a fantastic benefit in June 1979 called the *Secret Policeman's Ball*. Back at the beginning of 1976 Peter became involved in a series of legendary comedy shows for Amnesty International to raise funds for its research work in the field of human rights. The first, *A Poke in the Eye (with a Sharp Stick)*, took place in April, which brought together the four members of *Beyond the Fringe* for the first time since the 1960s. He also thoroughly enjoyed appearing in a Monty Python sketch in place of Eric Idle, who was away. A second one, called *An Evening Without Sir Bernard Miles* (the man who opened the Mermaid Theatre in London), took place in May 1977. Peter performed several sketches with Terry Jones, who was also part of the Monty Python team. These were both forerunners to the incredible *Secret Policeman's Ball*, which takes place over four consecutive nights.

Peter writes the sketches with the little-known comic Rowan Atkinson and John Cleese, who is also producing the show. It becomes one of the highlights of Peter's career. Some of the critics aren't as positive as he hoped after the first night's show and claim that it is merely a collection of old sketches. Peter is so furious he responds by writing a biting new sketch at high speed between the first- and second-night performances. The sketch is a brilliant and scathing satire on the judge's summing-up in the recent trial of Liberal Party leader Jeremy Thorpe. Thorpe has been charged with conspiracy to murder Norman Scott, a one-time male model, who claimed to be a former lover. Many thought the trial was fixed and a farce, and Peter's summing-up as the judge is achingly funny. He refers pompously to Scott, who is gay, as 'a self-confessed player of the pink oboe' and 'a man who by his own admission chews pillows'. He ends by telling the jury to 'retire ... carefully to consider your verdict of not guilty'.

The Secret Policeman's Ball is so successful that it leads to a TV special for Christmas 1979. The shows and its stars have a huge effect on modern British comedy. There are few comics today whose careers have not been heavily influenced by its anarchic and surreal humour. In addition it leads the way for other entertainers in subsequent decades to involve themselves in political and social causes.

Then, in 1980, Peter starts work on a one-off E. L. Wisty

special for ITV called *Peter Cook and Co*. Dudley stays in California and isn't involved. Instead Peter's co-writer is Bernard McKenna. Apart from the E. L. Wisty sketches, there are fifteen dancers, billed as the Wistyettes. Peter's guests include John Cleese, Beryl Reid, Rowan Atkinson and Paula Wilcox. One of the funniest sketches is with Beryl Reid as a plumber called Elka Starborgling, who, when she arrives dressed as a bee to cope with an emergency, says, 'I know. You weren't expecting a woman. Or a bee.'

Peter gives a series of interviews and makes a point of telling a reporter that he and I are back on good terms and refers to our problems and the injunction as 'a little local difficulty when we both lost our sense of humour'. He says that our marriage is 'as good as any marriage I know', but admits, 'There is no such thing as an ideal marriage.' I don't take that last comment seriously. Peter often says the first thing that comes into his head when he is being interviewed. I believe that overall our marriage is still strong, but I avoid dissecting it or examining each aspect under a microscope. Despite some destructive elements, we have a good relationship, and when he isn't drinking, we get on very well.

He is also quizzed about ambition. 'Ambition can lead to people taking pretty desperate measures at times,' he says. 'I am not that desperate.'

15

Town and Country Living

Peter keeps his word and buys me a second horse, Berry-B-Splendid, a Morgan filly. Having horses to ride and care for helps me cope with life, but I also need to get away from London. I ask Peter if he could perhaps buy a small cottage somewhere in the country where I could keep the horses. He says he will think about it.

He has started going to Stocks, the notorious Playboy mansion run by Victor Lownes, chief of *Playboy*'s British operations, which is situated near Aldbury in Hertfordshire. I am not happy about it – I don't know any wife or girlfriend who would be – but I know there is nothing I can do.

Victor bought the forty-two-room property, which was a former girls' school, in 1972 and it has become the scene of legendary champagne and sex parties. It is set in thirty acres and has a tennis court, swimming pool, giant whirlpool and stables to house some thoroughbreds. Inside, the décor is lavish and sultry. It has thick pile carpets, the corridors are dotted with erotic paintings, and many of the bedrooms have giant four-poster beds. There is also a viewing room where guests can watch films.

Although I disapprove of Stocks, it has become the place to be seen at weekends for anyone hell bent on pleasure and is regularly full of famous faces and tipsy tycoons. Visitors include John Cleese, *Superman* actor Christopher Reeve, singer Kenny Lynch, Keith Moon, Jack Nicholson, Warren Beatty and Tony Curtis. Victor loves throwing parties and ensures there is usually a funfair as well as a disco and masses of food and drink for his guests.

Stocks is also full of bunny girls. They are housed on the top floor of the mansion and prance about in their skimpy outfits, fake bunny ears and pom-poms on their bottoms, acting as hostesses to the countless men who flock to the freedoms they promise. Peter is perhaps inevitably drawn into this dubious hedonistic setting and even buys a T-shirt that says, 'Stocks House Regular'.

I briefly put aside my displeasure when a month or so later and, completely out of the blue, Peter says he's found a suitable country place for us in Hertfordshire, not far from Stocks. I am astonished he has moved so fast and go to see it. Mitchell Leys Farm is a sweet cottage set in three acres and has a stable yard. It looks perfect. The sellers have a German shepherd dog called Sweep and reveal they will have to put him down unless whoever buys the house agrees to have him. They also want the purchaser to keep their goat called Billy. We agree to take both animals.

The property is on the market for £70,000. I leave the negotiations to Peter and five weeks later, at the end of summer 1980, he tells me to pack my bags because the house will be ours – I notice he says 'ours' not 'yours' – by the weekend. He looks very pleased with himself when he says, 'I've got us the perfect cottage, and I can go to Stocks for the weekend and then come and see you. It's all sorted.'

He buys some inexpensive furniture and beds at a market in nearby Aylesbury to furnish it with, while I arrange transport for the horses and cats. They are my surrogate babies and I want to settle them properly. I only take one suitcase full of clothes for myself and leave everything else behind at the house. This includes a door on which I have done a full-size painting of Peter and written, 'I love you,' at the bottom. It was originally at Ruston Mews, but we transferred it to Perrins Walk when we moved and I subsequently sold Ruston Mews. I don't consider myself an artist, but it was fun to do. Once everything is ready, I follow the horsebox down to Hertfordshire in my car.

Part of me thinks that this cottage might be a fresh start for us, away from all the temptations in London, and I hope Peter doesn't find it too small. Peter has paid the price in full, so we don't have a mortgage, and he tells me to send my utility bills to his accountant, who will handle the payments. He also arranges for me to have £75 a week housekeeping money.

I move in and Peter comes down for three days. I'm pleased the cottage is an easy commute from London, but once he's gone back, I find being on my own very difficult. Although it is a modern house, it feels quite spooky, perhaps because it has been built on the site of an old farmhouse that burnt down. Being away from London helps me put things in perspective a little more. I feel sad that Peter has changed so much from the man I originally knew, and decide to write something down on paper to help me exorcise my negative feelings. I call it 'Twilight in Hampstead'.

> Let me take you into a dark room. The furniture is heavy. A makeshift coffee table piled high with papers, overflowing ashtrays, sunglasses and press cuttings. A large TV in the corner with a small library of well-worn blue movies. The atmosphere in the room is one of oppression. The power is generated from one man sitting alone in his darkness watching movies, unable to sleep. When he moves, it is to lift the glass of vodka to his lips, then chase it down with a lager.

The cigarette is sucked long and lovingly between the lager- wet lips. He is supping and smoking and watching. The whole body and head are geared to these compulsive addictions. The body stiffens before the deep inhalation of smoke. The smoke is drawn in with great speed and held there, before slowly spiralling out, causing a momentary relaxing of the body and a slight grimace of relief across the face.

Peter does what he said he would and spends the weekend at Stocks, then comes over to join me on a Sunday evening. He sometimes stays a week, other times just a day, depending on what he has to do. When we are not together we speak several times a day on the phone. I certainly don't see my move to the country as a separation, and Peter always refers to the cottage as 'our home'. The only basic difference between our life in London and the country is that I don't see him every day. It's as if he is commuting. We resume a sexual relationship, but I feel rather wary. I am not sure who else he is sleeping with; I am frightened of catching something and I don't want to take risks.

I have only been in the country for a few weeks when Peter tries to persuade me to move back to London to be with him. I decline and explain I want to give it a go in the country. Mucking out the horses, walking the dog and eating more healthily are giving my life a semblance of normality, and as a result I have seeds of hope. Although I am still very skinny and feel emotionally and physically battered, having to get up early in the morning to feed the horses, walk Sweep and take care of them all helps me get through the day. Sweep has really taken to me. He sleeps outside my door at night and yelps if I go anywhere without him. We have bonded quickly and he makes me feel safe. Peter likes him too.

One day some of Peter's fans turn up at the door wanting to know if Mr Wisty lives in the cottage. They obviously believe that Peter and one of his most popular characters are one and the same. Although I feel slightly worried about strangers approaching the property, because I spend so much time on my own, it is nice to meet some of Peter's admirers.

The next time Peter comes to see me, he unexpectedly offers to do some hard manual work. We have a makeshift pond with a natural spring in the field and he takes it upon himself to dig it out to make it a proper pond. He enjoys the labour, but admits the effort has knocked him out and doesn't volunteer to do anything like it again.

After a few more weeks I go back to Perrins Walk to collect some photographs and clothes, but nothing else. In practical as well as emotional terms it is not an easy trip. Making arrangements to come up to London is difficult, as I have to find someone to look after the animals. I also hate being reminded of the difficult times we spent there.

Late in 1980 Peter flies off for a brief trip to Los Angeles. He has agreed to play an English butler called Brentwood in a TV sitcom called *The Two of Us*. It is for the American channel CBS and he's thrilled because Dudley is in LA and it gives him a chance to compete with him again. He stays with the well-known actress Brenda Vaccaro, who in 1969 co-starred in *Midnight Cowboy* with Dustin Hoffman and Jon Voight. He rings me from her home every day, and once in the middle of what sounds like a lively dinner party. He always ends with the same comment: 'I miss you, Judes, and love you.' I don't know if he is having an affair with her, but she sings his praises on a couple of TV chat shows. It's not positive to wonder too much about how many times he might have been unfaithful to me. I don't torture myself by trying to separate rumour from fact, or one-night stands

244   Loving PETER

from something longer-lasting.

He returns just before Christmas 1980 in an ebullient mood. He has work to do, he has found me an idyllic place in the country, and he feels relaxed enough to bring down some of his AA friends to see me. They are always supportive even if he drinks in front of them. He doesn't however want Lucy and Daisy to come down. I don't challenge him, because I believe he wants to compartmentalise his life and just enjoy the peace of the countryside. I don't invite anyone from London down either and begin to make friends with people who are in one way or another involved with horses.

Peter decides to spend Christmas at Stocks and asks me to join him. I don't want to go and instead say I shall spend it with my animals. I never feel alone when they are with me. They make me feel I have a big family and I am so busy looking after them that time passes very quickly. Instead Peter persuades me to come to Victor's New Year's Eve party. Victor has invited the entire village, and there are some very respectable old ladies dotted around the crowded whirlpool saying, 'Hello, dear. How are you?' Just before midnight everyone joins in singing 'The Hokey Cokey'. I ask Peter if he is coming back with me that night or staying at Stocks. He says he wants to stay and takes me upstairs to show me his bedroom, which is decorated in deep red with matching velvet curtains and bedspread.

I go back to the farm on my own. It is a bright starry night and I walk out into the yard with my horses and look up at the night sky. It is very beautiful and I feel lucky to have such wonderful animals. Curiously I don't feel apart from Peter. I am pleased he knows exactly where I am. When Peter comes back the next day, he lets slip that it was Victor who found Mitchell Leys Farm, not him, and I suddenly realise I have been naïve and facilitated him leading a separate life in

London. With me out of the way in the country, he has the best of both worlds.

He returns to LA in the New Year to continue with *The Two of Us* and comes back when he can. On 3 April 1981 he turns up unannounced on my doorstep to tell me my mother died a few hours earlier of a heart attack. It is so unexpected that I break down in tears. I haven't spoken to her for two years. I couldn't cope with her and Peter's drink problems at the same time, and she kept ringing me when she was drunk and rambling on and on about how I didn't understand what she was going through with my father and that if I had helped her look after him, things might have been different. Her calls were invariably badly timed and usually occurred when I was preparing Peter's dinner. She was also guaranteed to rub me up the wrong way by beginning the conversation with 'What's Peter doing, darling? Is he drunk?' So when I moved, I asked Peter not to let her have my new phone number. The only people he gave it to were his close friends in AA, so they know where to find him. Meanwhile he kept in contact with my mother, and someone rang him instead of me when she died. I am profoundly shocked by what has happened and feel so bad that I didn't repair what went wrong between us or say goodbye to her.

Peter is wonderful. He sorts out all the funeral arrangements with my half-brother, then goes to Jersey for the funeral itself. I can't face it and stay in the country. I feel overwhelmed with stress and guilt, and know I am too fragile to cope. Her estate is divided between my half-brother and me, and I discover I have been left £130,000 (about £344,000 in today's money). When Peter hears this, he asks me for £35,000, which is half the cost of Mitchell Leys Farm. I give to him and tell the executors of the will what I have done. They tell me I can't afford such a gesture and advise me that in return for the money Peter must put Mitchell Leys Farm in my name. He agrees, then returns to Los Angeles.

I decide to use my inheritance to move closer to my roots, which are in Devon and where my father's family come from, as this will mean I can also ride on Exmoor, which I'd love to do. I tell Peter my plan. He is very enthusiastic and wants to know every detail of my property search. In a weird way it's as if we are just starting a relationship together. I look at the property adverts in *Horse and Hound* and find several that are in Somerset on the fringes of Exmoor and near the Devon border. I make an offer on one, Blagdon Close, in Wheddon Cross. It's the same price as Peter paid for Mitchell Leys Farm, but set in nine acres rather than three, and has central heating and an Aga. I buy the property and it's just as well I can make it warm, as the winter turns out to be the worst in years, with drifting snow up to the windowsills. I also buy another horse, called James, and give away the first one for breeding as it is not very good to ride.

Peter is pleased that I have bought a bigger house and more land for the same money, and two days before Christmas 1981 he flies in from Los Angeles to see it for the first time. A driver drops him off. He is totally drunk and has apparently been drinking nonstop from the moment he got on the plane. He barely glances round but declares that Blagdon Close is ghastly and in the middle of nowhere. He then demands some food and goes to bed. We have arranged to spend four days together over Christmas before he flies back to continue filming. I feel very anxious about how it will go, especially after the state he arrives in, but fortunately he is much calmer when he wakes up the next morning. We go for a walk and he agrees the rural setting is beautiful. I ask him what he thinks of James, my beautiful new Arab horse, and he says he reminds him of a prawn cocktail. He decides to call him Sir Jams after James Goldsmith, who sued *Private Eye*.

I don't have any alcohol in the house and he doesn't drink throughout his stay. He does, however, ask me for another £35,000. This time I have the guts to say no. I have no idea why he needs the money. He is still working, while I am not. Perhaps he has been gambling too much.

The phone rings for Peter. It is Dana Hill, who introduces herself as Peter's co-star in *The Two of Us* and says she'd like to thank him for the flowers he sent for her birthday. I say, 'This is Judy, his wife. I'll tell him,' and hear her draw in her breath. When I tell Peter she's called, he starts crying and tells me she is very young and sweet and that he has fallen for her. I am initially upset, but at least he doesn't actually say he is having an affair with her. I decide he is just a middle-aged man with a crush, and fortunately it is soon over. As is the sitcom. The ratings of the first series are not good enough to commission another and it is cancelled in March 1982. I feel relieved as I can tell the stress is getting to Peter.

By contrast Dudley is enjoying the fruits of his hugely successful romantic comedy *Arthur*, released in 1981. He plays the lead, Arthur Bach, a spoilt millionaire's son who spends his time getting drunk and chasing girls until he meets Linda Marolla, played by Liza Minnelli, a working-class girl with whom he finds an instant rapport. His family, however, have stipulated that if he wants to inherit the family fortune, he has to marry the woman of their choice. She is wealthy heiress Susan Johnson, played by Jill Eikenberry. Arthur does not love Susan, and when his family threatens to cut off his inheritance, Arthur asks his manservant, Hobson, who is brilliantly played by the great Sir John Gielgud, to help out.

The *New York Times* describes Dudley's timing as

'magical' and says that 'Miss Minnelli and Mr Moore play together with the kind of energising verve that one sees more frequently in the legitimate theatre than on film.' *People Weekly* writes, 'Dudley Moore has the angelic yet decadent look of a choirboy gone to seed. In this, his most brilliantly crazed performance, the five-foot two-inch actor proves that he can be a giant when it comes to comedy.'

The film grosses over $100 million. Sir John Gielgud wins an Oscar for 'Best Supporting Actor'. Dudley is also nominated for an Oscar and seals his place on the celebrity A-list.

Not surprisingly journalists keep asking Peter if he is jealous of Dudley. He says he is not, and that it is Dudley who has always wanted to be a star and not him, which isn't entirely true. He is not jealous of his fame as such. Instead there still remains a furious sibling rivalry between them that covers everything they do and say.

Peter even claims in a newspaper interview that when he did the pilot for *The Two of Us* he hoped it wouldn't work: 'I was told there was a one in five hundred chance of a pilot actually making it as a television series,' he says, 'and I thought, Great. I shall pick up some money from the one show and go home happy.'

He is caustic about Dudley and is quoted as saying, 'I have read newspaper cuttings on interviews with him for twenty years now and they all say at last he is happy. The thing about Dudley is that he is happy so long as he has friends and a lover. He doesn't read many newspapers or magazines and takes hardly any interest in what is going on in the world.'

He adds for good measure that unlike Dudley he doesn't want to live in Hollywood: 'English people over there talk about how much they like the weather and how you can always buy a record at three o'clock in the morning. Well, the weather bores me stiff, and who wants to buy a record at that hour?'

He also says that he wants to spend the next couple of months with me going for long walks, which I hope he means, and perhaps write a situation comedy. I believe he just wants to be home.

He meets up with Dudley in Los Angeles for a chat and they are persuaded to give an increasingly rare joint interview. Peter describes Dudley as 'selfish, greedy and vain – and therefore a fully rounded human being'. Dudley in turn says that Peter has 'a desire to shock like a flasher on Hampstead Heath. He wants to see the lady indignant but without any interest in molesting her.'

Peter replies caustically, 'I think Dud is delving deep into his own psyche and projecting it on to me. Once, during the *Beyond the Fringe* days, I observed that Dudley went from being a subservient little creep and a genial serf to become an obstinate bastard who asserted himself.'

I haven't seen Dudley for years, but I know neither of them will take each other's comments seriously. In fact Dudley would have been genuinely worried about Peter if he had been less biting.

Peter comes to Somerset quite often but, just like Mitchell Leys Farm, on an irregular basis. He sometimes stays for a weekend, other times for as long as a week. He plays golf and we go for long walks together. He even has a riding lesson at a local stables. When I ask him how the lesson has gone, he admits he spent most of the afternoon 'having a fag and a gossip' with the male riding instructor in the woods.

I have been slowly building up a menagerie at home. As well as my two horses, I now have four dogs, six cats, a goat and about fifteen bantams. It's difficult to know exactly how many bantams because they keep having babies. They roost around the rhododendron bushes, hay nets, in the barn and sometimes in the garage. The back door of the house is through the garage and so sometimes they manage to get into the kitchen too. Peter loves shutting them up in the henhouse at night. He rustles the bushes and calls them, then gathers them up with a teasing stick. He even gives them all names. This side of Peter is one no one knows exists, and I watch it blossom for a short time in an extraordinary way.

He is not drinking when he is with me and I have to make sure he has enough sugar in his system to prevent him having an epileptic fit. There is a lot of sugar in alcohol and it can be dangerous to stop having sweet things suddenly, so I give him lots of orange juice and glucose.

As a result when an elderly neighbour asks us over because she wants to meet Peter and give him her homemade sloe gin, I panic. She doesn't understand he should only have fruit juice and Peter is so well-mannered that he says we mustn't upset her by turning her down, so off we go. Each time she fills his glass we manage to distract her and I grab it and drink it. I am still not a drinker and think the gin tastes vile, but I will do anything to stop Peter having it. Fortunately she doesn't notice what I am doing, but of course Peter does and I see a look of love for me on his face. By the time we go home, I am so drunk I can hardly walk, but Peter is as sober as a judge.

So many people, especially in London, think our relationship is over, but it's not true. We are having a wonderful time together and are becoming increasingly close. He has even stopped going to Stocks. Victor was sacked by *Playboy* in late 1981 and in the late 1980s sold Stocks to cricketer Phil Edmonds, who in 1991 sold it on to Brigend plc and it was turned into a hotel.

Although our sex life is once again coming to a halt, we

are still very affectionate with each other, and Peter is more tender towards me than he has been for a long time. We sleep in separate rooms, but each night he sits or lies on my bed and gossips until he feels sleepy and then goes into the spare room. I would describe us as excellent companions, which is a rare and wonderful achievement in life and something to cherish. Most mornings are spent, as they used to be, with Peter reading as many newspapers as he can get his hands on, drinking coffee and being quiet. He loves reclining on the sofa and reading with a couple of dogs beside him and perhaps a few cats. We can sit together for hours not saying a word, both of us reading on adjacent sofas and then talking about what we have read.

He is so content that when I have to go to London for a medical appointment, he volunteers to look after all the animals for me. I worry whether he can do it, and leave him a detailed list of what time they all need feeding, what they eat and even exactly how to tie the hay nets for the horses so they are safe.

I start to feel anxious on my way home. Although I know Peter loves the animals, he doesn't like to be on his own and I worry that something might have happened to him or he has found it all too much and started drinking. When I arrive, though, Peter proudly takes me through every item on my list. He's been out with the dogs twice, given them food at 4.10 p.m. precisely and even washed up their feeding bowls. All the animals seem content, and Peter says he's had a peaceful day. It is little less than a miracle and shows how lovely he really is. It also makes me think how different our lives might have been if we had a child, not least because I believe I wouldn't have put up with a lot of his bad behaviour.

Working closely with the animals fires his imagination too

and he begins to talk about them as if they are human beings. We are together when the Falklands War breaks out, in March 1982, and watch the unfolding horror each night on television. It prompts Peter to enlist the animals into a make-believe Home Guard and they appear in the birthday card he sends me for my fortieth birthday in July. The card itself has an elderly man fly-fishing on the front, but inside he writes to remind me, in case I am absent minded, that it is my 87th birthday. He signs the card 'Lord Whirleypokes, Dr Groake, Professor Toad, Monsenior Newt and all the staff at the Blagdon Clinic for the terminally idle.' He then lists all the animals as if they are part of the Falklands War effort. Sweep is senior medical officer; Jade, another German shepherd, is Miss Tarty Nurse 1982; Sadie, a springer spaniel, is Miss Tarty Nurse 1981; Tiggs, a wirehair dachshund, is in public relations; Berry-B is Superbrat; Sir Jams is in catering; there is Basil, a bantam cockerel, in supplies; Bessie, another bantam, is a lay priestess; Flora, a bantam, is in the postal service and so on. While the war continues, they all have missions to accomplish, and he wants the Home Guard at Blagdon Close to be thriving and bring up the rear. Sadly, around this time, my beloved Sweep dies, but Peter buys me a German shepherd puppy we call Foggity and whom we both love.

Peter's parents, Margaret and Alec, come down for the day to see us. It is a special visit because Alec has recently been diagnosed with Parkinson's disease. His doctor put him into a nursing home almost straight away, but Peter took him out and has instead hired nurses to care for him round the clock at the family home in Milford-on-Sea. He spends a lot of time with his parents and is not only extremely dutiful but also makes them laugh.

Alec improves sufficiently to be able to make the journey

to see us. Margaret bravely drives all the way, but Alec doesn't travel well and gets fretful on the journey. Luckily it is a gloriously sunny day and everything goes well. Peter buys a salmon trout, which we cook in the Aga and serve with new potatoes and garden peas. After lunch I carefully help Alec upstairs so he can have a nap before tea and before Margaret drives them home. It is such an easy day that Peter and I treasure the memory for a long time. Peter is marvellous with his father, and as his condition deteriorates, he spends an increasing amount of time at his parents' home, on a rota basis with his sisters, Sarah and Liz, helping to care for him and keeping up the family's spirits.

I have learnt long ago that with Peter not everything is as it seems. Shortly after his parents visit I go to London to see him. I haven't been to Perrins Walk for a while and am shocked at how grubby and uncared for it seems. I see it in small details – for example, there is no toilet paper in the bathroom, and his pile of unopened mail is even higher than usual. I ask if anyone is cleaning for him. He is a bit evasive and then says he has a new Girl Friday. I am not sure whether this is a code to tell me he is having a relationship with someone or if he really has a cleaner but not a very good one.

I have managed to make arrangements for someone to look after the animals and planned to stay the night, but I can tell by his manner that he doesn't want me to. Perhaps he feels the house is his, rather than our territory now. I feel humiliated, but as I leave, he tells me what time he'll be arriving at Bladgon at the weekend, so I don't let myself think about it too much.

Towards the end of 1982 Peter goes off to Mexico to film *Yellowbeard*. It stars three of the Monty Python team – Graham Chapman, Eric Idle and John Cleese – as well as other comedy legends, including Spike Milligan and Marty Feldman, who tragically dies during filming. Peter writes much of the script and plays a gauche nobleman called Lord Lambourn. The film is a comic pirate romp, but it doesn't quite work. Peter's natural humour is spontaneous and instinctive, and doesn't seem to translate to the big screen. Critics say it is badly written, that its humour is laboured, and there are 'reams of unconvincing gung-ho'.

I think some of the puns are funny:

> BLIND MAN: I may be blind but I 'ave acute 'earing.
> SAILOR: I am not interested in your jewellery.

Peter comes back from filming with three different-coloured satin bomber jackets for Lucy, Daisy and me, and three Sony Walkmans, which are not yet easily available in the UK. He tells me that because I am the eldest I get first pick. He also suggests to my astonishment that we adopt a Mexican child. Apparently someone on the film has recently done so and he thinks it is a good idea for us. We haven't had the family we hoped for naturally, and although I long for a child, I know it is irresponsible even to think about adoption while Peter can't overcome his drink and drug problems. He is still taking all sorts of drugs and vacillating between being sober and nonstop drinking. He is in no state to take on the responsibility of a baby. I go against my instincts and dissuade him.

One afternoon he rings to tell me he has found a new therapist to help him stop drinking and asks if I'll come to London so we can both see him. I tell him brusquely that drinking too much is his problem, not mine. It is a spur-of-the-moment response and I realise too late that it is the wrong one. Both parties in a relationship share the problem

of addiction, and therapy can't be really successful if an alcoholic is treated on his own. I feel I have rejected an opportunity that might have led to a breakthrough in his drinking
and brought Peter and me back together permanently. It is a
big step for him to admit that he still doesn't have control
over his addictions, and an equally big one to find someone
to help him. I feel guilty that I have turned him down.

Peter goes on his own and doesn't seem to bear a grudge
that I don't come too. Instead he starts describing to me what
would be his perfect house in the country. This is an old
farmhouse with more land than we have at the moment and
a stream running through the garden. He suggests I try to
find it. I don't want to live in a house that Peter doesn't think
is perfect and after a while I find something I think he will
love. I describe it to him in a letter I send to Majorca, where
he is on holiday. He replies in a note addressed to Baroness
Blagdon saying that it sounds wonderful and he will make a
financial contribution. He signs it Lord Whirleypokes.

Unfortunately the house we have fallen in love with is
taken off the market before our purchase goes through, but I
feel happy because I have confirmation that Peter still wants
to be with me.

Peter doesn't work much over the next few years. This is
partly because he is looking after his father and partly
because he is not offered anything he particularly wants to
do. His film scripts haven't been a great success, and he is no
longer excited by television work. Instead he turns his attention to a neighbour, a rather eccentric character called
George Weiss, who prefers to be known as Rainbow George.
I met him briefly when we first moved to Perrins Walk in the
mid-1970s, as we passed in the street. At the time George
was spending a lot of time in Dublin, but now it seems that
he and Peter, who are near enough the same age, are

developing a friendship, getting up to mischief and drinking too much.

George's father was a diamond dealer and left him a considerable sum of money, which he is using to fund various hare-brained schemes, including setting up his own political party called Vote for Yourself Rainbow Dream Ticket. George begins fighting elections and by-elections all over the country. Peter helps with various suggestions about how to run the party, such as setting up a Ministry of Confusion.

Peter gradually becomes a regular visitor at George's house. He craves the company because he doesn't like to be on his own. He also knows George will join him in his bouts of drinking. Gradually George starts making recordings of his rambling and hilarious chats with Peter.

When Peter and I are not together, he calls me several times a day. He tells me about his life down to the smallest detail, but also filters out anything he would rather I didn't know. In 1983 it is left to a friend to warn me about an exposé in the *Star* by a black glamour model called Sandy Grizzle, who claims she met Peter at a party when she was sixteen and that he invited her to come back home with him. She describes how he wore huge dark glasses and was drunk and stoned and cracked jokes throughout their sexual encounter. Under the headline 'Captain Kinky – He and His Porno Pals Wanted a Gang Bang', she also talks about going to orgies held by Peter at our home. It is horrific to read and I finally acknowledge that this fills in the gaps about what's been happening at Perrins Walk while I have been out of the way, why it has such a weird atmosphere and why he hasn't wanted me to stay.

I ring Peter and ask him if it's true and he says it is. I am devastated and put the phone down. He calls me back that evening and arranges to come and see me that weekend. I don't say much on the phone, but deep down I feel betrayed by what has been going on in the place I still think of as home. It's humiliating for me to know so many people will read her story, and I also feel alone because there is no one I can talk to about it. Dudley is living the grand life of a movie star in America, and there is no point in me ringing him to say, 'Look what Peter has done to me now,' as he won't be at all surprised.

When Peter comes down the following weekend, he is apologetic and has a hangdog look. He hugs me affectionately, and we talk about everything except Perrins Walk and Sandy Grizzle. Instead we spent time as we normally do, looking after the animals, going shopping for food, and Peter lights the Pithy stove, which he had installed. He thinks it is a manly job and spends hours on his knees huffing and puffing to get it going and make sure there is a nice glow to come down to in the morning.

I feel so badly let down by Peter that shortly afterwards I begin a relationship of my own with a local man who is fifteen years younger than myself. I think, If he can do it, so can I. Being over forty is a dangerous time for a woman, and a younger man showing an interest in me makes me feel attractive again – at least for a short time. Of course, though, no one can measure up to Peter in any way and we never live together.

Peter continues to sound contrite on the phone and once again we become close. I tell him about my new relationship. He doesn't say much at the time, but not long afterwards he phones to say that the woman he described as his Girl Friday is called Lin Chong. He originally met her at Stocks, and she has worked as a PA to Victor Lownes. I don't take it too seriously and think of her as just another woman he's taken a liking to and who is doing a bit of light dusting.

Peter continues to come down at weekends, but as Christmas 1983 approaches and I believe he will be away, I make other arrangements and tell him I shall be spending the holiday with the local man. He sounds absolutely devastated, which I haven't expected. He then rings me several times a day wanting to know all about my young man and how I met him. He even asks if he can speak to him. I answer all his questions because I know that despite everything, we still love each other and I feel bad that I have hurt him. I don't give him the phone number, though.

He also sends me a number of touching letters, signing some 'truly thyne (sic) your own PC', calling me his bumble bee, and in one, he tells me he has loved me for a long time, and still has no wish for a divorce. He then sends a letter explaining that he will no longer be paying the utility bills as he has done in the past. It his reaction to me having another man in my life, but instead of upsetting me, this also makes me laugh because it is so typical of Peter.

Instead of spending Christmas 1983 with me, he goes to South Africa and sends me a bleak photograph of an empty swimming pool. In another letter he begs me to keep in contact and says how hurt he is when we are not constantly in touch. He tells me he thinks about me a great deal and realises that I am probably having a tough time too. He adds that even though we are no longer together as much as we used to be, he still feels close to me. He says I have always given him a feeling of wholeness and in a way we belong to each other. He admits that he is pretty hopeless at writing or talking at a deep level about how he feels, but that he longs to talk to me about anything, even our dog Monsieur Foggity's ears. He admits he feels diminished without me but doesn't want to whine and feel sorry for himself. He ends the letter telling me to look after myself and signs it with a doodle of himself similar to the one that he used for his column in the *Daily Mail*. This time the bubble that comes out of the side of his head tells me he loves me very much.

In addition he sends me countless telegrams, particularly when he can't reach me on the phone. They are often addressed to Mrs Rundle or Honey Rundle. He enjoys inventing names for himself and me just as much he does inventing characters in *Private Eye*. The bombardment of letters and my own feelings in response to them make me realise that my other relationship is on the rebound from Peter and I end it.

Even when Peter and I don't see each other very much, we continue to become increasingly emotionally close, at least over the phone. Neither of us holds back about what we think and feel, and I reveal my pain at what has happened between us and say that I am not coping very well. He tells me all sorts of things, from his appearance as King Richard III in the TV pilot of *Blackadder* to the details of his relationship with Lin, who is a Malaysian-born property developer. I am obviously not happy that he is involved with her, but I know that his liaisons often don't last long and I have no idea whether it is serious or not.

16

Complex Times

I assumed that because of everything that has been going on at Perrins Walk, Peter wouldn't want me any more, but his letters and phone calls make me realise that although he leads a double life, he remains devoted to me in his own way. I know too that I love him very deeply, and although many people might not agree, what Peter and I have is far more valuable than sex. We have become each other's confidant, and for me that is the deepest connection two people can have. So although some may think our relationship is unconventional for a married couple, it suits me. I have never lived a conventional life. I didn't with Sean, and I certainly don't with Peter. Instead I know that what we have is both profound and meaningful.

One afternoon Peter phones and asks me for the phone number of the father of the young man I was seeing. I have already told him he lives in a rented National Trust cottage and Peter calls him on another line so I can hear what he is saying, although not the response. He puts on a downmarket voice and offers to sell the property to him. From Peter's one way conversation I can tell the man believes him, and agrees to meet Peter at a destination on Exmoor to talk further. Peter has no intention of turning up. It's just a prank and I don't even know if the location actually exists. It is his way of entertaining me, getting me back as his audience and, most of all, letting me know he is still the top man in my life. It's confirmation of what I have always known – that Peter can make love to a woman mentally as well as physically.

In March 1984 Peter goes into a rehabilitation centre to try to dry out again and I put my house up for sale. I get an offer on condition I move quickly. I find another property called St George's, which is six miles away. It has four bedrooms, two bathrooms and is set in a lovely field. I can't discuss it with Peter because I know he is under sedation and not in a position mentally or physically to come and see it or make any decisions. He has also told me that Lin will be visiting him, and I feel it would be inappropriate for me to go too.

I decide to exchange contracts but keep the same phone number. When Peter leaves the centre, he rings me and asks to see the house. The moment he shows up, I know that things have changed between us. He is reserved and immediately asks if he can ring Lin to tell her he has arrived safely. I know in that instant that his relationship with her is not casual. He also reveals that he has had an epileptic fit in rehab.

He stays a week, and although he is pleased to see the animals again, there is a hesitancy about him and he doesn't relax even when we go to a local beach that is known for being wild and wonderful, and which normally he would love. He is the same at night. He still sits on the bed talking to me, but the warmth is no longer there and for the first time I cannot get it back. I am upset, as I have missed his laughter, advice and the way he has of easing my worries. More than anything I want us to get back to the great relationship we had at Blagdon Close.

Over the next couple of years Peter continues to visit me, but far less frequently. We still talk all the time on the phone, often as many as three times a day. He tells me minute details

of his life with Lin and how he is trying to get her to understand English humour. Sometimes he complains too: 'She has
come round and is sitting doing the vegetables. What I am
supposed to talk to her about?' he asks. The way he talks
about her makes me feel she is possessive.

On another occasion he rings sounding desperate and
jaded and says he thinks he is addicted to pornography, especially to oriental hardcore porn, as he can't stop watching it.
I try to calm him, but I feel very concerned. One problem
with Peter is that he is never at peace and always wants to
push back his boundaries. I fear that, as with his other addictions, he will need increasingly powerful amounts to give
him a high. He obviously needs help, not just from a doctor
but also spiritually. It is almost as if he has allowed himself to
be taken over by demons and needs exorcising. Although
everyone has some darkness inside them, Peter is yet again
delving too deeply into the dark side of himself.

He can no longer seek relief in his work. The early 1980s
are a fallow period and he is mainly appearing as a guest on
other people's chat shows, including those of comics Bob
Monkhouse and Russell Harty. Otherwise he watches
masses of television and occasionally is a panellist on Radio
4's *News Quiz*. His fragile state of mind isn't helped by the
fact that his father is increasingly ill and finally dies in
January 1986. Shortly afterwards, Margaret writes to me.

> I was so glad that Alec and I got to see you both in
> Somerset. He really enjoyed that day, and apart from
> his godson's wedding, it was about the last outing he
> had. After that he suddenly went downhill.
>
> I am so glad that neither of you want a divorce. It
> would make me very happy if you could get together
> again.

I am deeply touched by her words and so pleased that despite everything that has happened she feels that Peter and I make a good couple. Throughout my relationship with Peter she has never been anything other than supportive, kind and generous-spirited. She continues to ring me regularly and always enjoys talking about Peter's childhood. Peter is so distraught about losing his father that he makes a concerted effort to stop drinking.

He also, ill-advisedly, agrees to work with American comic Joan Rivers on her chat show *Can We Talk?* Joan is a tough, brassy comedian and wants Peter to add a touch of English class. The series is broadcast in March 1986 and is awful, both as a programme and particularly for him. He wasn't given enough time to build up any sort of comic relationship with Joan before the recordings were made at the BBC's Television Centre. There isn't even an opportunity for the two of them to indulge in some repartee at the beginning of each show. I don't think Peter could ever be comfortable with a woman who trades on a bitchy, self-mocking patter, and she is a far from natural vehicle for his talents. Joan does all the talking to her guests, while Peter is reduced to being her meeter and greeter, and I can't imagine anyone less suitable to being a straight man than Peter. It is deeply humiliating for someone of his talent and skill to be her sidekick, so it's no surprise that he comes across really badly. In one programme the comic Bernard Manning, who is a guest, says to him, 'You used to be very funny, Peter.' The reviews are terrible too and the *London Daily News* scathingly describes Peter as a man 'with a great future behind him'.

It seems now that both performers and critics can see that he is no longer functioning as he should. Publicly he explains his lacklustre performance by saying, 'I was there to help Joan out if she got into trouble, but she never thought she was in trouble, so I never helped her out,' but in private he is extremely upset by his reviews.

His gloomy mood isn't helped by the fact that Richard Ingrams resigns as editor of *Private Eye* in the same month, March 1986, a position he's held for twenty-five years. He didn't tell Peter in advance or even consult him on his successor. Instead he makes a unilateral decision to appoint Ian Hislop, who is only twenty-five. Peter already knows Ian, as when Ian was an undergraduate at Oxford University in the early 1980s, he wrote to Peter and asked if he could interview him for his humour magazine *Passing Wind*. Peter agreed and was quite impressed with him, so recommended him for a job on *Private Eye*. Now, though, he is furious with Richard for not consulting him and, after a lunch with a group of *Private Eye* rebel columnists, is given the task of telling Hislop he won't be editing the magazine after all. Unfortunately Peter gets so drunk that by the time he reaches *Private Eye*'s offices he has forgotten why he's come and Hislop keeps his new job. His grievance is soon forgotten, he and Hislop get along fine, and Peter continues to go to *Private Eye* to write jokes, but not as often as he used to.

He does, though, appear via satellite on an American production of *This Is Your Life* for Dudley. They are reconciled and shortly afterwards he flies out to Los Angeles to perform 'One Leg Too Few' with him for the US version of Comic Relief.

Later that year he rings on his forty-ninth birthday to say he has crashed his car into the back of a police car. He is furious that it has happened and is later banned from driving for a year.

I notice that he now keeps putting me off visiting him at Perrins Walk. I press him a couple of times and he finally admits I can't come because it will upset Lin. I try to hide that I am angry and upset, and once again acknowledge to myself that their relationship is more serious than I thought. I also notice, though, he doesn't ask for my keys back.

By the beginning of 1987 many of our phone calls centre round Lin. He is back drinking again, and shortly after one call when he sounds very drunk, Lin rings and says I shouldn't talk to Peter again. I put the phone down. She can't tell me not to talk to my husband. He rings soon afterwards to tell me he is going into a nursing home run by nuns in north London to try to dry out. It may seem bizarre, but despite the up-and-down nature of our conversations, we still find it very easy to talk to each other. This remains our binding thread for a while longer. Lin starts ringing me from her home too, particularly when she doesn't understand Peter's humour and asks me to explain it to her. It is a bizarre situation, but I am always polite. I regret getting involved. I should have left it entirely to Peter to sort out his relationship, but at the time I still loved him so much and thought I was doing the right thing. Nor did I know the full extent of their involvement.

Peter meanwhile tells me it isn't working with Lin and that he has asked Sidney Gottlieb to call her and tell her this. A week later he asks Sidney to get her to come back. One day in February 1987 he rings to plead with me to come and live with him in London and commute back and forth to the country. He explains that because I am not around, all sorts of bad things are happening. I don't say I won't come, but explain that I can't just abandon the animals, and if he genuinely wants me with him, I would have to employ someone full-time and I can't afford that without his help. He doesn't really answer, and I assume it is because of his drinking. He seems no longer to be able to function properly either physically or mentally. I am in a terrible dilemma, as part of me wants to be with him, and another part knows that for my own survival I need to stay away.

I contact an estate agent and go up to London to look at some flats and houses. It would be impossible to actually live with him. Not only because of Lin, but when he is drinking and taking drugs, life becomes too chaotic. Night becomes day, and his moods are completely unpredictable. I could, however, live close and be there whenever he needs me. I mention the properties to Peter when I return home and say that if I find somewhere, I will be available to look after him. He's obviously been drinking again and tells me he doesn't want me in London because it will upset Lin. It is an example of how he is inconsistent and can change his mind about something once he gets drunk. Looking back, I know that, realistically, living in London would have been the wrong thing to do.

In the end I stay put and we continue our daily phone calls. In another spate of calls he rings to say he and Lin have rowed all night, that he didn't sleep a wink and eventually asked a neighbour to come round to witness what was going on. I decide it is becoming too much for me to handle and tell him I won't phone him again. A couple of days later he rings me, this time to ask me to phone Lin to placate her jealousy. He also says he has told his children to have him committed if he marries her. I am not sure whether he is joking. Before I call Lin, she rings me. She is perfectly friendly and starts recounting an episode with Peter.

He must have told her about me hiding in a trunk to catch him out when he had the fling with the blonde nurse because she tells me she has behaved in a similar way. She describes how Peter went out and she let herself into Perrins Walk with her key but left everything untouched so that when Peter came back, he would think nobody was in. She then hid upstairs and waited. Apparently Peter returned with a woman and they were sitting chatting over a coffee when Lin suddenly exploded out of her hiding place. Soon after I have put the phone down on her, Peter rings and tells me the same story, adding that he was scared out of his wits. It's an utterly bizarre situation for me, but for reasons I am not entirely sure of, I continue to talk to her as well as Peter.

The most curious call comes one evening when she rings sounding very distressed. She tells me Peter is taking cocaine and is worried about his nose. She asks whether she should call the police. I tell her to call Sidney Gottlieb instead. I am shocked that Peter is taking such a dangerous drug, which really wasn't commonplace at the time. I wonder why Lin has told me, but I think she wants my advice because she, like me, doesn't have anyone to talk to about Peter and knows how close he and I are.

I meanwhile am slowly beginning to feel my wings in the world. I'm proud I've managed to find myself somewhere nice to live, yet at the same time I still want Peter to be part of my life and for our relationship to be affectionate and understanding.

It helps that by now I have things to occupy my time and mind. I am assisting a woman from the RSPCA to rescue dogs, some of whom are in very difficult situations and have been mistreated. It's always a delicate task and I have to use my wits. Having to cope with Peter's erratic behaviour and temper over so many years, I find that by comparison taking a dog away from its owner is relatively easy. In addition I take some of the dogs home to rehabilitate them and feel rather like a foster mother. I fence in my five-acre field and help them recover by throwing things for them to catch, taking them on long walks and riding with them. In addition I breed two litters of German shepherds, one of seven and another of four, to sell to the police when they are ready. Peter comes down to see them and we both fall in love with so many that it is hard to let them go. Luckily I am invited to their 'passing-out parades', before they officially become police dogs, by which time they have learnt to attack burglars. It is a wonderful occasion and I feel very proud of them.

It is tough coping with a family of animals on your own. If I don't feel well, I can't say, 'I won't walk the dogs today,' or, 'I won't muck out the horses.' There is a lot of physical work required in the house and garden, and I can't count on Peter for help. At least he remembers my forty-fifth birthday in July 1987 and sends me a tele-message that reads, 'Happy birthday, darling Mrs Rundle. Lots of love, Peter.'

Not long afterwards he rings to say he needs to come to talk to me because Lin wants him to ask for a divorce. I can hear he is drunk and tell him I'd like him to think about it when he is sober, and preferably when he has dried out. Over the following months Peter and I maintain irregular telephone contact and I keep myself busy with the dogs.

A few months into 1988 he rings to let me know me he is coming down to stay at Cedar Falls, a health farm just outside Taunton, which is quite near where I live and would like to talk about our divorce. We arrange that I will pick him up at Taunton Station. He has put on masses of weight and is very drunk. As soon as he clambers into my car, he starts weeping. I initially think it's because I am playing a Johnny Cash tape in which he sings 'I Walk the Line', which Peter loves, but it's not that at all. He explains that Lin has gone to Malaysia and his gas and electricity have been cut off and he doesn't know how to get them reconnected. He says he is paying her to take care of his bills and is dependent on her to run his house. It's quite obvious that he is now unable to cope with the most mundane of chores. He is so distressed that I drive him to the Cross Keys pub, just outside Taunton, where he has a beer and cheers up. We continue to the health farm and I help him unpack. At one point he pulls out a large bottle of Listerine and starts swigging from it. I say, 'Peter, you can't drink mouthwash,' but he laughs as he explains it contains alcohol.

He asks me to stay for a swim and for dinner, which I do. Shortly afterwards he introduces me to someone he has met in the smoking den, and the three of us have a chat. Anyone seeing us would assume we are a couple enjoying a break on a health farm, rather than experiencing a marital break-down. He is so obviously pleased I am with him and I know I could easily stay the night.

I don't want to leave him. We have had such a lovely time together, but I know it wouldn't be a wise thing to do. I feel torn, but for once my good sense wins. When I say I am leaving, he asks, 'What time will I see you tomorrow?' I tell him around lunchtime.

The following day, after lunch, we spend the afternoon together, and in the evening Peter goes to the village pub. When I go home and Peter returns to the health farm, he tells me he will spend most of the night in the smoking den. I reply that it's not what people normally do at a health farm.

The following day we are sitting chatting in the car when he suddenly asks me again if I want a divorce. I say, 'No, what about you?' and he replies, 'No.'

A little later, though, he has clearly changed his mind, as he says, 'I've come down to talk about a divorce.'

I nod and reply, 'It's your decision.' The whole thing is so strange, it's impossible to know how to handle it. I know on one level he is serious about wanting a divorce but on another it is difficult to take seriously because a few hours earlier he said he didn't. He then looks enormously relieved to have said what was obviously weighing heavily on his mind and immediately changes the subject. He instantly behaves as if nothing has happened and asks what time I will come and see him in the morning. It is bizarre and unreal. We get on so well, and he hugs and kisses me and chats away. I don't know anyone else who would behave similarly. Normally if you want a divorce you can't stand the person, but Peter quite clearly likes my company just as much as I like his. He stays at Cedar Falls for about a week. I am with him every day and he doesn't mention the word 'divorce' again.

Two days after he returns to London, though, he telephones to ask me to send him our marriage certificate. Alarm bells immediately ring in my mind. I know he wants it in connection with the divorce and decide I must get a solicitor before I do anything. I tell him I can't find it and then feel frightened. I've heard Peter when he's done deals over the phone for *Private Eye*. He is a very powerful man and can be quite lethal when he wants to get his own way. I worry that he could force through a divorce very quickly and I don't know my rights.

I find a solicitor in London, but he seems very absent-minded and chaotic. He makes arrangements for me to meet him, Peter and Peter's formidable show-business solicitor, Oscar Beuselinck, in his Soho office. When the day of the meeting arrives, we sit and talk in a windowless conference room. Peter has just come from a *Private Eye* lunch and is very much the worse for wear. He looks terrible, with unwashed hair, a T-shirt that doesn't cover his beer belly, a creased linen jacket and stained, crumpled trousers. He sits smoking a cigarette with one eye closed to help him focus on getting it in his mouth. After an abortive discussion about money he stands up and swears loudly at me. I notice that his flies are undone. When he sits down again, he appears to fall asleep.

After some time the solicitors suggest leaving us on our own for a short while to see if we can resolve the financial issue. It soon becomes clear that we can't, not least because Peter is too drunk, so instead I go for a walk around Soho. I bump into my lawyer on my way back and he says he had been looking forward to meeting the famous Peter Cook but that he's never seen anyone who is so well known look so appalling. Following our meeting he writes to Peter, who in turn rings me to say my lawyer is hopeless and advises me to find what he calls 'a proper solicitor'.

Luckily a friend recommends another lawyer, called Anthony Rubenstein, who specialises in divorce. I go to see him and he agrees to take me on, despite knowing I can't afford to pay his fees until everything is sorted, because he believes I have a bona fide case. Peter rings me regularly to see how I am. I know from experience that when Peter wants something, he is controlled, reasonable and devious until he gets it. I assume that it is why he is being extremely polite in his phone calls and deliberately making our conversations loving and friendly.

Anthony organises a meeting for Peter and me at his offices. It is like watching two Titans face each other. Anthony matches Peter both physically and mentally, and tells Peter what he knows about how *Private Eye* is financially managed. Peter is silent but looks very angry. I think Anthony wants Peter to grasp that when it comes to how much he will give me, he has nowhere to hide.

When he mentions the word maintenance, Peter reaches out his hand, takes mine and says, 'I want you to leave with me now, Judy.'

Taken aback, I say, 'No.' He repeats his instruction and I say no again. I've never done this to Peter. Usually I fall for his charm and decide I'll do as he says because it's easier, but on this occasion I can tell he is trying to manipulate me.

He then repeats something he once told me years previously: 'If ever we have to go to court, people will believe my word against yours.' In other words I am just a woman and no one will listen to me.

When the meeting is over, Anthony suggests that when I get home, I go riding and try to take my mind off things. I listen to his advice and it helps a little. Peter rings regularly and once even tells me that he likes Anthony and thinks he is 'a proper bloke'. He refuses to discuss maintenance, however, and Anthony suggests I go and see him at Perrins Walk and try to talk things through there.

Anthony prefers the option of going for a lump sum rather than regular payments because of Peter's poor health. He also warns me that he believes Peter won't want to settle out of court and will fight me all the way, and that if I lose my case, I shall probably have to give up my home and my animals.

In 1988 Peter becomes a regular caller on Clive Bull's late-night chat show on LBC, a London commercial news and talk station. It is a good outlet for him when he has trouble sleeping, and he usually calls at around 3 a.m. Peter adopts the character of Sven the Norwegian fisherman, who is calling from Swiss Cottage in north-west London. He has a Scottish accent, and his conversations are all about the state of fish and his disappointment that his wife, Jutta, whose family control the pilchard business in Oslo, has abandoned him and how it is her fault that he has resorted to picking up women in the local launderette. He pours out his heart, saying how lonely he is, and I wonder if he is feeling remorse about me. Some listeners take what he says at face value and ring up to offer advice.

He describes how in Norway the phone-ins are mainly devoted to fish and boasts about his knowledge of the effect of cannabis on fish: 'Well, they swim around in circles much as before, but luckily a bit happier ... From my experience, smoking fish is more harmful than cannabis.'

The character is a brilliant invention, and listeners don't know that Sven is really Peter Cook. Peter obviously enjoys the spontaneous chat, and I can tell by his manner and what he says whether he is feeling up or down and most of all if he is drunk. The calls continue on and off for about four years. Rainbow George goes on the programme too, but as himself, largely because it is almost the only outlet he can find to promote his political party.

It is finally arranged for me to go to Perrins Walk in the spring of 1989 to spend the afternoon with Peter and discuss the financial agreement between us. I dress quite smartly in a fine-check charcoal-grey Nicole Farhi jacket, white T-shirt and black trousers because I want to look my best. While we are talking, I notice a letter on the table addressed to Peter from a doctor, which informs him that his medical test is positive, that he has cirrhosis of the liver, and asks him to get in touch immediately. Cirrhosis is a serious chronic liver disease, usually caused by alcoholism, and leads to progressive loss of liver function. I am shocked and ask Peter what he will do if it really is serious. He replies, 'Nothing, except drink myself to death, because I'd be so frightened.' I discover he hasn't even contacted the doctor and feel anxious that he is ignoring such a life-threatening condition and, as is his habit, not facing up to reality. I then notice a large box of vitamins on the sideboard and I think how curious it is that at one level he is obviously trying to get fit. If he had been with me, I would have made him go to the doctor. I would have gone on and on, whenever I felt the time was right, as I did to get him to seek help for his drinking, until he agreed.

Luckily his mood that day is positive and he is both affectionate and supportive. I am glad because I can barely talk about our divorce with him face to face. I don't see why we need to divorce. I don't want it, and until very recently he hasn't wanted it either. I would settle to remain as we are. If I can't have all of Peter, being with him half the time is better than not being with him at all.

I watch with alarm as, despite the warning letter about his liver, he drinks an entire bottle of neat vodka straight from the bottle during the two hours we are together. He finally says he can afford to give me a lump sum of £150,000 and asks if that is OK. I tell him I think it is but I have to check with my lawyer. One of his phones ring and Peter becomes quite agitated. He says it is Lin, who wants to know if I am still with him. They don't live together. She has a property down the road. She calls again two or three times and each time Peter becomes more upset. He pleads with me to go and talk to her, saying she will be anxious if I don't.

I tell him I don't think it is a very good idea and in any case I have to get back to Somerset, but he finally persuades me. We walk down Hampstead High Street holding hands. Peter rings the doorbell, then lets himself in with his key. He removes his shoes in the hallway, as apparently is his custom. We walk upstairs to the sitting room together, but we are no longer holding hands. It is immaculately tidy and has deep-pile carpet, a black chrome coffee table and black chrome chairs placed against the walls. Peter sits on one, and I sit on another on the opposite side of the room. Lin comes in, gives us coffee, then sits beside me. She assures me Peter is in good hands, but admits that she is worried about how much weight he has put on. She says she is trying to look after him.

Peter sits slouched in his chair, drawing heavily on his cigarettes, before dropping off to sleep. Lin then asks if she can show me round her house. It's a bizarre offer, but I accept graciously. She seems particularly proud of her cocktail bar that opens at the touch of a button and has different types of glasses, cocktail shakers and, it seems, every type of alcoholic drink. My behaviour towards her is meticulously polite throughout.

By the time Peter wakes up I need to catch a train back to Taunton and Lin calls me a taxi to take me to Paddington Station. Peter comes to the door with me, gives me a kiss and stands waving. It's such an unreal situation. On my way home, I worry enormously about my animals. The ones that are still alive are old and difficult, and it is my responsibility to look after them. I want to keep them in comfort and it gives me something to fight for as we negotiate the divorce.

I ring Anthony the next morning and tell him about Peter's financial offer. He explains it is not enough for me to live on, especially as I have legal bills to pay, a house to run and no earning capacity. He also reminds me that I need something to put aside for my old age and suggests that an additional £50,000 would be more appropriate.

I ring Peter and ask for the extra money and he goes berserk. I try to make him listen to me, but he is cold and angry. I remember Anthony's pep talk, telling me that I mustn't be walked over, and somehow manage to say to Peter, 'You've got to face up to facts.'

Peter shouts down the line, 'You've never talked to me like this before. You've changed and I don't like it.'

His words give me a shock. He has been used to pushing me around and to a certain extent I've taken it and now I am suddenly standing up to him. I try to explain that I have bills to pay, and the quicker we sort it out, the better. But all he says is, 'Let it go to court.' He also tells me not to call him at Perrins Walk any more because Lin doesn't like it.

I am sure he believes I don't have the courage to face him in court, and that even if I do, he'll win because he is more articulate. He also has the advantage that he's been to court many times over cases that concern *Private Eye*, whereas I have never even been in a courtroom. Soon after my call Lin rings to say that if I ask Peter for more money, he will never speak to me again. It feels like emotional blackmail because she knows I want to stay in touch with him. It won't change anything anyway. The divorce and any money arrangements are strictly between Peter and me. Our divorce comes through on 5 April 1989, leaving the financial arrangements to be sorted out at a later date in court.

Shortly afterwards, to my great surprise, I see Dudley on the television in an advertisement for Tesco. He has a three-year contract worth millions and plays a Tesco buyer who undertakes a three-year worldwide search to hunt an elusive flock of French free-range chickens and on the way finds all sorts of other items the supermarket can stock. It feels strange to see him again, even if only onscreen. My life has changed so much since I saw him last, but I am pleased he is working and obviously earning well. The advertising campaign is a great success and kick-starts the store's rise to brand stardom.

On 18 November Peter rings me from Torquay to say he has married Lin ten minutes earlier. I ask where she is and he says she's gone shopping. I ask him what is the point of getting married for the third time, but he ignores my question. I get off the phone as quickly as possible. I feel desperate, humiliated and profoundly sad and lonely. I know the news will be in every paper and I feel so exposed and as if the

whole world can see my wounds. My life has been irrevoca-
bly changed and in such a public way. I want to hide so I
don't have to face people coming up to me in the street and
saying: 'I hear Peter has remarried.' For the next few days I
barely eat or sleep.

A week later Peter rings late at night wanting to discuss
whether I think the comedian Freddie Starr is funny. We used
to discuss different comedians and their various skills a great
deal, but it's no longer appropriate. I again ask where Lin is
and he says down the road in her house. They have not
moved in together even though they are now married. I then
say, 'How can you ask me about Freddie Starr when you
have just got married?' He has told me not to phone him, yet
he thinks nothing of continuing our chats when he feels like
it as if nothing has happened between us. The next day I send
him a postcard of a blackout of Minehead in Somerset with
just a naked light bulb shining but don't write anything on
the back. It expresses the blackness of what I am feeling and
I know Peter will understand. I also decide he can't use me as
a shoulder to cry on. There has to be an end to it and I
change my phone number so he can't call even if he wants to.

A week later, on 27 November, I receive a very caring note
from Peter's mother:

> Dearest Judy
>
> I've been meaning to write to you for ages, but
> there is nothing I can say. I feel so miserable about it
> all, but quite helpless.
>
> I do hope you are not too unhappy. I wish that I
> was not so far off. I had horrid sciatica the whole of
> last summer and I was not able to go far afield. Old
> age is very tiresome.
>
> With love and sympathy,
> Margaret

I feel so grateful to her, and her words console me.

Meanwhile affidavits from the lawyers fly back and forth. Some of Peter's are so wild and accusatory I sometimes feel he is trying to annihilate me.

17

The Final Split

I feel extremely stressed, and the only time I find any peace is riding on the moors or being with my animals. Sadly they are all rather old and won't be with me for much longer. I try to enjoy my time with them, and rather than be too house-proud, I let them go anywhere.

It is difficult when you are a stepmother to know what to do about stepchildren when the relationship with their father breaks down. Peter has been very good at handling us all and smoothing over any relationship difficulties because we all see him as the centre of the family, but since our divorce I am anxious not to create a potentially awkward situation between me, Lucy, Daisy and Wendy. My relationship with Peter can't have been easy for Wendy and although I love Lucy and Daisy very much, I can't bear the thought of resurrecting old hurts. Instead of trying to work out a way, I cut myself off from all of them.

Fortunately Margaret keeps in touch and writes to me again in March 1990. She knows instinctively how I feel and tries to explain how the divorce and Peter's marriage affects her.

> My dear Judy,
> It was nice to talk to you the other day – I am so glad that you are coming to terms with such a deeply

upsetting situation. I still find it hard to take, but as I said to you, I don't want to lose touch with Peter because I love him very much and I won't try to adjust my feelings ... I have borrowed a wheelchair to get around the house with (ankle still very painful ...).

I do hope to see you one of these days.

Much love from,

Margaret

Our case is scheduled for November 1991 in the High Court at the Aldwych and is expected to last a week. As well as Anthony Rubenstein, another lawyer, called Louise Spitz, is involved. My barrister is Florence Baron. I originally meet her in her chambers and Anthony warns me she is tough and won't give me an easy ride. He's right. She puts me through the sort of rigorous questions she thinks I might face from Peter's barrister. I find it gruelling, but it is a test to see if I can cope.

As part of the advance preparation, Peter and I both have to submit our bank accounts and outgoings over a three-year period, so the lawyers can see how we live, what we need and how we spend our money. I have to provide a GP's report on my health, which includes the fact that the whiplash injury I sustained in the car crash has triggered arthritis. I also have to get my house valued and include an estimate for repairs. Peter changes lawyers during these preparations, and shortly before the case is due to be heard, my lawyer makes one last request to Peter's solicitor to settle out of court, to save us both stress and expense. He turns us down.

In addition I ask the judge, through my barrister, for Lin not to be allowed in court while Peter and I are being questioned. It is agreed. Louise Spitz rings and asks what I am going to wear. I tell her my Barbour jacket because it represents everything I'm fighting for. I muck out in it every day; I ride in it; I walk my dogs in it. It represents my life, and when I put my hands in my pockets, I can feel oats, straw and hay and I feel in touch with the earth. She tells me it's a ridiculous idea and that she has seen a nice suit in a magazine that looks perfect for me and I should try to buy that. I refuse.

I am booked in to stay at the Cadogan Hotel in Knightsbridge for the length of the trial, and the night before it is due to start I have dinner with Anthony. I tell him I am frightened, particularly of being on the witness stand with everyone's eyes on me and being torn apart by Peter's barrister. Lawyers are clever at firing questions and ordinary people like me don't have the same ability with language to answer back skilfully. I fear I shall just stutter. He patiently tells me that if I am worried about a question, I should ask the barrister to repeat it slowly, that if I haven't heard it thoroughly, I should ask him to repeat it again, and that I should reply in my own time and not feel rushed.

I don't sleep a wink and turn up in court wearing my familiar Barbour, black trousers and riding boots, as I said I would. Peter and his legal team are talking in a huddle, and as I walk past them, they turn and stare at me, then start whispering among themselves again. It is very intimidating. I shiver with nerves, thrust my hands deep into my pockets and hang on to my bits of oats, straw and hay.

I am shocked by how Peter looks. He is so bloated that he reminds me of Elvis Presley shortly before his death. He is sweating profusely too, and as we move into court, I notice he keeps taking out a vial of pills from his pocket and swallowing several. I am first on the witness stand. Peter's barrister asks me detailed questions about my life, my horses and if I have a boyfriend. Each question feels like a punch to both my head and stomach, and I barely recover from one before he lays another one into me. He says, among other things, that as I was aware Peter was a drunk when I married him, I knew what I was letting myself in for. He also seems to want to present me as an idiot and gives the impression he'd like nothing better than to see me sobbing and agreeing I can't cope.

I feel dreadful, but then remember Anthony's words of advice. I ask him to repeat things I don't hear clearly and manage to slow down his rapid fire of questions. I answer each one carefully and as truthfully as I can. My barrister then questions me equally thoroughly. I'm on the stand for two and a half long days and notice that Lin brings Peter to court every day but, as requested, doesn't come into the courtroom itself. When I finally get down and walk past Peter, he reaches out to shake my hand.

It is now Peter's turn to be cross-examined by my barrister, but instead he breaks down and with tears falling down his cheeks suddenly admits he is addicted to cocaine, gambling and pornography and is an alcoholic. His conduct reminds me of how he behaved at AA meetings, when he stood up and said, 'My name is Peter. I'm an addict.' I find his confession so dramatic that I burst into tears too. My barrister turns round and says, 'Judy, do stop crying, for goodness' sake.' We adjourn, and when we come back, Justice Thorpe says the case is over, that it is obvious that neither of us wants to let go of the marriage but that nonetheless he is awarding me £230,000. Peter gives me the blackest of looks. His expression is one of hate and I can tell he is thinking, How dare she? It is intimidating to see him so angry and I confide in Anthony that I feel guilty and partly responsible for him bursting into tears. He tells me sharply not even to think about it.

We all leave by a side door to escape the press, but Peter

and I don't speak. Although the whole experience has been ghastly, I soon begin to feel elated. I have for once stood up to him, he hasn't had his own way, and my animals and I are now safe.

I catch the train home, and when I finally arrive, I close the door and make myself a cup of tea. I am enormously relieved but also very tired. Next morning I light a fire and shortly afterwards the press arrive and congregate outside my locked gates. One of the reporters shouts that they have seen smoke coming from the chimney so he knows I am at home.

Another shouts, 'Do you hate Peter?'

I shout, 'No.'

A third asks, 'Is it true you are a gold digger?'

I shout back, 'I am not talking. Go home.'

The following day's papers quote me as saying I am not a gold digger and that I still love Peter. They have made it up, but no one else knows that, including Peter's lawyer, who is straight on the phone to Anthony. Anthony then rings me to say that if I have talked to the press about the case, Peter will take me back to court. I explain I haven't.

The press stays clustered around my gate for four days. I feel imprisoned in the house but at least I am with my animals and can take them for walks around my field. As the days pass, I think back to the court case and feel increasingly upset by the way Peter has treated me. He behaved as if I was a stranger suing *Private Eye* rather than his ex-wife. There was no human contact or acknowledgement of how much we meant to each other for so long and it makes me feel very sad.

The money doesn't arrive and I become increasingly worried about my huge legal bills. Anthony warns me we may have to fight to get the money and that it might not be easy, partly because of Peter's reputation for not dealing with his mail and partly because his health is obviously so poor he may die first, in which case the money could be lost. We talk through various options and in the end decide to put an order on his house, which is valued at £400,000.

Coincidentally I get a letter from the nuns at the clinic that Peter has used when he wanted to dry out asking for help in obtaining money he owes them. I am shocked he hasn't paid because they were so caring. Fortunately once the order has been placed, my money arrives and the nuns are also paid. Dudley doesn't contact me and I have no wish to be in touch with him. That part of my life is over. Lucy and Daisy write to me and send me cards and I am really touched to hear from them. I also talk to Peter's sisters, Sarah and Liz. I am relieved that I can stay in the house for a while. I know it is too big and I can't afford to run it long term, but I want my animals to see out their days in familiar surroundings. Berry has already gone and I decide not to have any more dogs or horses because it is too expensive and too much work on my own. For the next year or so I feel I am running an old-age home for animals as gradually all my elderly pets pass away.

As for myself, instead of healing as I hoped, I begin to feel really ill. My immune system breaks down as a result of all the stress and I get several abscesses on my gums. My hair starts to fall out, and I develop a terrible skin infection. I feel wretched, have very little energy and during that time live a quiet, isolated life. I take antibiotics for two years and it takes me another year to feel I have fully recovered. It is a difficult period and I lose touch with Peter's family because I don't feel well enough to invite anyone round. I go out only when I have to and then keep my head down, my eyes averted and reduce all conversation to a minimum.

I have no direct contact with Peter, but it seems he isn't

doing much work. I occasionally hear him on the radio, and I watch him on television when he takes part in a 1993 Christmas edition of *Clive Anderson Talks Back*. Peter is the only guest. He appears as four different imaginary characters, and despite everything that has happened between us, I can't help but find him absolutely hilarious. His first character is Norman House, a quality controller in an Ipswich biscuit factory, who claims he has been abducted by aliens and is obviously based on Pete in *Not Only ... But Also*. When Clive, who is trying not to laugh, asks whether he was abducted to Mars or Venus, Norman replies, 'Ikea! They are people who arrived millions of years ago in cardboard boxes and were forced to assemble themselves ... without any instructions.'

The next character is Alan Latchley, a football manager who talks almost entirely in clichés. The third guest is Sir James Beauchamp, a 'notorious' judge, who is temporarily suspended for shooting a defendant in court and is a variation of Sir Arthur Streeb-Greebling, one of Peter's favourite characters. Clive asks if his behaviour has affected his relationship with his wife. He replies that his wife is 'slightly physically impaired'. That she either fell or was pushed off a horse, is partially paralysed and can serve drinks, but not peanuts at the same time.

I feel sure this unpleasant comment is directed at me. Peter often slightly alters names and situations when he writes a sketch, but the person it is aimed at knows absolutely it is about them. I feel so upset I barely listen to the last character, Eric Daley, a mega rock star with a band called Ye Gods, who breeds anchovies and 'can't get too much of the environment'.

I am amazed Peter has resurrected himself but happy that he is still able to make a living, even if it is only walk-on parts in other people's programmes. Although he has made me laugh, looking at him onscreen is like watching a time bomb. He is bloated as well as overweight and I think, How long has he got? I still care about him and I am sorry he feels angry that I won in court. It would have been so much better if he had been gracious and not tried to make me feel guilty for asking for a small share of his fortune.

Shortly afterwards he produces a rather disappointing video, *Peter Cook Talks Golf Balls*, which is based on his Clive Anderson appearances where he played an overbearing American commentator, a whisky-sozzled Scottish caddie, a retired major and a mad German psychiatrist.

In June 1994 I hear that Peter's mother has died, a month after she suffered a severe stroke. I know Peter will be devastated because they were so close, but I don't dare write to him. It is a misjudgement and one I regret. I know he will find it hard to cope with his grief and will drown his sorrows in his normal way. For me, her death underlines the end of my relationship with Peter.

I live quietly and uneventfully with my memories until the morning of Monday 9 January 1995, when my neighbour, Tina Farmer, rings to say she has seen on the news that Peter has died in hospital and wants to make sure I hear straight away. I am so shocked that when I go into the kitchen to make myself a calming cup of tea, I pour boiling water all over my hand. I ring another neighbour who lives across the road and she takes me to the local hospital, where my burns are attended to.

When I come back, I ask if I can sit with her for a while. I then go for a walk and don't speak to anyone else for the rest of the day. Peter was only fifty-seven and no matter what he said or did, I didn't want him to die. I feel wretched that I had no idea he was in hospital, let alone seriously ill. Apparently he was in intensive care for a week before his death. I can't bear the thought that I didn't know this. I would have loved to have held his hand and said to him that no matter what has happened I still love him. I so wish I could have said goodbye. I can't resist calling Perrins Walk just to hear Peter's voice on the answer phone one more time. I later discover Dudley does the same.

Over the next few days going out, even to the shops, feels as challenging as climbing a mountain. All sorts of people come up and talk to me. Some are friendly, others not so. I don't phone Wendy, Lin, Lucy or Daisy. I know I won't be able to hold a rational conversation with any of them, but Lucy and Daisy write very nice letters and I write back to them.

After a few days I manage to call Peter's sister Liz and she tells me Peter collapsed at home and was taken to the Royal Free Hospital in Hampstead, where he died of a gastrointestinal haemorrhage, caused by severe liver damage. Apparently he drank almost continually once his mother died and his whole bodily system collapsed. Despite the best efforts of the staff in the intensive-care unit, nothing could be done. Poor Peter. I know he was so frightened of dying. She also tells me that Peter had asked for my phone number when he was ill and badly wanted to get in touch with me, but no one knew what it was. I so wish I had given it to him. Liz and I stay in touch for a while and it is comforting to speak to her.

I also contact one of Peter's AA friends, who tells me that, to her surprise, Lin has invited her to his funeral. I don't get an invitation, and apparently Wendy hasn't been invited either. If I had been arranging Peter's funeral, I know I would have invited all his ex-wives. The funeral itself takes place on Saturday 14 January. I keep to my regular routine, which includes walking the dogs and shopping. I don't watch the news on television. It would be too painful.

There are fulsome obituaries and everyone is lavish in their praise of Peter. Dudley, who is obviously devastated by Peter's death, says, 'My life will never be the same because I felt so linked to him ... Peter had an extraordinary talent, but he ate too much, drank too much, smoked too much and did everything too much. At least he lived a full life.'

Jack Tinker, the renowned *Daily Mail* theatre critic, says, 'He gave every impression of a man who had enjoyed life entirely on his own terms. And which of us could ask for more?'

Jonathan Miller, who starred with Peter in *Beyond the Fringe*, adds, 'I had enormous admiration for Peter's comic genius, which, above all others, was the inspirational source for modern British comedy over the last thirty years. His death marks the end of an era.'

While Ian Hislop, editor of *Private Eye*, states, 'He was the funniest person I ever knew.'

Peter apparently asked to be buried in his parking space, but is taken to rest in the churchyard of St-John-at-Hampstead Parish Church.

A few months later, on 1 May 1996, a memorial service is held to celebrate Peter's life in St John's Church, Hampstead. Dudley is invited, but Wendy, Lucy, Daisy and I are not. Daisy is so upset that she asks Sidney Gottlieb to intervene on her and Lucy's behalf and eventually Lin agrees that she, Lucy and Peter's sisters can come to the service, although not the lunch afterwards. Instead there are lots of celebrities present, including John Cleese, Mel Smith, Jonathan Ross, Terry Wogan, Spike Milligan, Barry Humphries and Harry Enfield.

My life continues and in September 1999 I am greatly

upset to read that Dudley is suffering from progressive supranuclear palsy, a degenerative disease that destroys the nerve cells in the brain, and for which there is no treatment. It is so sad, particularly as his personal life is in such a mess. His third marriage was to actress Brogan Lane in 1988, but two years later it was over. He then married Nicole Rothschild, whom he met when she threw herself on the bonnet of his Bentley as he was driving down Sunset Boulevard. She gave birth to his second son, Nicholas, but their relationship was so tempestuous that they separated three years later, in 1998.

Their divorce is acrimonious, and during the hearing she accuses him of spending £64,000 on prostitutes and drugs. I am shocked to discover he has a chronic addiction to drink and drugs, and has frittered away a fortune of £10 million. He disapproved and argued all the time with Peter over his drug-taking and now he has totally succumbed and is using, among other things, amphetamines and ecstasy.

After his divorce from Nicole he sells his Californian beach house and moves to New Jersey for daily treatment at the renowned Kessler Institute for Rehabilitation. He doesn't improve, and in 2001 he makes one of his last trips to London to receive a CBE from Prince Charles. It is deeply upsetting to see him in a wheelchair. He can no longer play the piano, and his illness has now deprived him of the ability to speak. Apparently one of his last coherent instructions is to forbid Nicole from attending his funeral.

He becomes so ill that Nicole drops her £7 million custody battle and Dudley's friend Rena Fruchter, who is also an accomplished pianist, and her husband take him under their wing and care for him. He apparently has very limited resources, as his medical bills and battle with Nicole have eaten into his capital.

He dies aged sixty-six on 27 March 2002, three years after his diagnosis, following a bout of pneumonia, a side effect of his illness, and I read that his last pleasure as he lay on his deathbed was to listen to music and Rena playing his album *Songs Without Words*, which he composed in 1991.

It marks the end of an era, and although I was close to Dudley, it seems a long time ago and I don't regret not having been in touch with him. I don't have the same feelings for him as I do for Peter. My current life in the country is a world away from the one I shared with both Peter and Dudley.

Epilogue

Writing *Loving Peter* has at times been painful, as I've been forced to confront so much, in particular the reality of Peter's drinking and behaviour with women. I've had to open dark cupboards in my mind and I've not always enjoyed what I have found, but overall it has helped me gained more perspective on what happened and find peace. It has certainly enabled me to separate the sometimes awful way Peter behaved when he was caught in the vice-like grip of alcoholism from the life-enhancing Peter who was sober.

Peter had three major rejections in his life by the three people who were closest to him: his mother, by not being with him nearly enough; by Dudley, who ultimately wouldn't continue working with him because of his drinking; and by me, by all accounts the love of his life, because in the end I couldn't cope with his addictions.

In addition we were both very sensitive and the harsh realities of life hit us hard. Peter sometimes found the world unbearable without resorting to alcohol to soften its blows. I understood his reaction and, because of my own background, tried in whatever way I could to help him. It is something I believe made me an enabler to his drinking.

The truth is that Peter remains part of my psyche. I spent my best years with him; he coloured my life, gave me countless insights and we had the same sense of humour. Looking back over the life we shared for more than twenty years has been an extraordinary process of laughter and tears. It has also helped me remember so much, from tiny gems to acts of great significance.

There weren't many normal times because Peter wasn't a normal person. He had a rare talent and a unique way of looking at things. His humour was deliciously naughty and wonderfully vibrant, and when he wasn't drinking, he had such an upbeat approach to life. I was always proud of what he achieved – how many people can, for example, leave a legacy that influences every generation of comedians since his death? I always tried to encourage him as best I could, but without doubt I loved the man even more than the performer. There are thousands of moments of complete hilarity we shared, but I shall refer to just two special recol-lections. One is when we were in Nutmeg Drive in the States and he dressed up as Groucho Marx, complete with mous-tache and false nose, to cook on the barbecue. The other is when we were in Blagdon Close and the countless times when we'd be up half the night trying to put out one of Peter's special bonfires, which usually ended up with him hopping about on the top with a hose and trying not to burn his feet or get them too wet. He also had the ability to make me laugh at myself, which I shall never forget. I regret that I didn't manage to maintain some sort of career and have a family, but I have come to terms with both. Nor am I in touch with Peter's children, but I think about them with enormous fondness.

I now live in a modern bungalow in a peaceful Somerset village. The days pass quietly. I enjoy long walks in the coun-tryside, tending my small garden and reading. I miss Peter, his humour, his intelligence and his company. I regularly wish I could speak to him to ask his opinion, share something amusing or just so he can make me laugh. We were always able to pick up where we left off and I am sure we would start talking as if we had spoken only yesterday.

Peter was the love of my life and I have never been as close to anyone, before or since, but I had to learn to share him with a lot of other people, because that was part of who Peter was. It was worth it. Just as it was worth preserving our relationship through his affairs and addictions.

When I look back, I can see the good times far outweighed the bad, and I know Peter would laugh to hear me say that I think my mother was right when she said, 'He's very nice to go out with, darling, but don't get married to him.'

He was an impossible act to follow. I feel very lucky to have been part of his life for such a long time. Others have written about him but it is now my turn and I believe I knew him better than anyone.

Index